The Professional Marketer

TIM MATTHEWS

Embarcadero Press

San Francisco   New York   Dublin   Tokyo

ISBN 10: 0692232850
ISBN 13: 9780692232859

Table of Contents

Preface

I wanted to buy this book, but couldn't find it. So, I wrote it.

As I write this paragraph, I am sitting in my home office looking at four shelves chockablock with marketing books. Wonderful books. Insightful books. Landmarks in the marketing profession. I have read all of them. But the book I need isn't there—a practical book to refer to when faced with questions on day-to-day marketing tasks. I need a book I can hand to someone on my staff who has a question on how to measure a direct mail campaign, size a market, write a press release from scratch, and the dozens of other tasks marketers perform every week.

The marketing canon contains books on marketing strategy, like *Crossing the Chasm*, that are must-reads, but don't help a marketer on a tactical basis. *Ogilvy on Advertising* has very practical advice, but is limited to advertising. Lon Safko's *Social Media Bible*, weighing in at seven hundred pages, is probably more than you need if you are not a social media specialist. *The Professional Marketer*, on the other hand, is a compendium that summarizes key skills in marketing and can be used as a quick reference for applied marketing skills.

Why was I looking for a book like this in the first place? I had a realization one day, after answering a pretty basic question from a senior marketing staff member: Most marketers are never trained. Many receive on-the-job training from excellent managers. But just as many—if not more—are just thrown in and fend for themselves. The result is a very narrow and limited understanding of marketing. Most are competent in their own patch, but lack an understanding of other marketing domains, inhibiting not only their ability to work cross functionally but also their career growth toward becoming a CMO.

Enter this book. It contains, in my estimation, the minimum set of skills a marketer needs to master to be considered a *professional* marketer. Anyone who aspires to a career in marketing should be conversant in all of them. The inspiration for the title came from my wife—a former professional chef—and her training manual from the Culinary Institute of America, *The Professional Chef*. Anyone who graduates from the institute is trained on all of the fundamental building blocks of food preparation, resulting in a basic fluency that can be applied no matter where and what they cook.

The book is organized into six sections, starting with marketing strategy, moving on to awareness, then to demand generation, spending time on working with direct sales and channel partners, and ending with concepts key to running a marketing department.

Section 1 – Marketing Strategy and Science – Peter Drucker, The Four Ps, Ted Levitt, Crossing the Chasm; Positioning and the Brand; Market Segmentation; Marketing Planning

Section 2 – Getting the Word Out – Public Relations; The Press Release; Social Media and WOM Marketing; Product Reviews, Case Studies, Awards, Studies/Surveys

Section 3 – Building Demand – Direct Marketing; Marketing Lists and Databases; Leads Opportunities and the Funnel; Events; Advertising

Section 4 – Arming Sales – The Website; Collateral and Other Assets; Speaking and Presentations; Sales Training and Enablement

Section 5 – Marketing via Channels – Marketing and Selling through a Channel; Partner Programs

Section 6 – Marketing Management – Test and Measure; Showing Results – ROMI, Dashboards, and other Metrics; Marketing Budgets; The Marketing Department

Each chapter covers a key marketing discipline and is designed to be self-contained. Most include a case study. Where prior understanding of an important concept is needed, a back reference to a previous chapter is provided. For the ambitious, I've included a reading list of my favorite works.

I don't expect anyone to read the book in one sitting, or even cover to cover. But I do hope it sits near your desk, or at the ready on your e-reader, as a trusted reference. Mastery can come over time. Once you have mastered the concepts in all twenty-three chapters, I would consider you a professional marketer.

Lastly, not all of the examples are from this year or last year. I travel through the last five decades (and in one case go back almost two centuries) both to illustrate how modern marketing came to be and also because so many of those examples are just, well, better. Marketers have an unhealthy predisposition for the now. New innovations in marketing technology happen every week, but there are also long-running truths in marketing—don't ignore the past. I could see any of the new crop of vodka marketers getting inspiration from Pyotr Smirnov's ingenious tactics that I cover in chapter 7.

I've always hated long introductions, so I hope this has whet your appetite for a full course of marketing. I trust that you will find this book useful and that it will contribute to your mastery. Bon appétit.

Chapter 1

Drucker, Levitt, the Four Ps, and the Chasm

Think of the most successful and widely recognized brands—Coke, Walmart, Microsoft, Nike. In any field, they likely have one thing in common: great marketing. These companies prosper and expand by combining a few fundamental business concepts and practices:

- An acute understanding of customer needs

- An astute awareness of their markets

- The right price

- Great salespeople and partners

- Successful introduction of new products

Not coincidentally, all of these features are essential elements of marketing.

Marketing is much more than Pantone colors, social media backlinks, and visually appealing direct mail pieces. Marketing is strategy. Marketing is science. Marketing is the engine that creates customers and drives business. Although these ideas might seem obvious, in reality, many marketers do not embrace them. This failure hurts both the marketers and the organizations they work for.

But where did these ideas come from? Modern marketing stands on the shoulders of many great thinkers. This chapter focuses on the writings of five particularly influential marketing giants—Peter Drucker, Ted Levitt, E. Jerome McCarthy, Geoffrey Moore, and Everett Rogers. If your goal is to create a successful brand—and, of course, to craft a successful career in marketing—then understanding the power of marketing through the eyes of these giants is essential. Let's begin by examining the writings of Peter Drucker.

Peter Drucker

Peter Drucker is widely recognized as a seminal figure in modern management, so it may seem strange to begin a book on marketing by examining his work. The German-born Drucker is perhaps the best-known and most influential thinker on management theory and practice. Among his many accomplishments, he

- was one of the first writers to discuss corporate divisional structure;
- coined the term "knowledge worker" before Bill Gates entered kindergarten;
- created the concept of management by objective (the MBOs many marketing managers' bonuses are based on today); and
- predicted the rise of outsourcing as a viable business strategy.

This list barely scratches the surface of the major contributions contained in his thirty-nine books, but Drucker's views on marketing are direct and without pretense. The fact that they come from a respected business management thinker, and not a marketing specialist, gives them added weight outside marketing departments, which is why I am starting with his work.

Let's face it—many business executives are dismissive of marketing. Few executives truly understand what marketing is and the power it holds. To them, marketing is the department that keeps the website current and pays an agency to create attention-getting ads. Given the ubiquity of marketing in modern businesses, why do so many executives fail to appreciate its true value? One possibility is that these individuals are simply unaware of all the work that goes into making the phone ring, encouraging a shopper to reach for your product, or enticing a prospective customer to respond to your online ad. An alternative explanation is that the marketing they see practiced in their organizations is too tactical or poorly executed, which reinforces their (mis)impression of marketing's role and contributions.

Drucker flips this perception on its head. Rather than focus on the effect, he looks at the cause, which marketing has a lot to do with. In "The Purpose and Objectives of a Business" (chapter 3 in *The Essential Drucker*), he argues that the purpose of a business is neither to make a profit nor to maximize revenues by selling more product. Those objectives are *measures* of a business, but they are not its *purpose*. Rather, according to Drucker, business exists for only one reason—to serve the needs of its customers. He goes one step further: "There is only one valid definition of business purpose: *to create a customer*."[1] Marketers can relate to this definition. After all, does any other department spend as much time strategizing to identify, reach, appeal to, and maintain customers as marketing?

Drucker agrees with this assessment of the critical role of marketing. In his own words: "Because the purpose is to create a customer, the business enterprise has two—and only these two—basic functions: marketing and innovation." True marketing, he argues, starts out with customers, their wants and their needs. Truly understanding these needs and then working to deliver on them are the keys to creating customers.

Drucker also debunks a common misconception concerning the relationship between the sales and marketing departments. Most VPs of marketing have heard their VPs of sales tell them that sales is marketing's customer. This is actually a polite way of saying that sales should be free to make demands on marketing, and marketing should give sales what it wants.

In fact, as Drucker explains, the *customer*—and not the sales department—is marketing's customer. Marketing's job is to understand what the customer needs and to feed that information back into the organization to help it meet the needs of the customer.

Drucker takes this idea a step further: "The aim of marketing is to know and understand the customer so well the product or service fits him and sells itself." He continues: "The aim of marketing is to make selling unnecessary."

(I strongly recommend you do not present this argument to your VP of sales!) Although this concept seems quite provocative, it is essentially sound: If a company can understand the market, meet its customers' needs perfectly, innovate technically or economically to create the product or service, and then reach those customers, then how much selling is actually left?

Drucker had a talent for examining what was right in front of us and presenting it in a plainspoken, straightforward way that was accessible to anyone, regardless of his or her function. His reputation as a management guru may help you convey the role of marketing to your executives.

Ted Levitt and Marketing Myopia

Sitting in the boardroom of a Boston-area software company years ago, one of my marketing colleagues, pounding the table, exhorted, "Remember, we're not in the railroad business, we're in the transportation business!" What on earth was he talking about? We were not in either of those businesses.

He was offering, as it turned out, an analogy, utilizing Ted Levitt's most famous example of *marketing myopia*. Levitt created this term to refer to a highly restrictive view that many business executives hold and the damage it can cause. Levitt argued that had the railroad industry stepped back and taken a broader view—that it was actually in the transportation business—it could have rescued itself. The rest, of course, is government-subsidized history. In our colleague's mind, the high-growth gravy train our software company rode was about to end, because we, too, were taking a limited view of our market. In *Marketing Myopia*, Levitt sums up the fate of the railroad industry:

> Less than 75 years ago, American railroads enjoyed a fierce loyalty among astute Wall Streeters. European monarchs invested in them heavily. Eternal wealth was thought to be the benediction for anybody who could scrape together a few thousand dollars to put into rail stocks. No other form of transportation could compete with the railroads in speed, flexibility, durability, economy and growth potentials.

Even after the advent of automobiles, trucks and airplanes, the railroad tycoons remained imperturbably self-confident. If you had told them 60 years before that in 30 years they would be flat on their backs, broke and pleading for government subsidies, they would have thought you totally demented.[2]

Unfortunately, that is essentially what happened. Today, in the United States, Amtrak survives only due to generous handouts from the US government. The hubris of their success blinded the railroad barons to the competition generated by other means of transportation, such as automobiles and commercial airlines. And that word—transportation—is fundamental to Levitt's thesis that the railroads defined themselves too narrowly, as players in the railroad business, and not more broadly, as players in the transportation business. This myopia ultimately prevented them from viewing the market more broadly.

Underlying marketing myopia are two basic tenets:

- Companies stop growing not because the market is saturated but because management fails to adapt to market conditions.

- An industry is a customer-satisfying process, not a goods-producing process. (Recall Drucker's philosophy.) Businesses will be more successful if they concentrate on meeting customers' needs rather than on simply selling products.

Levitt cites Hollywood as another case of myopic management. Hollywood moguls, who perceived themselves as strictly in the movie business, viewed the introduction of television as a threat. "Hollywood scorned and rejected TV when it should have welcomed it as an opportunity—an opportunity to expand into the entertainment business."[3] Another example of an industry that defined itself too narrowly and therefore missed an opportunity to broaden itself. As Levitt noted at the time of his writing, the TV business is bigger than the movie business ever was. Going further, rather than learn from this error, Hollywood, in fact, repeated it, first with the advent of the VCR and again with the introduction of DVDs. Even today, Hollywood remains myopic, as exemplified by its failure to fully embrace online streaming of movies over the Internet. Based on this history, we have no doubt that some new disruptive innovation just over the horizon will once again cause agita for movie execs.

Myopia stems from a belief in—and a reliance on—the concept of a growth industry. Growth opportunities do exist, and smart companies organize to take advantage of them. However, there will ultimately come a time when growth slows or stops. At this point, companies that have assumed that their industry—meaning their product—is the key to their success will begin to decline. As Levitt explains: "The history of every dead and dying growth industry shows a self-deceiving cycle of bountiful expansion and undetected decay." He identifies four conditions that typically assure this cycle:

- The belief that growth is assured by an expanding and more affluent population

- The belief that there is no competitive substitute for the industry's major product

- Excessive faith in mass production and the advantages of rapidly declining unit costs resulting from increased output

- Preoccupation with a product that lends itself to carefully controlled scientific experimentation, improvement, and manufacturing cost reduction

To prevent myopic decision making that leads to decay, companies must first be cognizant of these misleading assumptions. Simply relying on a growing population, or even expansion into new regions, is not adequate for long-term survival. Neither is cost cutting if the compensating demand is not there. Rather than focusing exclusively on their immediate competitors (those in the same industry), companies should be constantly on the lookout for new competitors that offer a substitute product or service—trucking over rail cargo transport, airplanes over trains for leisure travel. Finally, improvements in manufacturing alone won't guarantee success.

At this point, you might be thinking, all of this sounds fine, but how is a company to know where it should move and how it should broaden? Levitt addresses this issue in his accounts of primary examples—the railroads, Hollywood, petroleum, automobiles. In each case, the companies suffered because they were product oriented and not customer oriented. Adopting a customer orientation enables companies to think like customers, understanding their needs and trade-offs.

In terms of marketing, Levitt argues that the emphasis on *production* leads to an emphasis on *selling*—a phenomenon that modern marketers can identify with. This approach exacerbates the problem: "The difference between marketing and selling is more than semantic. Selling focuses on the needs of the seller, marketing on the needs of the buyer."[4]

Companies that avoid the pitfall of myopia come at things from the perspective of the customer. They offer not what they have to sell, but what the buyer wants. Again, although this may sound like a semantic difference, it is truly fundamental in a go-to-market plan. Levitt supports this contention by debunking a popular misunderstanding about Henry Ford, a manufacturing and entrepreneurial legend:

> We habitually celebrate him for the wrong reason—his production genius. His real genius was marketing. We think he was able to cut the selling price and therefore sell millions of $500 cars because his invention of the assembly line had reduced the costs. Actually he invented the assembly line because he had concluded that at $500 he could sell millions of cars. Mass production was the *result*, not the *cause* [my italics], of his low prices.

For an example of a company that truly understands its market, consider the case of Apple. The company was originally named Apple Computer, and, as its name suggests, it focused exclusively on selling computers. Over time, however, it broadened its vision to embrace other innovative products, such as music players, phones, tablets, and lots of music and movies online. To reflect this transformation, in 2007, the company changed its name from Apple Computer to simply Apple. By 2011, Apple sold more than four times as many iPods, iPhones, and iPads as Macs and MacBooks.[5] Moreover, its market cap and brand valuation hitall-time highs.

Levitt shined a light on what now seem like obvious failures of management. We often wonder how and why large companies or entire industries fade or fail. More often than not, the fundamental reason is a preoccupation with production, cost cutting, and selling, rather than understanding the evolving needs of customers. With such a seminal work at our disposal, the most egregious example of myopia may simply be the failure to read this piece and heed its warnings.

McCarthy and the Four Ps

What is marketing? Ask one hundred marketers, and you are likely to get one hundred different answers. Consult the dictionary, and you find stolid definitions like the following: "The commercial functions involved in transferring goods from producer to consumer."[6] But, what does that really mean? And what exactly would a head of marketing be in charge of?

In his 1960 book *Basic Marketing: A Managerial Approach,* E. Jerome McCarthy, a marketing professor at Michigan State University, created a simplified model and mnemonic for the key elements of marketing. His model is known as the Four Ps: product, price, place, and promotion. McCarthy's model was a simplification of earlier work on the key marketing ingredients, or "marketing mix," by Neil Borden from Harvard Business School.

Let's take a closer look at McCarthy's Four Ps.

> Product – Refers to the actual goods or services and how they relate to the end user's needs and wants. The scope of a product also includes supporting elements such as warranties, guarantees, and customer service.

> Price – Refers to the process of setting a price for a product, including discounts. Although most often price is described in terms of

currency, it doesn't have to be. What is exchanged for the product or services can be time, energy, or even attention.

Place – Indicates how the product gets to the customer, for example, point-of-sale placement and retailing. Also known as distribution, "place" can refer to the channel by which a product or service is sold (e.g., online vs. retail), the geographic region (e.g., Western Europe), or industry (e.g., financial services), and the target market segment (e.g., young adults, families, businesspeople).

Promotion – Refers to the various strategies for promoting the product, brand, or company, including advertising, sales promotion, publicity, personal selling, and branding.

In practice, the Four Ps should be thought of as four levers. To grow a business or to fix a faltering business, you need to employ one or more of the Four Ps. Moving those levers up or down as needed will have a direct impact on the business.

McCarthy's Four Ps are perhaps the most important concepts a marketer can master. You will be hard-pressed to find a more concise and durable definition of marketing. The Four Ps will serve you well when you need to determine whether you are working on the right things.

Crossing the Chasm – Geoffrey Moore (and Everett Rogers)

Geoffrey Moore is well-known in high-tech marketing circles. Many experts treat his seminal book, *Crossing the Chasm*, as the bible for bringing high-tech products to market. His identification of the "chasm" in the selling process is perhaps his most valuable contribution, and it has earned him his status as a modern marketing guru.

Just as McCarthy's model was based on Borden's prior work, *Crossing the Chasm*, published in 1991, is a refinement of the theories proposed by sociologist Everett Rogers. In his 1962 book *Diffusion of Innovations*, Rogers popularized the concept of the *innovation adoption life cycle*, also known as the *technology innovation lifecycle.* Diffusion of innovations is a theory that seeks to explain how, why, and at what rate new ideas and technology spread through cultures. Rogers's diffusion, or lifecycle, model is illustrated in figure 1.

Figure 1: Everett Rogers's diffusion of innovation model

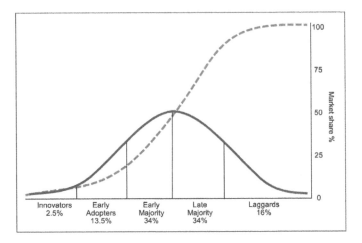

Interestingly, Rogers created the innovation adoption lifecycle to describe attitudes toward the purchase of hybrid seed by farmers in Iowa (though there is some dispute over whether the roots lie in corn or potato seeds). Therefore, although Moore popularized this model within the context of high technology, it can be applied to any industry where innovations are introduced.

Rogers's model displays a bell curve (the solid line) that covers five distinct categories of buyers, each of which makes up a percentage of the total market. The dashed line shows the eventual 100 percent saturation of a market. The categories are the innovators, early adopters, early majority, late majority, and laggards. Rogers defines an adopter category as a classification of individuals within a social system on the basis of innovativeness. An early adopter is more innovative than an early majority, for example.

Below is a summary of representation of Rogers's five categories.*

Innovators – Pursue new technology products aggressively. They sometimes seek out these products before the company has launched a formal marketing program. Technology is a central interest in their lives, regardless of what function it is performing. Although they represent less than 3 percent of all customers, winning them over at the outset of a marketing campaign is essential, because their endorsement reassures the other players in the marketplace that the product does, in fact, work.

Early adopters – Buy into new product concepts very early in their lifecycles, but, unlike innovators, they are not technologists—the kind of people who like new technology or inventions for their own sake. Rather, they are people who find it easy to imagine, understand, and appreciate the benefits of a new technology and to relate these potential benefits to their other concerns. Because they rely on their own intuition and vision, they are key to opening up any high-tech market segment.

Early majority – Share some of the early adopters' ability to relate to technology, but ultimately they are driven by a strong sense of practicality. They want to see well-established references before investing substantially. Because there are so many people in this segment—roughly one-third of the whole adoption lifecycle—winning their business is essential for the manufacturer to realize any substantial profits and growth.

---

* For the curious, Rogers's work contains richer psychographic profiles that are quite interesting.

Late majority – Share all the concerns of the early majority, plus one major additional one: Whereas people in the early majority are comfortable with their ability to successfully learn and use a technology product, members of the late majority are not. They wait until a product has become an established standard, and they tend to buy from large, well-established companies. Like the early majority, the late majority comprises about one-third of the total buying population.

Laggards – Simply don't want anything to do with new technology, for a variety of reasons, some personal and some economic. Sellers often dismiss laggards as not worth pursuing.

Moore's primary innovation to Rogers's model is in the introduction of gaps—or "three cracks and a chasm," as he puts it. The concept of gaps posits that companies do not smoothly sail from one adopter category to the next, effortlessly riding the bell curve to increased market share. Rather, the differences between the various categories constitute gaps that companies must jump over. They are not barriers that prevent passage. However, companies must make a concerted effort to jump from one category to the next. Moore's revised technology adoption lifecycle, which includes the cracks and the chasm, is illustrated in figure 2.

Figure 2: Geoffrey Moore's technology adoption lifecycle

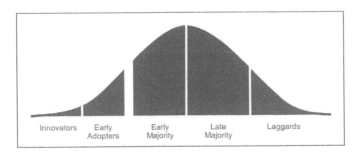

The first crack is a relatively small one between innovators and early adopters. It occurs when a new technology or innovation cannot be translated into a beneficial product. Moore offers Esperanto (the international language) and neural networks (the computer representation of the human brain) as examples. Both are technically fascinating, but neither offers any proven usefulness to the buyer. Esperanto was never widely used, and neural networks have still not provided the promised advances in artificial intelligence. These products only appeal to innovators because they tend to love technology for technology's sake.

The second crack occurs between the early majority and the late majority. Simply put, the late majority may not be willing to tolerate or work around product deficiencies and therefore may not buy the product. Moore uses programmable VCRs and desktop scanners as examples of products that struggled at this stage. Both were relatively mature products that offered features the late majority didn't necessarily value or care to learn to use. Devising a strategy to bring utility to this group by investing in the right things—simplification, integration, repackaging, whatever—is vital to a product's success.

In contrast to these relatively minor gaps, the chasm represents a formidable obstacle to companies looking to leap from the early adopter to the early majority. The early adopters look to technology and innovative new products as a change agent. They are willing to be champions in the face of opposition. In short, they are willing to go out on a limb and tolerate product flaws for a jump on the competition. By contrast, the early majority are looking for an incremental benefit, an evolutionary approach. The product needs to be more complete and mature to jump this chasm.

As the title suggests, Moore spends most of his efforts discussing how to cross the chasm from the early adopter to the early majority. He outlined a method that follows the steps below. Moore uses the WWII Allied invasion of Normandy, D-Day, as an analogy. In his view, crossing the chasm and entering a new market is an act of aggression, often with life-or-death consequences for the companies mounting the attack.

- Target the attack – You must choose a niche to use as a beachhead. As a start-up or new market entrant, you aren't likely to have the resources necessary to focus on a large market, so it's better to be more effective in a smaller one.

- Assemble an invasion force – Create a "whole product" that provides a solution to the customer's problems in its entirety. Early adopters might be happy stitching together different pieces, but early majority users are less likely to want to do so. Moore cites the PalmPilot as a whole product that provided advanced functionality without too much complexity. Focus not just on the product but also on support, training the entire customer experience. Apple's iPhone—which is part PDA, part phone, part music player, part computer—vanquished its competition (who themselves vanquished Palm) through a complete customer experience that to some just feels like magic.

- Define the battle – Create positioning to demonstrate that you are the leader in the segment you are attacking.

- Launch the invasion – Leverage a direct sales force, which is the best channel for selling high-tech products and for crossing the chasm.

It is essential for marketers who are looking to bring a new product to market to understand the technology adoption lifecycle. Specifically, they need to make a clear-eyed assessment of each market stage. If you find yourself on the wrong side of the chasm, then following Moore's guidance is the best way to cross. And, if you are not in the high-tech field, you can still benefit from this strategy. Remember Everett Rogers and his seeds.

Putting It into Practice

What can you do with all of this marketing wisdom? I certainly don't recommend running around your organization like a marketing pedant (though occasional table pounding is allowed). I do recommend that you internalize these lessons and look for opportunities to put them into practice.

Step back from the minutia of marketing execution from time to time to see the bigger picture. Take into account customer needs, market dynamics, the relationship of price to your product, and whether customers are ready for what you are building.

With this understanding, think of the levers at your disposal, and ask yourself whether ads and press releases (promotion) are truly your best strategy. Alternatively, should you focus on something more fundamental about your product or routes to market? Finally, if your department is restricted to creating direct mail pieces, press releases, and advertisements, then ask your CEO why your department is only in charge of one P when Drucker, Levitt, McCarthy, Moore, and Rogers knew better.

Learning More

+ Peter F. Drucker, *The Essential Drucker* (New York: Harper Business, 2001).

+ Theodore Levitt, "Marketing Myopia," *Harvard Business Review*, September–October 1975, 26–44.

+ William D. Perreault, Stanley J. Shapiro, and J. E. McCarthy, *Basic Marketing: A Managerial Approach* (Irwin Professional Publishing, 1986).

+ Geoffrey Moore, *Crossing the Chasm* (New York:Harper Business, 1991).

Chapter 2

Positioning and the Brand

When people hear your company name, what images or ideas come to their minds? More importantly, are these images the ones you want people to have? What people think about your company is perhaps the most important element not just in marketing but in business in general.

Positioning and its close cousin—brand—are the two of the most important assets your organization owns. *Positioning* is the place (or position) your product, service, or company holds in the mind of a customer. *Brand* is how they feel about your product, service, or company. Positioning is more cerebral, while brand is more visceral, even emotional. Take how men might choose a beer in a bar. Heavy or light? Budget or premium? A beer's positioning is how it is viewed in the context of all the beers on display. A beer's brand can convey a lot of other things—sportiness, exclusivity, worldliness, to name a few.

Marketers need to understand both positioning and brand to help sell their products. I like to think of positioning as making sure your product is in the running, and the brand as the deal closer. A strong brand attracts buyers. Brand loyalty is a long-term strategic asset that will continue to drive your business.

Despite this reality, many companies do not pay sufficient attention to their brand—what it means and what is required to maintain it. This behavior seems strange, because most businesspeople are envious of highly successful brands like Apple, Coke, and Mercedes. The problem is that, although brand is vital to market success, it is a topic that falls somewhere between elusive (for those being kind) to soft (for the cynics who like to make or count things). Most CMOs melt into a puddle when asking a gimlet-eyed board of directors to fund branding, because they are not able to effectively articulate its unequivocal value.

Understanding the importance of positioning and the brand and effectively conveying this understanding to your organization's leaders is imperative, because these elements create strategic advantage in the market. This chapter will cover both in detail and explain how companies can use them to get an edge on their competition.

Positioning

Positioning is sometimes referred to as the fifth P, along with product, price, place, and promotion. (Recall our discussion of McCarthy's model in chapter 1.) A product or company's position is how potential buyers perceive that product or company. Positioning is expressed relative to the position of the product or company's competitors. In marketing, positioning has come to mean the process by which marketers try to create an identity in the minds of their target market for their product, brand, or organization. As the masters of positioning Jack Ries and Al Trout explained, positioning is the process of creating an impression in a consumer's *mind*.[7]

The "positioning era" began in the early 1970s. Somewhere between the influential article "Positioning Is a Game People Play in Today's Me-too Marketplace," by Ries and Trout in *Industrial Marketing* in 1969, and an ad placed in the *New York Times* in 1971 by advertising giant David Ogilvy that proclaimed, "The results of your campaign depend less on how we write your advertising than on how your product is positioned," a fundamental shift had occurred, one that focused more on the position a product staked out in the market rather than simply the image it sought to convey.

To understand the impact of this shift, we need to briefly review the evolution of modern advertising. In the 1950s, advertising was very much focused on the product itself, as well as its features and benefits. With the increase in products and advertising generated by post-WWII prosperity, however, advertising the product was no longer sufficient. There was a glut of similar products in the prospective customer's mind. Efforts to address this problem led to the emergence of the "image era" of advertising, starting in the 1960s. In the image era, successful companies found their reputation, or "image," was more important in selling a product than any specific product feature. Ries and Trout identify David Ogilvy as the "architect of the image era."[8] Ogilvy saw each advertisement as an investment in the long-term image of a brand. Two of his more notable accounts that employed this strategy were Rolls-Royce and Schweppes.

But with too many companies jumping on the image bandwagon, an "image glut" formed in the marketplace, with no real distinction among similar products. Ries and Trout noted that "just as the 'me-too' products killed the product era, the 'me-too' companies killed the image era. As every company tried to establish a reputation for itself, the noise level became so high that relatively few companies succeeded."[9] As a result, there was a pressing need for a new approach. An answer to that need emerged: positioning.

Table 1 lists some common approaches to positioning. Note the use of superlatives—best, fastest, most.

Table 1: Common approaches to positioning

Approach	Example
The best / Best quality	Stradivarius violins
Best value ("Bang for the buck")	Ikea
Aspiration / Most luxurious	Rolex
Must-have	American Express
Fastest	Domino's

Positioning is the relative competitive comparison a product or company occupies in a given market as perceived by the target customer. Consequently, if a product is the leader in an existing category, then it has the leadership position. If it is not, then it can be positioned as the up-and-comer. Or, the company can create a new category in which the product can be the leader. An example of a company that employed this strategy with great success is Volvo. Realizing that they were entering an extremely crowded market, Volvo created a new category for its product—the safest car. Not the fastest or the most luxurious. But the safest.

Ries and Trout also emphasize that the mind has limited capacity; that is, it contains only a finite number of slots or positions for products to occupy. Among the vast number of products on the market, yours needs to occupy one of these slots.

To combat this crowding problem, sometimes a marketer needs to create a little room in the customer's mind—elbow his way in, so to speak. This approach is called *de-positioning* and refers to efforts to change the identity of competing products, relative to the identity of your own product, in the collective minds of the target market. Some marketers prefer de-positioning to positioning, and usually do so by claiming that some significant change in the market has transformed their product into the new number one.

A great example of effective de-positioning is the competition between Apple and Microsoft. Apple's 2006 "Get a Mac" campaign featured two actors named "Mac" and "PC" who anthropomorphized their computer namesakes. Mac was a younger, thinner, casually dressed twentysomething who was able to accomplish things easily. In contrast, PC was heavier, stodgier, wore glasses, and was more than a little dorky. Anything Mac could do would take PC longer, if he could do it at all. Apple used the campaign to change the definition of the personal computer, from simply one designed for use by an individual to one that had to be easy to use. Put simply, Apple added the dimension of ease of use to the equation. Apple was easy. PC was hard. Ease of use was paramount. Apple was number one. The Mac's market share increased 42 percent during the time the campaign ran.[10] In 2009, *AdWeek* named "Get a Mac" the campaign of the decade.

Table 2: Examples of positioning relative to competition

Company A	Position A	vs.	Company B	Position B
Subway	Healthy fast food		McDonald's	Value
Nike	Athletic performance		Vans	Hip, "Off the wall"
FedEx	Peace of mind		UPS	The logistics experts
BMW	Driving pleasure		Volvo	Safe and secure

Developing the Positioning Statement

A *positioning statement* is a short statement that demonstrates the value of what you offer, how it differs from your competition, and how it has a meaningful impact on your target audience. The positioning statement is an internal tool that you use to communicate your positioning. It codifies the customer benefit and the uniqueness of your product, service, brand, or company. It is the basis for all of your marketing messages and communications, including the development of a tag line. Other groups within your company can use the positioning statement to help them with their work. Your advertising team or agency, for example, can utilize the positioning statement as input to develop your advertisements. Understanding the target buyers, the value they see in your product, and how your product or service differs from competing products or services are essential components in creating a tag line that your target customers can identify with.

Developing a positioning statement requires a lot of hard work. The individuals involved need to question basic assumptions about their product or company, exchange opinions, resolve differences, and, most difficult of all, arrive at a final decision on a specific direction. Companies that lack the discipline needed to develop positioning and stick to a direction—and to the strategy that supports that direction—risk diffusing their marketing effort. The result is wasted time and, ultimately, wasted market opportunity.

The usual process for creating a positioning statement combines internal meetings and interviews with key stakeholders. Key stakeholders can include executives, founders, sales reps, and anyone you think really understands your customers and market. But even more important, and often missed, are interviews with customers, partners, and even prospects, if you can find them. Because the ultimate goal of positioning is to create a position in the mind of your customers or the market at large, understanding how your customers feel is essential to creating an effective statement.

Going further, you need to pay particular attention to your customers' needs—what they are seeking in a product like yours—and how they perceive your product as different. A very difficult challenge in the positioning process occurs when customers feel differently about your product, service, or company than your executives do. Who is right? Do the customers just not get it? Or, is the company not delivering? Perhaps the company has never clearly articulated its position. As difficult as these discussions can be, this process can be a crucible from which something better can emerge.

After you have collected all of this feedback, the process of crafting the statement starts. Ideally, you should appoint a small group to complete the task. Otherwise, the process may never end. In the initial meeting, the group should collect as many ideas on the position of the company as possible. Its next task is to take a stab at crafting the actual statement.

The positioning statement should be an honest reflection of your product, service, or brand. The key to a good statement is specificity: capture what your company delivers and how it differs from the competition. In addition to being informational, the statement can also be aspirational. For example, if your company has a three-year plan to add features to a product, grow your footprint, capture market share, or achieve some other objective, the positioning statement can reflect these goals.

There are two widely used templates for positioning statements:

> For (*target audience*), (*product/service/ brand*) is the (*frame of reference*) that delivers (*benefit/differentiator*) because only (*product/service/brand name*) is (*reason to believe*).

> For (*target audience*) who wants/needs (*reason to buy your product/service/brand*), the (*product/service/brand*) is a (*frame of reference*) that provides (*your key benefit*). Unlike (*your main competitor*), the (*product/service/brand*) provides (*your key differentiator*).

The positioning statement must convey the purpose and impact of your business quickly yet convincingly. For this reason, both templates are short and concise. The second template more directly addresses your key differentiator and the contrasts with your competition.

Both templates include the basic components below. The second template is more explicitly aimed against a competitor and breaks out its name and the differentiator.

- Target audience – The demographic or psychographic description of your desired customer. This is who your product, service, or brand is intended for, and it includes customers who most closely represent your product, service, or brand's most fervent users.

- Product/service/brand – What you're marketing. This might seem like a simple step, but take a few moments to reflect on exactly what you are attempting to position. Is it the product or service itself? Or, is it your company?

- Frame of reference – The category or market in which your product, service, or brand competes. Establishing a frame of reference helps provide context for your brand and relevance to your customers.

- Benefit/differentiator – The most compelling and motivating benefit your brand offers your target audience relative to your competition.

- Product/service/brand name – The name of the product, service, or brand you are positioning.

- Reason to believe – Proof that your product, service, or brand delivers what it promises.

Here is how I position this book:

> For *professional marketers* who *need to learn fundamental marketing skills, this book* is a *professional development tool* that *provides easy-to-understand and pragmatic advice to help them get their job done.* Unlike *searching through blogs or reading dozens of marketing texts,* The Professional Marketer *boils it down to provide a convenient and authoritative overview* that can be applied directly to the job at hand.

After you have crafted your statement, it is essential that you test it. If the statement is going to inform your go-to-market plan and guide your marketing efforts, then it has to hold up. To ensure that the statement works, you need to ask a number of critical questions:

- Is the statement clear?
- Does it focus on and motivate the core target audience?
- Does it provide a distinctive and meaningful picture of your product, service, or brand?
- Does it differentiate your brand from the competition?
- Is it credible?
- Does it allow for future growth?

The Brand

Now that we've covered positioning, let's talk about brand. Exactly what is a brand? This sounds like a simple question. After all, it's a term that's bandied about in marketing conversations all the time. However, people frequently don't truly appreciate what a brand is, what it isn't, and how it impacts marketing and sales.

Brand is one of the most misunderstood terms in marketing. In addition, it has multiple interpretations. Brand is frequently confused with positioning. The two terms are closely related, perhaps even two sides of the same coin. Nevertheless, there is a distinct difference between the two. Positioning is the place (or position) your product, service, or company holds in the mind of a customer. Brand is how they feel about your product, service, or company. Here's how Marty Neumeier, author of *The Brand Gap*, explains it: "A brand is a person's gut feeling about a product, service, or company."

As illustrated in figure 1, a brand needs to be unique, valuable to a customer, and defensible. It also has to be genuine, which, in my opinion, is the most important component. A brand has to feel right; it must be believable. Equally important, a brand needs to make an emotional connection with a buyer. For instance, consumers make an emotional connection with Coke, Mercedes, Rolex, Starbucks, and other great brands.

Figure 1: Characteristics of a brand

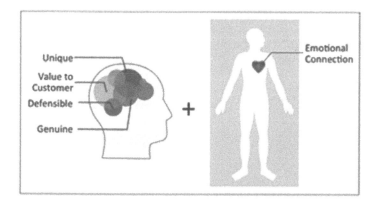

Another way to understand a brand is to think of a person. A person has a physical body. He or she also has a personality, reputation, beliefs, and a certain character. When you think of a person, you no doubt think of all of these things, probably unconsciously. Products and companies are much the same. There is the physical instantiation of a product—its "body"—that can be anything from a bar of soap to an aluminum can filled with soda to a fast convertible. In your mind you probably have already associated products with these examples. Ivory, Coke, and Porsche, perhaps? That's the power of a brand.

Like people, brands have personalities. Some are serious. Some are playful. Some are a bit boring but reliable. Brands have reputations, too. They can be friendly, customer oriented, on time, or any number of other things. Note that we are highlighting positive characteristics. However, brands can inherit negative characteristics over time, due to inattention or poor business execution by the brand's creator. Finally, brands, like people, can age. They can become old, tired, and irrelevant, which is why they need to be maintained. The Oldsmobile brand—the name itself a liability—was retired by General Motors in 2004.

Before proceeding with this discussion, we need to distinguish between a brand and a logo, because even many marketers confuse the two. A *logo* is a symbol or other small design adopted by an organization to identify itself, its products, or its services. A logo is a part of the *brand identity*. Along with supporting colors, fonts, and other graphical elements of the brand identity, a logo helps a consumer spot Starbucks from a mile down a Hong Kong street, or makes an advertisement feel as though it was created by Apple. Although a logo can be the most recognizable component of a brand, there is much more to a brand than a logo. You don't feel the way you do about Apple because of the logo.

We are all influenced by brands. When we purchase products, we make decisions that reflect our feelings toward particular brands, what we know of them, and what we've come to expect if we have already purchased a product or service from that brand.

Two important concepts related to brands are brand promise and brand equity. *Brand promise* refers to what people have come to expect from a product or company. It is the sum of people's interaction and experience, or what they have heard from others if they are not a customer. It's what convinces customers to keep coming back or perhaps to try a product for the first time. It's also what might keep them away. On May 11, 1996, ValuJet Flight 592 from Miami to Atlanta crashed into the Everglades. The DC-9 disappeared from the radar and into the wilds of the Everglades, resulting in the loss of 110 people. The company is now known as AirTran. The damage to consumer confidence was so bad the company renamed itself.

Brand equity is the set of assets (and liabilities) linked to a brand's name and symbol that adds to or subtracts from the value of a product or service. These assets are grouped into four major categories:

- Brand name awareness
- Brand loyalty
- Perceived quality
- Brand associations[11]

Having strong brand equity means that people have heard of you, will buy from you again if they are existing customers, will consider buying from you if they are not, and will remain loyal as you extend your brand with new products.

It's clear that brands are valuable. But, how can this value be measured? Interbrand, a global branding consultancy, pioneered brand valuation. They created a process that takes into account the financial performance of the brand—either a company or a product—the role of the brand in the purchasing process, and the overall strength of the brand, measured using a methodology from Interbrand or other brand monitoring firms. Table 3 displays the values of the top ten global brands, based on Interbrand's 2011 report. Are these the brands you expected to see? Why or why not?

Table 3: Ranking and value of top ten global brands

Rank	Previous Rank	Brand	Country	Sector	Brand Value ($m)
1	1	Coca-Cola	US	Beverages	71,861
2	2	IBM	US	Business Services	69,905
3	3	Microsoft	US	Computer Software	59,087
4	4	Google	US	Internet Services	55,317
5	5	GE	US	Diversified	42,808
6	6	McDonald's	US	Restaurants	35,593
7	7	intel	US	Electronics	35,217
8	17	Apple	US	Electronics	33,492
9	9	Disney	US	Media	29,018
10	10	hp	US	Electronics	28,479

Source: Interbrand, "Best Global Brands 2011"

Building and Maintaining a Brand

Every organization needs to pay attention to its brand. The degree to which your organization's management values its brand will depend primarily on two factors: the size of your organization, and the industry you are in. Smaller organizations tend to devote less attention to their brands than larger organizations. Consumer products and service businesses tend to appreciate their brands more than other businesses.

How should an organization build and maintain its brand? A basic approach is for management to insist on manufacturing or providing great products or services and to ensure that every employee is living up to the organization's values. For people looking for a more structured approach, David Aaker, a marketing professor at the University of California at Berkeley, and the author of *Building Strong Brands*, has developed a comprehensive brand-identity planning model, which we reproduce in figure 2. The planning starts with a strategic analysis of customers, competitors, and the company itself.

At the heart of Aaker's model is a fourfold perspective on the concept of a brand. To help ensure that a firm's brand identity has texture and depth, Aaker advises brand strategists to consider the brand as:

- a product;
- an organization;
- a person;
- a symbol.

Each perspective is distinct. The purpose of Aaker's system is to help brand strategists consider different brand elements and patterns that can help clarify, enrich, and differentiate an identity. Once a company has defined its brand, the marketing team should create a detailed brand identity document and communicate it to other members of the organization, including the CEO and other executives.

Figure 2: Aaker's brand identity planning model

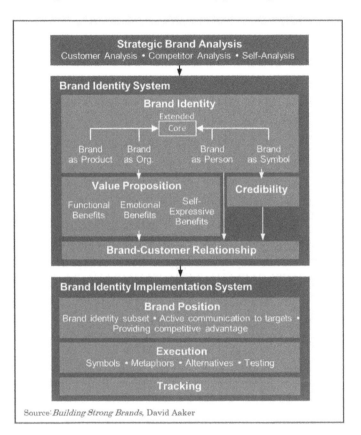

Source: *Building Strong Brands*, David Aaker

To understand how Aaker's system works, look at the "Brand Identity" box and think of a famous brand. Let's use Harley-Davidson* as an example. Can you visualize the product—a Harley-Davidson motorcycle—and think of what makes it unique? You could probably fill a page. How about the organization? "Independent" and "American" come to mind. In addi-

---

* Harley-Davidson is not a bad example. Interbrand's 2012 report ranked it ninety-sixth with a brand worth $3.8 billion.

tion, there is a certain type of person you associate with a Harley—tough, independent. And, of course, we are familiar with the Harley-Davidson logo, which many customers tattoo on their bodies. Talk about brand loyalty!

Maintaining your brand requires a lot of work, across many disciplines, across multiple departments, inside and outside of marketing. It involves a lot more than simply advertising or public relations. In fact, it's not just about marketing. It's about your product, how your customers feel about your salespeople, whether they got a good deal, and how often they hear about you. If you think about it, maintaining your brand focuses on how your customers experience the Four Ps we discussed in chapter 1.

One reason that maintaining your brand can be so challenging is that there are so many factors that can impact your brand. Figure 3 presents the most critical factors in a visual format. The different sizes of the boxes represent emphasis—or importance—which will vary depending on your business. Reliability might be the most important factor for an airline or broadband Internet supplier. Advertising is probably more important than product quality for bar soap. Companies that sell to other businesses through a direct sales force need to make sure their salespeople are well informed and responsive.

As you think about managing your brand, don't forget about groups like technical support or customer service. How they treat customers is a reflection of your brand. Finally, bad customer experiences can have a dramatic impact on your brand. As an often-invoked Warren Buffett caution goes, "It takes twenty years to build a reputation, and five minutes to ruin it."

Figure 3: What makes a brand?

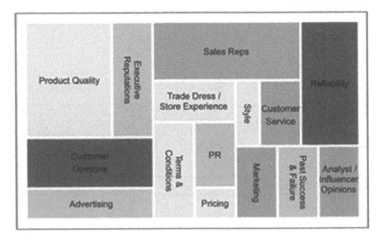

Finally, with the rise of social media, consumers have a much greater voice than ever before. Companies can no longer control their message and their brand image via conventional PR and advertising. Rather, marketers need to devise strategies to mediate and influence consumers who write or comment using social media. Some marketers refer to this process as "managing the dialogue" about the brand, which is very different from controlling the brand image. Companies have taken to monitoring social media, looking for potential influencers, and "putting out fires" with unhappy customers as fast as possible. Good customer service and a small gift or waived fee can turn even the angriest customer into a champion. We will discuss this concept further in chapter 7.

Identity Systems

An *identity system*, sometimes called the *corporate identity*, codifies the visual expression of an organization's brand. The logo constitutes the bulk of the identity, and it should be able to stand on its own. However, the full identity encompasses far more than the logo. The following list identifies the key components of an identity system.

- Logo – An image, like the Nike "swoosh," or a *wordmark,* like the script Coca-Cola, that represents a brand, company, or organization.

- Visual elements – Additional graphical elements—whether lines, shapes, icons, or cartoon characters—may be part of the identity and can be used across a range of media.

- Color palette – Consistent use of colors is important to an identity. Imagine if McDonald's turned blue or Starbucks suddenly became red.

- Sounds – A *jingle* is a short tune used in advertising and for other commercial uses. Though less common today, some jingles, like Roto-Rooter's, have survived long enough to become critical to the identity. More recently, a short sequence of notes—referred to as chimes or tones or audio trademarks—has become popular. Intel's five-note tone, NBC's three-note chime, and ESPN's six-note *da-na-na, da-na-na* are unmistakable.

- Package design – Sometimes the package itself is distinctive enough to support the identity. The most famous example is the Coca-Cola "contour" bottle, which is trademarked. Coke even prints it on their soda cans!

- Document design – The physical appearance of reports, white papers, letters, e-mail templates, data sheets, and brochures reinforces the identity. For this reason, it should be specified. Critical design elements include margins, logo placement, acceptable and unacceptable types of graphics, and fonts. Some companies even have a font created exclusively for them.

In addition to these basic components, business identities can incorporate other features. For example, restaurants, airlines, and other service businesses express their brand with their uniforms. Store design—including lighting and music—can reflect the corporate identity. For retail businesses, the design of the signs, storefront, and store interior constitutes what is known as *trade dress.* Trade dress is so critical to brand identity that it is legally defined as defensible intellectual property.

Applying the identity system consistently is very important. Marketing teams should create a style-and-usage guide that clearly specifies how to accomplish this task. Guides should contain the following information:

◆ The proper and improper use of logos, in a variety of applications, such as print, online, and signage

◆ How and where visual elements are used

◆ When certain colors of the palette are used

In addition, they should include as much additional detail as the organization feels appropriate. Marketing communications, corporate communications, and/or the branding team usually have responsibility for maintaining the proper use of the identity. This role has earned these departments the affectionate nickname "brand police."

Case Study

Virgin America is a California-based airline that has a declared mission to make flying good again. Launched in 2007, the airline's goal was to disrupt the airline industry. Though hypercompetitive, the airline industry had become sclerotic. According to the American Customer Satisfaction Index, in 2011, the American airline industry had lower customer satisfaction than the IRS and US Postal Service.[12] This presented an opportunity for an airline that would emphasize customer service and the flying experience.

Flying Virgin America is like flying no other airline. From the moment you check in, you notice the difference—rock music plays at the self-service check-in kiosks. The planes have pink mood lighting (a seemingly small but important part of the Virgin America brand identity that was important enough to take the time for regulatory approval). The safety video is clever and funny. It has over five hundred thousand views on YouTube. Think about that—no one pays attention to safety videos on the plane, but someone put

Virgin America's on YouTube, and it has been viewed by half a million people! (Creating buzzworthy content is discussed in chapter 7.)

According to Virgin America VP of Marketing and Communications Luanne Calvert, the goal was to disrupt the industry and differentiate the airline from all others. Brand was key to this. Virgin America extended its branding to every bit of the customer experience, including elements like music, mood lighting, and humor. To achieve its mission of making flying fun again, Virgin America sought to let people take their on the-ground experience up in the air with them. Why couldn't air travel be relaxing, comfortable, and fun? Music, lighting, leather seats, and humor were important elements.

Virgin America had another, unique challenge. The airline inherited some brand elements from its parent company, Sir Richard Branson's Virgin Group (technically, due to US government restrictions prohibiting foreign control of US airlines, Virgin Group is a minority owner). Branson himself has cultivated a sexy, adventurous brand with a bit of cheek that works well for many of its businesses. But Virgin America had some unique requirements.

According to Calvert, the airline ran the risk of seeming exclusionary or aloof if it did not add friendliness to the brand's personality. Stressed-out or fearful flyers also respond well to friendly staff. Obviously, based on ACSI's findings, friendliness was on the wane in the airline industry.[†]

The company also cultivated two additional brand personality elements—being clever and provocative. The safety video and mood lighting serve as examples of Virgin America's cleverness. Its ads seek to provoke change in the industry, asking questions like, why can't airline food be as good as food you can get in the airport or at a local restaurant? This provocateur stance suits the upstart airline.

The brand torch is carried throughout the entire organization. Every employee understands the importance of the brand, from the airport staff to the flight crew to the executive team. Calvert's brand management team oversees

---

[†] United, the largest airline in the United States, perhaps had a part to play in opening up an opportunity for Virgin America. It dropped its "Friendly Skies" campaign in 1997, after thirty years. It was revived, perhaps due to Virgin's success, after United and Continental merged.

the brand and helps maintain its key elements of being friendly, clever, and provocative.

The team and Virgin America's agency also create unique digital and live experiential showcases to let potential customers experience Virgin America. Because so much of the Virgin America brand *is* the airport experience, Calvert's team has been working on ways to bring that experience to prospective customers outside the airport. These efforts include an interactive online video called "VX Experience" that is half party, half airplane, and the Virgin America Club Level at AT&T Park, home of the San Francisco Giants, where the signature Virgin America mood lighting creates a unique atmosphere.

The results have been impressive. Since launching in August 2007, Virgin America has captured a host of travel industry best-in-class awards, including: "Best Domestic Airline" in *Condé Nast Traveler*'s Reader's Choice Awards for five consecutive years, "Best Business/First Class" in *Condé Nast Traveler*'s Business Travel Poll for five consecutive years, "Best Domestic Airline" in *Travel + Leisure*'s World's Best Awards for five consecutive years, and #1 in Class in Zagat's Global Airlines Survey in 2008, 2009, and 2010.

Calvert says the company also measures Net Promoter Score (also covered in chapter 7) among its Elevate frequent-flier program members. Virgin America is number one by a long shot over their closest competitors, JetBlue and Southwest.

Learning More

- David Aaker, *Brand Relevance: Making Competitors Irrelevant* (San Francisco: Jossey-Bass, 2011).

- David Aaker, *Building Strong Brands* (New York:Free Press, 1996).

- Seth Godin, *Purple Cow* (London:Penguin Books, 2007).

- Marty Neumeier, *The Brand Gap* (Berkeley:New Riders, 2006).

- Al Ries and Jack Trout, *Positioning:The Battle for Your Mind* (New York:Warner Books, 1982).

Chapter 3

Market Sizing and Segmentation

There is a common sin that marketers frequently commit. In their rush to build a website or create an attractive logo, they forget something very important: who is the buyer? These marketers are firing without aiming. They are being tactical and not strategic. Sometimes they are simply shooting to make it seem as if they are doing *something*.

To build an effective marketing strategy, you need to understand who will be buying your product. This means, among other things, that you need to calculate how big the potential market is for your product or service and how much of that market will be contested by your competitors. And, if you are really good, you will learn not just *who* those buyers are but *why* they purchase the goods and services they do.

Market Segmentation

A *market* is a place where trade takes place. Markets are dependent on two major participants—buyers and sellers. *Market segmentation* is what the name suggests—understanding the overall potential market for your product and determining which subsets, or segments, of that market are most likely to buy from you.

This chapter covers both business-to-business (B2B) and business-to-consumer (B2C) markets. Some businesses sell only to other businesses, while some sell only to *consumers*—individuals who buy products or services for personal use. Some, like Dell, sell to consumers and to other businesses.

Businesses and consumers are both buyers, and once they have purchased, both become *customers*.

Market segmentation varies somewhat depending on whether you are selling B2C or B2B. Regardless, most of the core concepts are the same. You will just be segmenting using different criteria.

For B2B markets, there are three fundamental characteristics of the customer that your company should know: location, company size, and industry. Let's take a closer look at each one.

> Location – Where is the company located? Most commonly, marketers perform this segmentation at the country level. For smaller businesses with less reach, or for certain types of products or services, however, segmentation can be performed on the level of a state, a province, or even a city. In some cases, segmentation considers whether the target company is located in a major metropolitan area, a suburb, an exurb, or a rural area, although this level of segmentation is more common for B2C markets.
>
> Company size – Is the company a small business, a midsized business, or a large enterprise? This information is valuable, because it helps the seller determine whether its products meet the target company's needs and the target company can afford them. Although definitions of these three segments vary, the most common breakdown is:
>
> ◆ small businesses have fewer than 100 employees;
>
> ◆ midsized businesses have 101 to 1000 employees;
>
> ◆ enterprises have more than 1000 employees.
>
> Some marketers divide one or more of these categories into subsegments. For example, the small office / home office (SOHO) segment is a small business with fewer than ten employees. Other marketers add segments; for example, large enterprises for companies with more than five thousand employees. (FYI: all of the Forbes Global 2000 fall

within this subsegment.) Which system you adopt depends on the nature of your organization, its products and/or services, and its goals and strategies. The most basic rule is to use segments that make sense for your business.

Industry – Different industries have different needs, and knowing which industries need your products and services is a critical aspect of segmentation. You can obtain lists of industries—and subindustries—from a number of sources. The most common source is the Standard Industrial Classification (SIC) code. The US government created the SIC codes in 1937 to establish a standard system that all federal agencies and departments would use to classify industries. All SIC codes consist of four digits. For example, the industry SIC code for Metal Mining is 1000. Within this industry are numerous subindustries, such as Gold and Silver Ores (1040) and Miscellaneous Metal Ores (1090).*

For B2C markets, marketers typically employ a different set of characteristics. Because these marketers are targeting people and not companies, they need to adopt a more granular and more "human" approach to segmenting. To accomplish this task, they focus on four sets of characteristics: geographic, demographic, psychographic, and behavioral.

Geographic – This segment largely parallels "location" in business-to-business marketing. In the case of consumers, however, the marketer might place greater emphasis on whether a person lives in an urban, a suburban, an exurban, or a rural area. Marketers of some products and services (e.g., bathing suits, snowmobiles, ignition block warmers) may also be interested in climate.

---

* In 1997, a new six-digit system called the North American Industry Classification System (NAICS) was introduced. NAICS codes have largely replaced SIC codes, although most people still refer to the codes as "SIC codes." NAICS was jointly developed by the United States, Canada, and Mexico to facilitate trade among these nations following the creation of NAFTA. The codes for Gold Mining and Silver Mining are broken out in NAICS, 212221 and 212222 respectively.

Demographic – There is a whole list of characteristics that you will likely want to know about your buyer, including age, gender, marital status, education, occupation, income, ethnicity, and religion. In the case of age, for example, marketers have identified different cohorts, ranging from Baby Boomers (born in the baby boom between 1946 and 1964) to Generation X (the disaffected and directionless generation that followed) to the Millennials (aka Generation Y, they grew up with digital technology). In some cases, marketers create segments by combining two or more demographic characteristics. A well-known example is DINKS (dual income, no kids). With two incomes and no child-related expenses, DINKS represent a vital market segment for luxury products, such as international travel and two-seater luxury sports cars.

Psychographic – Psychographic segmentation groups customers according to their lifestyle. Basic psychographic characteristics include activities, interests, opinions, attitudes, and values. The tool that marketers most frequently use to create psychographic profiles is the activities, interests, opinions (AIO) survey, which is sometimes called a "lifestyle survey." Significantly, critics charge—with some justification—that psychographic segmentation can come across as marketing hocus-pocus. The fact remains, however, that identifying and understanding psychographic characteristics are essential if you want to understand your buyers' behaviors. A seminal lifestyle survey in the early 1970s by Joseph Plummer found that male users of bank credit cards saw themselves as modern, risk taking, and upwardly mobile. Plummer encouraged banks to promote these aspects of their cards while also using marketing to change traditional concepts of money and the perceived limitations of the typical conservative lifestyle to bring on new customers.[13] Credit card companies took this to heart, and we have all seen credit card usage move from the occasional large or "emergency" purchase to the everyday purchase in our lifetime. Table 1 summarizes the most common elements of AIO surveys.[14] Marketers can create questions that probe various elements to look for new insights or test hypotheses.

Table 1: Elements of activities, interests, opinions (AIO) surveys

Activities	Interests	Opinions
Work	Family	Themselves
Hobbies	Home	Social issues
Social events	Job	Politics
Vacation	Community	Business
Entertainment	Recreation	Economics
Club membership	Fashion	Education
Community	Food	Products
Shopping	Media	Future
Sports	Achievements	Culture

Behavioral – This segmentation is based on actual customer behavior toward products. Behavioral segmentation focuses on a few fundamental factors, including, but not limited to:

+ brand loyalty;
+ whether the customer is a first-time or repeat buyer;
+ the benefits the customer is seeking;
+ holidays or events that affect purchases;
+ the customer's readiness to buy.

Behavioral segmentation is most closely related to the product itself, and it is a fairly straightforward approach to segmenting. Consider, for example, repeat buyers with high brand loyalty. No matter where they are or what they believe, they are a highly desirable market segment.

Market Sizing

Clearly, identifying the viable markets and market segments for your products and/or services is essential to your company's success. Regardless of the markets in which you operate, however, it is essential that you have an accurate knowledge of their size.

It's probably safe to assume that everyone wants to do business in a large and fast-growing market. However, it is possible to make money in a niche or a nascent market. You can also be successful if you introduce a revolutionary product that is just the tonic for customers who are fleeing a declining market. The point is, you can make money in all types of markets.

How can you determine how large your target market is? There are several standard metrics you can use to measure markets.

Total available market (TAM) – This is the total size of the market. It is also referred to as *total addressable market.*

Served available market (SAM) – Also known as *served addressable market,* the SAM is the total size of the market that is currently being served, or sold to. It is a portion of the TAM, and therefore it is always smaller. For example, according to the research firm IDC, 659.8 million smartphones were shipped in 2012, up 33.5 percent from the 494.2 million units shipped in 2011.[15] Assuming all of these are sold, then the SAM is 659.8 million, plus the smartphones previously sold, minus the number taken out of service. A big number, but nothing compared with a potential TAM in the billions if every adult in the world owned one.

Share of market (SOM) – More commonly referred to as *market share*, this is the percentage of the market that a given company owns.

Market growth – This is the rate by which the TAM is growing. It is typically calculated on an annual basis and expressed as *compound annual growth rate* (CAGR, pronounced "ka-grr").

Figure 1: Market sizing graph – composite TAM, SAM, SOM, and CAGR

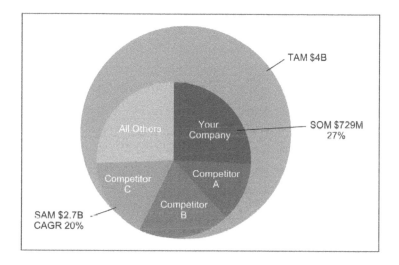

You can obtain many of these numbers from analysts who follow your industry or product. If you are selling something new, you may need to extrapolate or combine research to create an approximation, or "comp," of your market.

A bit of advice to those of you who create marketing plans: Never walk into the boardroom with only the TAM. From personal experience, I can tell you this is one of the fastest ways to get thrown out of said boardroom. You need to understand the market dynamics—what your competitors are doing, price pressures, the strength of your brand—better than that. Also, never say the following: "This market is so big; if we captured only one percent of it, we'd all be rich." I know more than one venture capitalist who stops listening to your pitch at that point. No one goes into business to get a 1 percent share, and presenting this argument suggests that you don't have a very sound strategy.

An accurate knowledge of market size is critical to understanding the dynamics of a market—current or new—and assessing whether there is room for growth. Good markets are typically large and have a gap between the TAM and the SAM. This gap represents sales opportunity for your business. Opportunity also arises when the vendor with the largest SOM is vulnerable and your company feels it can take away market share based on an advantage in your product, price, or distribution. Another strategy for stealing market share is aggressive promotion. One of the best examples of this strategy is the market share gained by online insurance companies such as GEICO and Progressive. With essentially the same product, offered for a bit less via direct sales as opposed to agents, aggressive promotion via television advertising enabled these companies to dramatically increase their market share. As of 2011, GEICO is the third largest auto insurance provider in the United States, and is growing at 7 percent, while the CAGR for the overall auto insurance market is only 1 percent.[16] GEICO is stealing market share.

The best way to size markets is to perform both a top-down and a bottom-up analysis. Find analyst reports that provide the TAM, growth rate, and market share, if they are available. Then, balance that top-down approach with your own bottom-up calculations based on your price, manufacturing capacity, and sales reach.

The Buyer Persona

Thus far we have established that to create a successful marketing campaign, you need to become familiar with both the composition and the size of your market. Knowing your *market*, however, is not the same as knowing your *buyers*. It is one thing to know which country buyers live in, which industry they operate in—even their age. But, what does that tell you about what they think and what motivates them to buy?

In B2B scenarios, marketers are guilty of targeting companies and departments within companies without truly understanding who the actual buyers are. Even when B2B marketers know the titles of their target customers, what else do they really know about them? How do these customers view products such as yours? How do they buy? Do they even have the authority to buy? Are there any other obstacles in the way?

In B2C marketing, knowing the age, gender, and hometown of your buyer tells you only so much. Even knowing their interests may be enough to segment them adequately. For example, consider all the cohort of female twentysomethings in your area who like to read. Beyond this single common characteristic, they could be completely different individuals. If you are trying to sell them an e-reader, like Amazon's Kindle, knowing what they read, how often they read, and if they travel would be very useful. High-income voracious readers looking to lighten their load on business trips would be a good persona to target.

How can marketers acquire a better understanding of prospective buyers and their behaviors? One effective strategy is to create a composite profile, or archetype, known as the *buyer persona*. The buyer persona clarifies who the buyers really are, what motivates them, how they think and talk, and what issues they face in their jobs, for B2B, and everyday lives, for B2C. Marketing that takes these factors into account will be more effective.

The best way to start the process for a B2B market—assuming you are working for an established business with existing customers—is to interview a few salespeople to find out whom they typically sell to. If you sell via retail to consumers, then you may need to talk to the sales associates on the floor. If you are a new company, or if you are bringing out a new product with a different buyer, you will need to make some assumptions based on your knowledge of the market. You can also analyze competing or similar products to obtain insight into the behaviors of the people who purchase them. In each scenario, you are looking to identify the profile that most often buys your product. Knowing more about these individuals will make your marketing more effective in many ways—buying the right lists, creating meaningful tools, speaking their language, and teaching new salespeople the traits of their prospective customers.

Interviews are critical to developing a good buyer persona. Actually speaking with the buyers can uncover insights that would never come to light otherwise. Yet, many marketers never take this step. Why not? One obvious reason is that contacting real buyers is a difficult and challenging task. You need to find buyers who are willing to talk, as well as sales reps who are comfortable allowing their marketing people to speak directly to their customers. Another challenge is the potential embarrassment associated with asking questions that the buyer assumes you should know. (So, why did you buy our product?) You need to make a concerted effort to overcome these challenges. Rest assured, the results are worth it.

One vital rule in conducting effective interviews is to make certain that you are speaking to the actual buyer. This might sound obvious, but not all sales reps know who these individuals are. Especially at larger accounts, where one salesperson may be in charge of the relationship for his or her company, he or she may deal only with the top person, and this person may not be the decision-making buyer.

Interviews should be conducted by the marketing team without the sales rep present (if possible). You don't want a sales rep jumping in and answering questions you put to the buyer. Interviewing buyers over the phone and face-to-face are both fine. It is always better, however, to have a dedicated notetaker present so that the interviewer can focus on developing rapport with the buyers. Here are some sample questions for B2B buyers, organized by theme:

Role and Responsibility
- What is your role? What responsibilities do you have?

- What department are you in? What does your reporting structure look like?

- What is the biggest challenge to getting your job done?

Key Initiatives and Objectives
- What are your key initiatives? How do they relate to your business?

- What are the major hurdles to your accomplishing them?

- How does your organization measure success?

Buying Process and Decision Criteria
- What made you decide to buy a product like ours? What factors drove that decision?

- Take me back to the day you decided to start looking for products like ours. When was that, and how did it happen?

- What was it that finally convinced you to buy our product?

- Who else got involved in the decision and why?

Wild Cards
- If you could change one thing about your job, what would it be?

- How do you think your role compares with those of your peers?

- What advice would you give to college graduates looking to land a job like yours?

The questions you ask can take any form you think will give you the background and insight you are looking for. You will likely not get through all of them in an interview. Asking open-ended questions and listening carefully are essential to getting beyond merely courteous answers. You should probe and ask deeper second-level questions to get to the heart of the matter. Most important, just get the subject talking, telling his or her story. After you have conducted half a dozen interviews, you probably will have accumulated enough material to build a profile. How many interviews you conduct, and if you segment by market or geography, are decisions you will need to make based on the nature of your business.

The buyer persona should be compiled into a short document that other members of the sales and marketing teams can reference. Content—insights—is more important than format, but a good B2B persona should contain the following:

- ◆ Profile – A brief description of the person—what the person's title or role is, whom he or she reports to, typical career path, age range, and other useful details. Some people choose to name their personas for easy reference and to get to "know" them as a person. In my experience, I have found that this strategy more often than not causes cynicism on the part of those outside the process. A common mistake is to spend too much time on this piece of the persona, and not enough on the items below, which are where the real insights come from.

- ◆ Role and responsibility – What is this person's job, and what is he or she responsible for? Understanding this completely, even in areas that don't directly pertain to your product, can offer critical insights.

For example, a nurse might make a recommendation to a doctor on a new piece of equipment, unofficially, and have some influence.

+ Career aspirations – Who does this person want to be when he or she grows up? Perhaps your product can help this person get there. This can be the most powerful insight you gain from the interview. People always act on their personal motives.

+ Purchasing process – Where does this person find information about products like yours (you should be advertising there), and how does he or she buy products like yours (make sure you have the right channel)?

+ Blockers – What makes this person's job difficult (time in the day, people, process), and what rivalries might exist with others? It is amazing what you will find out, and removing these blockers with your product or process can help ramp up your revenue.

Buying Center

In B2B sales, there is rarely just one person—or persona—involved in the buying process. The *buying center* is a formalization of that concept. Many people with different roles and priorities participate in purchasing decisions. Unlike consumer buying, where the consumer, either alone or with assistance or influence from acknowledged opinion leaders, makes his or her own purchase decisions, in business buying, a group often determines which products or services the business purchases.

A typical business buying center includes a variety of participants:

+ Initiators – people who begin the purchase process by defining a need (These individuals are sometimes called the "champions," and they serve as coaches to the sales team throughout the process.)

+ Decision makers – people who make the final decisions

+ Gatekeepers – people who control the flow of information and access to individuals in an organization

- Influencers – people who have input into the purchase decision

- Purchasing agent – the person who actually creates the purchase order

- Budget owner – the person whose budget is paying for the purchase (There can be multiple owners if several departments are funding the purchase.)

- Users – people who ultimately use the product or service

In many situations, people play more than one role in business purchasing decisions. Depending on an organization's structure and the importance of the decision being made, a buying center can include few or many layers of management. Sometimes, buying centers are formal committees created to make a purchase decision. Some members of a buying center will participate throughout the decision-making process, whereas others will be involved only briefly. Technical staff may evaluate potential products for purchase and influence the decision, but then leave the actual purchase to the decision makers, budget owner, and purchasing agent.

Every company has a different buying process and therefore a different buying center. But, eventually, a pattern will emerge. Ensuring that your marketing efforts take into account all of the players in the buying center is very important. For example, ads may need to reach not only users but also budget owners. As another example, your sales team may need to have different conversations with different members of the buying center. In general, the fewer the people in the buying center, the faster the sales cycle. Aligning your product so that the decision maker, budget owner, and user are the same can also be a very effective strategy. The CEO might be the initiator, decision maker, budget owner, and user of a new private jet.

Case Study

A 2005 article in the *Washington Post* revealed that the consumer electronics firm Best Buy had jumped on the buyer persona bandwagon.[17] In an effort to increase retail sales, Best Buy had profiled its customers and then used this information to identify four customer archetypes. The company also decided that there were certain unprofitable customer types whom they would stop reaching out to.

So, meet Buzz, Barry, Ray, and Jill, Best Buy's four personas:

- Buzz – the young tech enthusiast
- Barry – the wealthy professional man
- Ray – the family man
- Jill – a soccer-mom type who is the primary shopper for the family but usually avoids electronics stores

What makes Best Buy's program interesting is how far the company took the concept. Not only did the company tailor its marketing efforts and advertising to appeal to the four personas, the company also modified its store design and sales training to take Buzz, Barry, Ray, and Jill into account. Here's what they did.

The first step was to redesign, or reconfigure, each store to appeal to one or more of the personas. For brevity, we'll focus on what they did to appeal to Jill.

Best Buy analyzed local demographics and store purchase histories to determine which of the four personas would be the best customers for that location. Stores where Jill would be the target customer showed *The Incredibles* and *SpongeBob SquarePants* on the display televisions to appeal to the children Jill brought with her. They also turned the background music down a notch and included Jill's favorites, like James Taylor and Mariah Carey. In addition, they set up nooks to look like dorms or recreation rooms where Jill and the children could play with the latest high-tech gadgets at their leisure. Finally, the stores placed a higher concentration of kitchen appliances on the floor.

In addition to modifying the store design, these stores assigned a specialized sales staff, known as personal shopping associates, to assist Jill. These assistants wore pastels instead of the royal blue shirts that other salespeople in the store sported. They were stationed at an island in the center of the store that was decorated with fake purple flowers and stuffed animals. The personal shopping associates were trained to understand Jill—that she shops for electronics only a few times a year, but she spends a lot of money when she does. Because the Jill persona typically does not understand electronics well, or does not have all the details, the associates asked basic questions and then provided recommendations.

This creative strategy produced immediate results. In one of the pilot stores, less than a year after the redesign was rolled out in October 2005, Jills increased their spending by 30 percent. This increased spending helped boost the store's revenue to what was expected to be $75 million to $80 million in the year, up from around $50 million a year before the redesign. In addition, it helped push the customer loyalty rating of the store to among the top five in the country.

Nationwide, such "customer-centric" stores experienced an 8.4 percent increase in sales in the second quarter, compared with the same period in the previous year. Stores designed for the other three personas showed similar gains.

Learning More

◆ Adele Revella, *The Buyer Persona Manifesto* (Friday Harbor, WA: Buyer Persona Institute, 2011), e-book

Chapter 4

Marketing Planning

Creativity is a trait most people would include in the psychographic profile of a marketer. After all, we are the ones responsible for slick advertising, eye-catching graphics, and clever promotions. However, there are other traits that successful marketers need to possess. For example, marketers need excellent planning and communication skills. In addition, we are increasingly being pushed to be more strategic. As a result, marketing plans have become more important than ever. Marketing plans help organizations synthesize, communicate, and execute their strategies.

In practice, a marketing team will need a set of plans. An *annual marketing plan* that captures the key objectives and initiatives is a must. Individual marketing departments should also have their own annual plans, which should align with and expand upon the annual marketing plan owned by the VP of marketing or CMO. This chapter will also cover essential cross-department plans in this chapter, including the *go-to-market plan* and the *message platform*.

I will also spend some time defining key marketing activities, including *campaign, launch*, and *program*. Many marketers do not understand these terms and, worse, use them incorrectly. Confusion results. People get perturbed. Execution suffers. To help avoid these marketing ills, I will stake a claim on proper usage of marketing lexicon.

To begin, table 1 shows the six essential marketing plans and where they fall in the strategy, execution, communication spectrum.

Table 1: Hierarchy of marketing plans

What	Document
Strategy	Go-to-market plan, marketing requirements document
Execution	Annual marketing plan, launch plan
Communication	Message platform, PR plan

Strategy – Go-to-Market Plan

The *go-to-market strategy*, or *plan*, is one of the most important things you will do in marketing. It will determine your likelihood of success, as well as your potential profitability. Also known as GTM or G2M, go-to-market strategy refers to the way you plan to sell your product to customers who are ready to buy. Phrased differently, your strategy should include what you are selling, who you are selling to, and how you are selling to them—in essence, the product and place of marketing's Four Ps.

Your go-to-market plan can be as complex and detailed as you feel is necessary, but should not be complicated at the expense of agility. As you create your plan, keep in mind that you may need to change it quickly if things are not working out. No matter how detailed the plan, however, there are some key elements you need to include:

> Market sizing and segmentation – This is the market segment or segments that are most suitable for your products or services. Recall from the discussion in chapter 3 that markets can be segmented based on a range of criteria, whether industry, geography, demographic profiles, or other.

> Product – What product do you plan to sell to a given market segment? Your GTM may call for you to emphasize different products in different market segments. In the case of a go-to-market strategy for a single product line or service, you might design a specific model, variant, or package for a particular market segment.

Buyer – The person or group of persons who will purchase your product. In consumer marketing, the buyer frequently is an individual consumer. In contrast, business-to-business marketing targets the buyer persona or buying center.

Routes to market – Will your product be sold direct by salespeople, directly online, through resellers, or through retailers? These channels are the typical *routes to market*. You might decide that certain channels are more suitable for certain market segments or buyers than others. In other cases, a mix of channels is appropriate. A typical example of a mix for business-to-business products is to employ direct sales in a company's home country and resellers in other countries. Alternatively, you can have direct sales service large customers and let channel partners and your online store handle smaller orders.

The better your go-to-market plan, the stronger your other marketing plans will be. A well-crafted GTM plan enhances your ability to identify and scope the marketing support that is necessary to make your plan effective. It also helps you to understand what the buyers are looking for when they make a buying decision. You can utilize this knowledge to create on-target supporting messages, advertising, and other materials. Equally important, you can direct your salespeople or channel partners to the most likely buyers to help them in their efforts.

Similarly, the more carefully targeted your GTM strategy is, the more effective it will be. Despite what some people might believe, trying to sell as many products to as many people through as many channels as possible is not necessarily the best strategy. Keep in mind that even large enterprises have limited marketing resources. An organization may find itself spread too thin, unable to create enough demand to be of interest to channel partners, or enough noise to attract the attention of potential buyers. In addition, marketing a product to the wrong segment wastes valuable time and money. For example, a product that appeals to a large company might be too expensive or too difficult to use for a smaller company. Exercising discipline in a go-to-market strategy is a major challenge, but it is well worth the effort.

Execution – The Annual Marketing Plan

After you have developed the go-to-market strategy, the next step is to create the annual marketing plan. The purpose of the annual marketing plan is to identify the tactics that will generate the necessary awareness and demand for the product among the desired buyers in the target market segments. Depending on the organization, the plan may also include training and awareness for salespeople and reseller partners. Finally, the plan should identify specific goals and metrics that the marketing team will use to measure success.

Creating the Marketing Plan

Marketing plans are typically generated annually, because they are tied to specific annual revenues. They may also be generated around a significant event, such as a product launch or geographic expansion. These are called *launch plans,* which are discussed later. Large organizations typically have one annual marketing plan and multiple individual launch plans for products introduced during that year. Organizations should review their marketing plan on a quarterly basis to assess whether the plan has achieved its goals and metrics, and to make any necessary course corrections if it has not.

Marketing plans can contain all kinds of tactics: advertising, the website, trade shows, public relations, analyst relations, channel incentives, promotions—you name it. They can also take many different forms. At the most basic level, however, all marketing plans contain the list of programs and the activities and associated costs necessary to drive them. This combination of activities is commonly referred to as the *marketing mix.*

Although marketing plans can take on a number of forms, and marketers have access to literally hundreds of templates, all plans should include a few common elements:

- market sizing and segmentation
- go-to-market strategy
- awareness and demand-generation targets

- marketing programs
- budget

Market sizing and segmentation were covered in detail in the previous chapter. Because of their complexity, we'll examine marketing budgets in greater detail in chapter 22.

The Launch Plan

As we mentioned above, the launch plan is a subset of the marketing plan that focuses on the introduction of a single product or service. Depending on your company size, you may have either one or several products or service launches in a given year.

The launch plan will look more like a project plan than the annual marketing plan. It should summarize the target market, the buyer, and the launch objectives, whether awareness objectives or specific revenue objectives. Most importantly, however, the launch plan should list all of the activities that have to come together for you to meet the target launch date.

Here are some elements you will want to include in a launch plan:

- Product availability – If you are introducing a new product, when will the product be ready? If your company sells through retail, when will the product be available in stores? In some cases, a company will launch new products before they actually ship, typically either as part of a market stall strategy or because the company wants to take advantage of an industry event. A market stall is when a company intentionally announces a product well ahead of availability so that customers wait until that product is available rather than buy a product from a competing vendor. Larger companies are notorious for "stalling" markets at the expense of their smaller competitors.

- Marketing assets – A detailed list of assets, such as data sheets, brochures, and new web pages or microsites, that need to be ready at the launch. If you are in charge of a global launch, then don't forget to leave time for translation.

- Public relations and influencer activities – Details on customers who have used the product or an early version, analysts who may be quoted, reporters to brief, and release date and time. If you are holding a press conference, then the launch plan should include the logistics. It should also specify the activities designed to reach out to important customers, bloggers, and other influencers.

- Advertising – Specifics on when ads will be ready and where they will run. Any additional keywords needed for search engine marketing should be included.

- Sales, support, and channel enablement – The biggest mistake you can make is to launch a product and surprise your sales team and partners. They don't like to be caught flat-footed. Make certain that your salespeople are briefed, armed with tools, and properly trained. Also, don't forget to develop mindshare among channel partners, who likely have other things going on. Customer service and technical support reps may get asked questions about the new product when they are helping customers with other things.

- Internal communications – How will you make certain even your receptionist knows what the launch is about? Internal communications can include frequently asked questions (FAQs) documents, employee webcasts, training events, e-mails from executives, and even signage for your lobbies and cafeterias. Launches are also an opportunity to get the whole organization excited.

- Launch events – If you are holding a launch event—whether at your headquarters, a trade show, or another venue—then the launch plan should contain details on when, who needs to be there, and a detailed schedule, or "show flow," so everyone knows his or her part. You may also want to include key talking points for your executives and spokespeople to ensure that they stay on message.

Communication – The Message Platform

The average customer receives hundreds, if not thousands, of messages every day. In every medium, from home to work and back again, companies are trying to sell something. So, if you think customers are waiting around waiting to hear what you have to say, think again. This is not a new problem. Even in 1997, when the web was nascent and Twitter, Facebook, and the iPhone were not yet born, consumers were overwhelmed:

> Consumers today are surrounded by advertising. There are various estimates, but most range from hundreds to low thousands per day. David Shenk, in his book *Data Smog*, states that the average American encountered 560 daily advertising messages in 1971. By 1997, that number had increased to over 3000 per day. The average consumer today sees more ads in one day than his predecessor of fifty years ago.[18]

Be fascinating!

Given this glut of information, a successful marketing campaign needs to say something interesting, relevant, and meaningful. And, it needs to say it over and over again. Remember: frequency, consistency, and simplicity. Marketers refer to the collection of carefully chosen words and phrases that they use to describe their offering as a *message platform.* For a message platform to be convincing, each element should be concise and compelling. Keep in mind that the words and phrases in your message platform will be used by other members of your marketing team—from PR to advertising to the web team to social media—when they write about your product, whether for a launch, a campaign, or any other activity. The message platform is the master document on which a lot of other writing will be based. All communication should conform to the message platform.

There are many ways to format a message platform, and content may vary from company to company. Regardless of the specifics, however, a proper message platform should contain at least the following six elements:

- ◆ Buyer priorities and needs – This element summarizes your buyers' top priorities or needs. Market segmentation and buyer profiles will yield this information, and it should be limited to the "short list" of what your buyers care most about. An acute knowledge of needs and priorities will help writers and other marketers better understand your buyers and the context in which they make decisions.

- ◆ Positioning statement – As we discussed in chapter 2, a positioning statement is a short statement that demonstrates the value of what you offer, how it differs from competing products and services, and how it has a meaningful impact on your audience. The positioning statement can cover an entire company, a product line, or an individual product.

- ◆ Key messages – Recall that the positioning statement is intended to help internal audiences understand your desired position in the marketplace. Obviously, however, you also need to convey this message to the external marketplace. To accomplish this task, marketers create key messages, which are short statements that phrase your product's value in terms the buyer will understand.

- ◆ Proof points – Proof points are the supporting evidence that validate and give credibility to the key messages. Whereas key messages are complete sentences, proof points are bullets. Each key message should be supported by two to three proof points. Well-crafted proof points will make your messaging more powerful and help cut through the cynicism and inattentiveness toward marketing messages that "data smog" has fostered.

- ◆ Value proposition – The "value prop" is what—hopefully—your salespeople will be repeating every time they meet a new prospect. It describes what you have, thecustomers for whom it is intended, and what benefits they will gain from using it. Although this sounds straightforward, think of all the times a salesperson has tried to explain to you what he or she is selling. Five minutes into the monologue, you still have no idea what the product is or why you should buy it. Somewhere, a marketing person did not do his or her job of arming the field staff with a value proposition.

* Copy blocks – Copy blocks are fleshed-out messages, in full sentences, that can be dropped into marketing assets, whether direct mail, e-mail, advertising, or some other medium. The best practice is to provide short, medium, and long versions, usually twenty-five-, fifty-, and hundred-word blocks that describe your company and its offerings.

Figure 1 below shows how all the pieces of the message platform fit together, starting with buyer priorities and needs on the more strategic end, and finishing with completed copy blocks that can be used as is on the delivery end.

Figure 1: Message platform components

Buyer Priorities & Needs Target buyer personas and their needs in brief			Strategy
Positioning Statement Statement that summarizes desired positioning and differentiation			
Key Message 1 Short statement that summarizes benefit	Key Message 2 Short statement that summarizes benefit	Key Message 3 Short statement that summarizes benefit	
Proof Point 1 Support for key message	Proof Point 2 Support for key message	Proof Point 3 Support for key message	
Value Proposition One sentence that summarizes what you bring to a target buyer			
Copy Blocks Longer 25-, 50-, and 100-word descriptions of your offering and organization			Delivery

A critical element of an effective message platform is *differentiation*. The most common reaction that customers—consumer or business—have to a sales pitch is to associate the product or service with something they already have. After they have done this, they want to know how your product is different from—and better than—the product they already use. This is where differentiation comes in. If the answer to this question is not in your positioning statement and key messages, and is not backed up with proof points, then you need to go back to the drawing board.

As you've probably concluded by now, testing the message platform is critical. It is imperative that you get feedback from people outside the group that developed the messaging to confirm that your messages are credible and differentiated and that your product's value is clear. Depending on your resources and access to participants, testing can range from presenting the message to a few friendly customers, partners, and salespeople to showing draft messaging to industry analysts, trusted customers, and, in some cases, focus groups for feedback. There is really no right way to conduct testing. Whatever method you employ, however, you should follow a consistent format for presenting the messaging and collecting feedback. This strategy will ensure that you are getting the best possible input. As you collect feedback, keep a lookout for ideas on wording and insight into how buyers perceive your organization and what value they see in what you do. You can use this feedback to improve your messaging.

Finally, because the message platform is intended to be consumed by other marketing and sales personnel, a well-designed platform will contain variants of the key messages and value propositions—the copy blocks noted above. Because you need to achieve consistency of message, you should create short, medium, and long versions, and they should be easy to cut and paste from the documents. As the creator, you will benefit from these efforts when you are not asked to write a hundred words for every press release, award submission, and third-party website. And success? When you overhear a salesperson from across the country parroting your words to a nodding customer, you know you've got a winner.

Other Important Marketing Documents

In addition to the documents we have discussed, a marketing plan can encompass any number of subplans and documents. Two that are worth considering are the PR plan and the marketing requirements document.

The *public relations plan*, more commonly called the *PR plan*, should outline awareness goals, press releases to support product launches, placed/bylined article submission opportunities, speaking opportunities, blogs, and other media, such as Twitter and Facebook. I like PR plans because they force PR teams to think proactively, and outside the blocking and tackling of press releases, to support product announcements. PR plans should include calendars for social media posts, because they improve internal communication and keep internal bloggers informed of when they will need to post, what the overall strategy is, and what conversations or topics they should be monitoring. I discuss the PR plan in greater detail in the public relations chapter.

As the name suggests, the *marketing requirements document (MRD)* describes the requirements of customers in the market. The task of creating the MRD is usually assigned to product marketing. The MRD should be revised annually to reflect significant changes or shifts in the market. Be careful not to confuse the MRD with the *product requirements document*, or *PRD*, which product or brand managers create to prioritize specific feature additions to their product. MRDs should identify issues and needs at a higher level—family sizes are growing and need bigger cars; more families are getting into stand-up paddleboarding; companies are struggling to stay secure in the face of mobile phone use; small businesses cannot keep up with paperwork requirements imposed by new government regulations; and so on.

Speaking the Same Language

Many marketers use the terms *campaign*, *launch*, and *program* interchangeably. This gets very confusing when you are trying to communicate with other team members, outside agencies, heads of sales, and CEOs. These three terms are clearly related, and there are variants or extensions of each term that can make one term look like the other. Nevertheless, they are distinctive concepts, and marketers need to understand what each one means. I will also describe how *promotions* and *activities* fit in with all three.

Let's begin with the *campaign*. Exactly what does this term refer to? Basically, a campaign is a coordinated set of activities, associated with a theme, designed to promote a product or service. A theme can be a topic, a subject, a motif, or an idea. Campaigns have a longer duration than launches, typically encompassing a season or a fiscal year.*

Whereas a campaign covers an entire fiscal year, a launch involves the introduction of a new product or service, with associated activities to promote it. The launch typically takes place on a given day, with everything lined up and ready to go, and it is generally tied either to product availability or to the announcement of availability. A campaign, by contrast, can be independent from the launch and have greater longevity.

Of course, in practice, the distinction between launches and campaigns can become blurred. For example, marketers sometimes conduct "rolling thunder" launches—taken from the sound of echoing thunder—where the launch is succeeded by a steady drumbeat of activities. These activities consist of a series of tactics deployed over time to sustain attention, or "noise," about the new product or service. At this point, launches can begin to resemble campaigns. Also, in some cases, companies launch a new campaign concurrent with a product launch, further conflating the two concepts.

The next concept, *program,* is a grouping of common marketing activities, including reputation, demand generation, sales enablement, and market intelligence. *Reputation* includes brand or corporate advertising, public relations, and loyalty programs. *Demand generation* includes any tactics that will capture leads. *Sales enablement* is the training and equipping of your sales team and partners. Finally, *market intelligence* consists of information about your customers, markets, and competitors. A common mistake is for marketers to refer to tactics as programs, as in "social media program."

The individual actions that companies take to achieve a marketing outcome are known as *tactics* or *activities.* Common marketing tactics include events, direct marketing, telemarketing, direct-response advertising, online advertising and search engine marketing, promotions, social media, content

---

* The "Campaigns" tab in many popular sales-and-marketing automation applications, which is generally where programs or tasks are tracked, confuses the matter greatly.

syndication, and tactical PR activities such as press releases and product
reviews.

Finally, *promotion* is the publicizing of a product or service to achieve
market awareness through the media, customer communication, and/or advertising. These activities can range from the high-level act of promoting all
of your products—the fourth P in McCarthy's model—to a narrowly targeted
effort to promote a specific product, typically with an associated promotional offer. In the context of the annual marketing plan, "running a promotion"
typically means creating an incentive to sell more of a given product.

Figure 2 below depicts the relationship among campaigns, launches, programs, and tactics/activities.

Figure 2: Marketing activity taxonomy

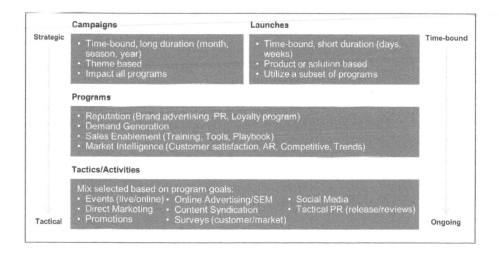

Prescribing a hierarchy of campaigns, launches, programs, promotions,
and tactics/activities is challenging, if not impossible. There is no one-size-
fits-all solution. Every company is different, and the different divisions within
a company may have different needs. While one division is launching a new
product with a fresh go-to-market strategy, another division may be introducing an existing product into a new geography, and a third may be running a
price promotion to spur sales of a sputtering product. Success is defined as

having the appropriate level of marketing plan in place that achieves the following objectives:

- It demonstrates strong ties to corporate goals.
- It is measureable so that the marketing team can show progress.
- It has room for promotions, launches, and campaigns to tie in.

Remember that a well thought-out plan gives the marketing team (both internal and external) clear targets, and it increases the likelihood they will achieve their objectives with the highest degree of success. It also provides invaluable help when budgets are being set and/or reevaluated, because it clearly articulates the expected results associated with various items.

Lastly, I would be remiss if I did not mention the growing "Agile Marketing" trend. Adapted from a popular software development methodology, agile marketers set goals and objectives monthly and work on them in monthly "sprints." The idea behind Agile Marketing is to adapt quickly and achieve results fast. It is suitable for companies that are in rapidly changing, perhaps highly competitive, markets. Even if a company chooses to work in this way, an annual plan that sets the "arc" for the year is still a good idea. Also, almost every company has an annual revenue target that marketing will need to support.

Case Study

The vision for IBM's "Smarter Planet" campaign was laid out in a November 17, 2008, speech by IBM chairman and CEO Sam J. Palmisano. "The world will continue to become smaller, flatter…and smarter," he said. "We are moving into the age of the globally integrated and intelligent economy, society and planet. The question is, what will we do with that?"

The speech emphasized how the world's systems and industries were becoming more instrumented, interconnected, and intelligent, and that leaders and citizens could take advantage of this state of affairs to improve these systems and industries.

IBM is a $100 billion company with thousands of computer hardware and software products, ranging from mainframes to disk drives, databases to retail point-of-sale systems. A campaign had to be expansive enough to include all of them, and it had to be credible and relevant to customers.

According to Michael Paterson, creative director at Ogilvy & Mather, IBM's agency of record, "The 'smart planet' thought was sparked by Palmisano's speech, but the challenge in executing the campaign was coming up with imagery that would vividly illustrate abstract concepts. At the agency we began noodling around with ideas based on this, and one day one of our junior art directors came up with this beautiful graphic icon of a planet with little 'think rays' popping out of the top. It looked like the planet just got smart."

The Smarter Planet campaign was rolled out in 2008. Ogilvy went with a concept they called "op-ads" a takeoff off newspaper op-ed opinion pieces— that featured a provocative headline, a think-ray-inspired image, and copy that presented a viewpoint from IBM. The campaign was rolled out first to the *New York Times* and *Wall Street Journal*, then to other leading papers in major economies around the world.

A good campaign has a theme and has the durability to last a year or more. Based on those criteria, Smarter Planet is a great campaign. As of the writing of this book, the campaign has been running for five years. It not only provides a theme but a unique "visual vocabulary" that is instantly recognizable. Smarter Planet succeeds on a number of levels:

- Awareness – The imagery, or visual vocabulary, is immediately recognizable, unique to IBM, and the op-ad format allows room to present the IBM viewpoint.

- Agenda – Building on Palmisano's speech, the campaign sets a business agenda that describes IBM's opinion on where the industry is going.

- Motivation – Part of the reason for the success of the campaign is that it is so much more than advertising. It is an ad campaign, but it is also a mandate, and a vision. The campaign works to motivate customers, employees, and partners alike.

- Conversation – The campaign acts as a conversation starter for IBM's sales reps. "We think this is a business-building platform. We know our clients are looking at this time as a time to drive transformation and change, and the prospect of making their industry smarter, we believe, couldn't come at a better time," said IBM's head of corporate marketing, John Kennedy.

- Organization – IBM uses Smarter Planet not just in advertising but in product and solution marketing. The IBM website, and the Smarter Planet microsite, neatly organize the large and diverse set of products IBM sells.

Smarter Planet won the Effie Award in 2010. The Effie Awards are the American Marketing Association's awards program to recognize the most effective advertising efforts in the United States each year. Smarter Planet has had a measurable impact on IBM's business. According to IBM's marketing team, by presenting a unified vision across every IBM channel and touchpoint, the campaign changed perceptions and drove a 37 percent increase in revenue, with a campaign that paid back media dollars ten times in profit.

Learning More

- Erik Peterson and Tim Riesterer, *Conversations that Win the Complex Sale* (New York:McGraw-Hill, 2011).

Chapter 5

Public Relations

*P**ublic relations** (PR)* is the practice of managing the flow of information between an organization and the public. The goal of PR is to influence public opinion. As long as people have walked the earth, they have tried to convince others to see things their way. PR is the formalization of that human need, acting on behalf of a company, government agency, nonprofit organization, or famous person, and using all manner of media.

In far too many cases, PR is the only thing that an organization's leaders know about marketing. Although this attitude demonstrates an incomplete view of marketing as a whole, it underscores the importance of PR and the support it gets from people outside marketing. One of the most famous remarks that speaks to the importance of PR was allegedly uttered by Bill Gates, one of the most successful entrepreneurs in US history: "If I was down to my last dollar, I'd spend it on public relations."

This chapter discusses the importance of PR to the overall marketing mix, covering a bit of the evolution of the practice into what we now know as modern PR. I will also cover PR agencies and how to work with them, the importance of working with influencers, and how the effect of PR can be measured, ending with one of the most dramatic examples of PR impact in modern history. I save the mechanics of the press release until next chapter, in order to emphasize the importance of PR strategy and influence.

The Evolution of Modern Public Relations

The evolution of public relations is a fascinating one. PR developed as a marketing practice long before other components of the marketing mix. Formalized PR efforts date back to the seventeenth-century Catholic Church. The leaders of the French Revolution subsidized editors and sent agents throughout the country to advocate their cause. The legend of Davy Crockett stemmed from the work of his press agent and was created to win votes away from the incumbent president Andrew Jackson.[19]

The dawn of modern public relations stemmed not from politics but from industry. The so-called "battle of the currents" between Westinghouse, who advocated alternating current power, and Thomas A. Edison's General Electric, who advocated direct current transmission, is one of the earliest examples of how public relations was first conducted in the United States by powerful economic interests. Using former newspapermen as their publicists, the companies fought each other tooth and nail for media attention, political influence, and marketing advantage. We all know who won that battle, though Edison would have several victories himself over the years. Trade associations also caught the public relations fever in the late 1800s. The Association of American Railroads claims it was the first organization to use the term *public relations** in its 1897 *Yearbook of Railway Literature*.[20]

Public Relations Agencies

Suppose you issue a press release and no one cares? What if not a single editor or reporter expresses any interest in it, and not a single story regarding the news you are announcing appears anywhere in the media? Your CEO may pound the table in a fit of pique, but that won't do much. Other than the occasional Google search hit, you won't be getting much awareness for your

---

* Edward Bernays, profiled in the case study at the end of this chapter, also claimed to have coined the term. Bernays did coin the term "public relations counsel" in his first book *Crystallizing Public Opinion*, seeking equal stature for this new professional as an organization's legal counsel.

effort. Working with a PR agency is essential if you want your news to have maximum impact.

The nation's first public relations agency, the Publicity Bureau, was founded in Boston in 1900 by George V. S. Michaelis, Herbert Small, and Thomas O. Marvin. In 1906, the bureau came into prominence when it was hired by the nation's railroads to oppose adverse regulatory legislation that was then in Congress. Remember, the goal of PR is to influence public opinion, and railroads at the turn of the twentieth century were concerned about government impact on their business.

PR agencies can contribute to a successful marketing mix in a number of ways. Agencies are made up of people who understand how news gets made. In fact, some agencies employ former reporters and editors who really know their stuff, having been in the shoes of a reporter who continually faces deadlines.

How exactly can an agency assist you in your marketing efforts? The first thing an agency can do for you is advise you on how to craft news. What is the hook or interesting angle? Is there enough substance to your news to generate a compelling story? Is it something that would catch the eye of reporters or their editors? When you sign with an agency, you reap the benefits of their years of experience. These individuals know how to package the news to maximize its chances of getting picked up.

In addition to crafting the press release, agencies will also help you build a list of potential outlets for your news. Agencies maintain databases of reporters and editors, and they track their comings and goings as well as their areas of interest. Because they know the preferences or tendencies of many editors and reporters, they can help position or package your news for maximum effect.

An agency will then "pitch" your news to the press. Even if you have interesting news and a killer angle and have sent it to all the right people, it may still not make it into print or over the airwaves. Why not? There are several possibilities. Perhaps there is more interesting news on the reporter's "beat." Perhaps the reporter never heard of your company before and therefore is not certain whether you are a credible source. Or, perhaps the reporter is extremely busy—which most reporters are—and doesn't have time to take a chance on your press release. This is where a PR agency can be so valuable.

A good agency will have a relationship with the publication, editor, or reporter that you can leverage to get your news considered. PR agencies and the press have a symbiotic relationship: The agencies provide newsworthy stories, and the media provide the publicity. Although there may be a certain amount of contempt for PR "flacks,"[†] reporters understand that agencies are valuable news sources. Further, once an agency provides a reporter with a good news story, the reporter will likely trust the agency in the future. As a marketer, you are benefitting from this relationship. In fact, it's part of what you're paying for.

Another important benefit of working with an agency is that they look out for your interests by monitoring what the media are planning to cover. For example, agencies examine editorial calendars—annual plans for feature stories published by magazines—to find potential fits for your company or product. They also monitor the news and social channels related to your business to identify trends, keep track of influencers, and find opportunities for your spokespeople to comment on articles, blogs, and posts. I liken PR agencies to business development for news. You are paying them to be constantly on the lookout for opportunities to broadcast your message.

How to Pick a PR Agency

Given how important an agency is to getting your news into the media, picking the right one is extremely important. Here are things that you should look for. You can get answers to these questions by asking the vendor directly and checking with a few of their clients. An agency that is a fit should:

- have experience in your industry;
- Have worked with companies like yours—similar size or structure;
- be a good fit for them; a big agency is, generally, not a good fit for small businesses, as their focus is on large clients;

---

† After the "energetic" movie publicist George Flack, and nothing to do with shrapnel or criticism.

- have consistently delivered results for a number of clients;

- work the way you want to work; some marketers like to do the strategy and want the agency to just pitch; others want the agency to bfigure out both strategy and pitch;

- be comfortable with the schedule/pace of your company; some companies are good at planning ahead, while others are always having "fire drills";

- be good at the things that are your priorities—traditional press, industry analysts, financial analysts, working with bloggers, tracking social media, etc.

- feel right; don't underestimate the importance of working with people who you get along with and are comfortable with.

- let you meet the staff you will be working with; be wary of the firms who send in the senior people for the sales pitch, then hand you off to a junior person to work with you from then on.

Working with Influencers

Managing the flow of information between an organization and the public involves more than drafting a press release and sending it to the media. Your assertion that your news is important does not guarantee the media will see it in the same way. You must substantiate your claim, a process that requires third-party validation. *Influencers* are third parties outside of the news media that help you promote and substantiate your cause. The most common types are industry and financial analysts, newsletter publishers, bloggers, celebrities, and customers.

Industry Analysts

Reporters frequently seek out analysts for their expert opinions on a market trend or a new product release. To craft a successful marketing campaign, it is critical that you establish and maintain good relations with analysts in your product market.

As the title suggests, industry analysts typically follow certain industries. Analysts are particularly common in high technology and consumer electronics. They are paid to follow your industry and to offer advice to both vendors and prospective customers. Industry analysts also provide opinions and commentary to the media, both as part of their job and to burnish their credentials. Some analysts also measure market size and rank vendors. The Gartner Magic Quadrant is probably the most influential vendor rating report in the high-tech industry. Customers often consult these reports when they are making purchases. Gartner illuminates a given technology market by segmenting the various players into four sections, or quadrants:

- ◆ Leaders – Well-established firms that are generally achieving their objectives

- ◆ Visionaries – Companies that understand market trends, but do not effectively adjust to them

- ◆ Niche players – Businesses that are successful within a small market segment

- ◆ Challengers – Organizations that are currently successful, but do not appear to grasp market trends (Contrast with visionaries.)

Developing and sustaining viable relationships with industry analysts is essential, but it is not sufficient. Rather, it is vital that you *influence* these individuals to share your (positive) image of your company and/or product. Most marketers probably understand that to convince analysts to rank your company highly in their reports, you need to faithfully complete the required submissions for these reports. What many marketers don't realize, however, is that you also need to influence the criteria in your communications with, and messages around, the analysts. (Analysts read the articles and bloggers too.)

Analysts also have a good handle on what customers are asking for. Therefore, they can be of great assistance in positioning your product or company, crafting messages, and performing other key marketing activities.

Financial Analysts

Another field in which analysts are highly prominent is the financial industry. As you probably suspect, publicly held companies try to influence financial analysts—the researchers who work for banks and provide insights into company stock prices and futures. Most public companies have a specialist team called "investor relations" that specifically deals with financial analysts. Perhaps this team's most critical function is to review the quarterly earnings press releases and then set up teleconferences with financial analysts to discuss the results. It is important to keep this team apprised of what PR is doing to ensure that your company generates consistent messages and optimizes communications opportunities.

Other Influencers

In addition to industry and financial analysts, there can be any number of influential people in your industry. Specialty newsletter publishers are a good example. As their title suggests, these professionals write; however, they are not like beat reporters. They quite often influence opinions regarding companies and products, and they are sought out by other media for their expert insights. Their entire publication can focus on a single industry. Newsletter topics run the gamut—from stock picking to search engines, from the weather to wine—and there will almost certainly be a few related to your product, company, or cause.

With the explosive proliferation of the Internet, bloggers have also risen to prominence. In fact, some newsletter writers have moved to blogging as their medium. In addition, there are many other bloggers you need to become familiar with. Moms who test baby food can have a huge following. The same applies to "geeks" who spend weeks exploring every nook and cranny of a new computer model or disassembling every new Apple iPhone model. You name it. These are people whose opinions are sought out by others. Therefore, as with industry and financial analysts, you need to influence them. In his book *The Tipping Point*, author and journalist Malcolm Gladwell labeled these people "mavens." Mavens are intense gatherers of information and impressions who are often the first ones to detect new or nascent trends. Make certain you don't forget about mavens when you send out news. Include them in the process.

Influencers can also be famous people—such as athletes and actors—whom the public trusts. Clothing and accessory manufacturers send huge amounts of free goods to these individuals in the hope that they will wear them in public—and get photographed or filmed doing so. Professional athletes get paid millions to wear sneakers for a reason. In addition, there are professional pundits, style mavens, and countless other influencers. As a marketer, you need to use your imagination here. The basic rule: you should consider *anyone* who might influence your customers as part of your PR strategy.

Customers

Finally, your customers can be influencers. Your marketing and PR team should cultivate relationships with customers who are willing to speak with the press. Moreover, PR should help "sell" your customers on the idea that speaking with analysts or directly to the press is a benefit to their companies and their careers. Making customers into "stars" can make them happy and be an asset to your marketing mix. Working with customers who blog or actively use social media can deliver great results.

Gaining Publicity from Placed Articles and Speaking Engagements

Many publications, especially trade and special-interest magazines, accept article submissions bylined by subject-matter experts or other people with specific knowledge on a topic. This is another great way to attract media attention, and it will give you the opportunity to shape the entire article, not just a press release and your spokesperson's commentary. Some publications also seek out editorials or point-of-view (POV) pieces when they are looking for an influential person's take on an issue, industry, or trend.

PR agencies can help with this process. They will work with you to create an abstract of your idea and pitch it to the press. In addition, if the spokesperson or company executive has limited writing prowess, the agency may also be able to ghostwrite your company's publications. Good PR agencies will also come up with story ideas—or "angles"—to get your name in print.

PR agencies can also enhance your marketing campaign by helping to place speakers from your company at industry trade shows and conferences. Getting a spokesperson to present at an influential industry event is a great way to influence hundreds, sometimes thousands, of people at the same time. In some cases, the media will cover the event or seek an interview with the spokesperson afterward. Good PR firms routinely scrutinize trade show calendars for "calls for papers" or "calls for abstracts," and they can actively pitch executives or subject-matter experts to event organizers. As with placed articles, agencies can draft an abstract and bio for the speaker to optimize his or her chances of being selected.

Crisis Communications

Crisis communications is a subspecialty of public relations. As the name suggests, it is designed to protect the reputation of an organization that is confronted with a public challenge. This could be anything, such as an industrial accident, a criminal allegation, a government investigation, a lawsuit, or any number of other scenarios involving the legal, ethical, or financial standing of the entity. Crisis communication is sometimes referred to as "damage control." Famous examples of crisis communications are the seven deaths in 1982 from tampered Tylenol, the 1989 environmental disaster caused by the *Exxon Valdez* tanker oil spill, and the 2010 BP oil spill in the Gulf of Mexico.

When events like these happen, the media firestorm can quickly overwhelm the ability of the entity to effectively respond to the demands of the crisis. Companies facing such a threat will often bring in experienced crisis communications specialists to help prepare and guide them through the process.

Although every crisis will be different, organizations should have a crisis communications plan in place in case an incident occurs. The best practices for managing a crisis include designating a team and spokespeople, developing positions and answers to challenging questions, and being proactive with communications.

Measuring Influence – Share of Voice

Share of voice (SOV) is a term used both in public relations and advertising. SOV refers to the exposure of your company or product (your share) compared to that of your competitors. Back in the print-only world, people sometimes talked about "column inches" of coverage. In PR, SOV is measured by the number of stories written or aired about your company or product. These stories can appear in all types of media, including newspapers, trade publications, television, radio, and, increasingly, blogs and other online media. Regardless of the particular media, your objective is to ensure that your voice stands out among all the other voices promoting similar products or ideas. Figure 1 shows an example SOV report for Acme Corporation versus its competitors.

Figure 1: Share of voice (SOV) example

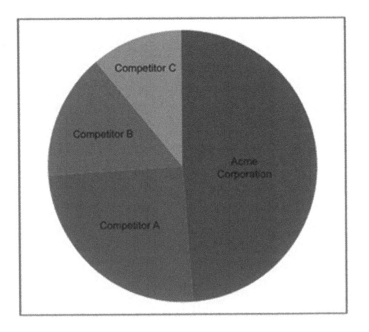

An important element within SOV is sentiment, or tone. You need to be concerned with not just how much is being written or broadcast about your company but *what* reporters are writing or saying. Some marketing wit years ago termed this "tonnage versus tone-age." Exxon, no doubt, led in SOV (tonnage) among oil companies in March and April of 1989, but that was because its tanker the *Exxon Valdez* struck Bligh Reef and dumped more than 250,000 barrels of crude into Prince William Sound in Alaska—one of the worst environmental disasters in recent history.

Sentiment is usually measured using a simple scale with three ratings: positive, neutral, and negative. Some measurements also include strongly positive and strongly negative, as in figure 2 below. These ratings can be somewhat subjective, but are a useful indicator of the overall attitude toward your organization. Figure 2 below is an example SOV chart with sentiment from my time at Symantec. Note that while our competitor, EMC, received more total coverage than we did during the period, almost half of it was unfavorable (shown in darker shades).

Figure 2: Share of voice with sentiment

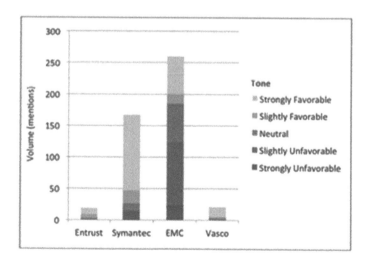

Most PR agencies offer share-of-voice measurement services to their clients. In fact, I would recommend making this service a prerequisite for any agency you hire. SOV charts with sentiment are a valuable tool for discussion among the PR team, as well as a convincing metric to use when you are justifying the PR budget. In the event your agency does not offer SOV measurement, or if you want a second opinion, there are a number of media-monitoring companies that provide self-service and human-assisted measurement, including BurrellesLuce, Cision, and Vocus, to name a few.

Ethics and PR

The history of PR is complicated and leaves many marketing professionals feeling conflicted. The profession we know today grew from promoting many ethically questionable causes. The press release was, in fact, written for crisis communication—not a new product promotion, but the exigency of a troubled railroad. Edward Bernays, as you will read below, employed novel techniques for causes some might find repugnant. His seminal work, *Crystallizing Public Opinion*, was reportedly followed by one of the most odious propaganda figures of all time, Joseph Goebbels, the Nazi propaganda minister.

Certainly, PR has been used for many more noble, or at least mundane, purposes. But for many, the taint is still there, and whether the caterpillar has transformed to a butterfly, or remains a grubby business, is still an open question.

Given the historical bias, it is especially important for PR professionals to be honest and ethical in their work. The Public Relations Society of America has a code of ethics members are required to follow. The code requires public advocacy, honesty, responsible use of expertise, objectivity, loyalty to clients, and fairness in dealing with clients, employers, competitors, peers, vendors, the media, and the general public. Given how different times are today, PR professionals stray from this code at their own reputational risk.

Case Study

One of the giants in the history of PR in the United States is Edward Bernays (1881–1995). Many experts credit him with almost single-handedly creating the craft we now know as public relations.[21]

In addition to pioneering the field of PR, Bernays was also a polarizing character. Although he helped define, legitimize, and grow the public relations trade, his critics consider many of the methods he employed, and the products and causes he promoted, to be morally questionable. Below, I recount one of his most famous PR campaigns because it was brazen, original, and highly effective. I will leave it to you to judge its morality.

The case involved work that Bernays performed for the American Tobacco Company. As told in Larry Tye's *The Father of Spin*, Bernays would stop at nothing to make his client successful.

The American Tobacco Company had achieved outstanding success by positioning its major cigarette brand—Lucky Strike—as the smoke of choice of US troops in WWI. During the 1920s, the company's president, George Washington Hill, became obsessed with breaking open another market—female consumers. At that time, smoking by women was still considered taboo, although some cracks in this tradition were beginning to show. To exploit these small openings in changing social mores—and, not coincidentally, to increase his company's profits—Hill hired Bernays to create a PR campaign to make smoking by women socially acceptable. He informed Bernays, "If I can crack that market, it will be like opening a new gold mine right in our front yard."[22]

Hill's strategy was to capitalize on the slimness trend that was coming into vogue, specifically by associating cigarette smoking with a trim waistline. Picking up on this theme, Bernays launched a campaign of enlisting experts to reinforce slimness. He included actors, athletes, society women—even male dancers who preferred svelte dance partners. Bernays also enlisted the former chief of the British Association of Medical Officers of Health to warn women of the dangers of sweets and to convince them that the right way to finish a meal was with fruit, coffee, and a cigarette.

Bernays did not stop there. He urged hotels to add cigarettes to their dessert lists. Bernays even distributed sample dessert menus, prepared by an editor at *House and Garden,* that included Lucky Strike cigarettes. His efforts were so pervasive and successful that he received complaints from candy makers and sugar manufacturers, among others. But, that was just the first act. While women began to smoke in greater numbers in private, Hill wanted them to feel comfortable smoking in public, estimating that would double his market.

Bernays called in psychologist Dr. A. A. Brill, a disciple of Bernays's famous uncle, Dr. Sigmund Freud. Brill maintained that as women had become "emancipated," many had suppressed their feminine desires and increasingly sought equality with men. It was Brill's characterization of cigarettes as "torches of freedom" that sparked Bernays's imagination.

Bernays arranged a parade—a march, really—of thirty debutantes in New York City. He carefully orchestrated this parade on Easter Sunday, down Fifth Avenue. No detail was left to chance. Women would "join" the parade as it passed by prominent churches in New York, including Saint Thomas Church and Saint Patrick's Cathedral. American Tobacco, of course, supplied the cigarettes. Marchers would ask other women for a light in a show of sisterhood as they joined the parade. Bernays hired his own photographer to document the parade and provide pictures to the press.

Bernays's parade proved spectacularly successful. During the following days, women took to the streets, "torches of freedom" in hand, in Boston, Detroit, and San Francisco. The flames of controversy were ignited, with editorials and articles arguing pro and con for weeks. As Bernays summed up in his memoirs, "Age-old customs, I learned, could be broken down by a dramatic appeal, disseminated by a network of media."

Learning More

• Larry Tye, *The Father of Spin: Edward L. Bernays & the Birth of Public Relations* (New York:Crown, 1998).

Chapter 6

The Press Release

The workhorse of public relations is the press release. Written in the form of a conventional news story, a press release alerts the media to an organization's news and presents it in that organization's point of view. Editors and reporters use facts, quotes, and other information contained in releases to flesh out their stories.

Given the importance of the press release and the process of creating and disseminating a good one, I have dedicated an entire chapter to the topic. I begin by recounting the origins and history of press releases, then move on to discuss how to create, format, and distribute them. The chapter concludes by examining some important parts of the release process, including media alerts, press conferences, press briefings, and selecting and training appropriate spokespeople.

Origin of the Press Release

The first organizations to utilize the press release were the nation's large railroads. The first press release was issued by Ivy Lee, a founding father of PR.[23] At the time, Lee's firm, Parker and Lee, was the public relations agency for the Pennsylvania Railroad. After one of their trains jumped the tracks, resulting in a wreck in Atlantic City in 1906, Lee did something new. He drafted a statement—the first press release—that openly disclosed information to journalists before they could hear different accounts from other sources. His goal was to avoid inaccurate rumors. Lee's release was created as a tool to help with crisis communications, which we discussed in the last chapter. The *New York Times* actually ran the story verbatim, without any revisions, and is shown below in figure 1.

Figure 1: The *New York Times* story that reprinted Ivy Lee's 1906 Pennsylvania train wreck story

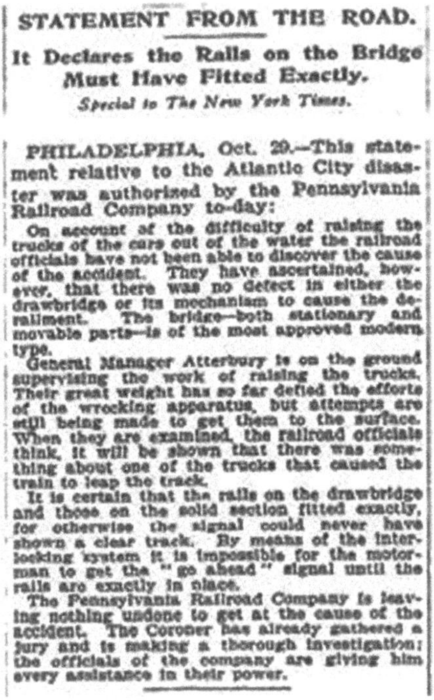

STATEMENT FROM THE ROAD.

It Declares the Rails on the Bridge Must Have Fitted Exactly.

Special to The New York Times.

PHILADELPHIA, Oct. 29.—This statement relative to the Atlantic City disaster was authorized by the Pennsylvania Railroad Company to-day:

On account of the difficulty of raising the trucks of the cars out of the water the railroad officials have not been able to discover the cause of the accident. They have ascertained, however, that there was no defect in either the drawbridge or its mechanism to cause the derailment. The bridge—both stationary and movable parts—is of the most approved modern type.

General Manager Atterbury is on the ground supervising the work of raising the trucks. Their great weight has so far defied the efforts of the wrecking apparatus, but attempts are still being made to get them to the surface. When they are examined, the railroad officials think, it will be shown that there was something about one of the trucks that caused the train to leap the track.

It is certain that the rails on the drawbridge and those on the solid section fitted exactly, for otherwise the signal could never have shown a clear track. By means of the interlocking system it is impossible for the motorman to get the "go ahead" signal until the rails are exactly in place.

The Pennsylvania Railroad Company is leaving nothing undone to get at the cause of the accident. The Coroner has already gathered a jury and is making a thorough investigation; the officials of the company are giving him every assistance in their power.

After their initial use by the railroads, press releases rapidly became the norm in all corporations and large organizations. Early in the twentieth century, for example, Ohio Bell Telephone discovered that if it handed out "canned" news in this form, newspaper reporters would stop attending hearings on telephone rates to acquire the information in person. This strategy minimized uncomfortable press inquiries concerning rates and related matters. The origins of the press release can seem cynical attempts to control the news. The modern press release, however, is more often used to attract the media's attention to consider writing articles, to attend press briefings, and to request interviews with an organization's spokespeople.

Today, organizations large and small, from every industry and the public sector, write and issue press releases. Some prefer the term *news release*, feeling the word "press" is not broad enough to cover television and radio editors and reporters. Anachronistic or not, I prefer *press release*—and I would point to the White House Press Corps as evidence of the inclusiveness of the term.

Though the format of a press release has changed somewhat from the one Lee wrote, the aim remains the same—to get coverage. The content still must provide news reporters with the basic information they need to write their stories.

Writing the Press Release

How can you be reasonably certain that your press releases will contain the requisite information in an appropriate format? The answer is that there is a standard structure for press releases. Your organization will still need to create news and find an interesting angle, but using the standard format assures you have everything the media will need. In this section, we examine the basic elements of the standard release structure.

> Identifier – When creating a release, you should place the words "PRESS RELEASE," in all caps, bolded, at the top of the first page. Though this might seem obvious, how is an editor or reporter to know what the document you or your agency sent them is? Significantly, organizations also release a standard PR document called a *media alert* to invite or alert media representatives to an upcoming event, such as a press conference. A media alert contains many of the same elements as a press release, so people can confuse the two. The "PRESS RELEASE" label clearly distinguishes your news from a media alert. (Media alerts are covered below.)

Timing – Press releases typically state "For Immediate Release" at the top left, bolded. This statement informs editors that the story is publicly available—on the wire or via your website—and that they can report it. If your story will be released at a future date, then the press release should say "For Release on [fill in your date]." Organizations use this approach when they give releases to the media in advance of the public release date—a common practice that we will discuss later in this chapter. If you want to make the point more strongly, you can substitute "Embargoed until [fill in your date]." Even if you do label a release as embargoed, it is best to have a conversation beforehand with the journalists to ensure they understand and will honor the embargo.

Contact information – The contact information informs the reporters and editors who supplied the story and whom they should contact if they have questions. This information should be right justified and placed above your headline, with the word "Contact" in bold situated directly above it. Include the contact's name, company, phone number, and e-mail address. If you use an agency, the contact may be someone from the agency. In some cases, press releases include both the agency and issuing company's press contact information. Generally, the company contact should not be your spokesperson. Rather, you should list either the PR manager or the marketing person responsible for the announcement, because you may not want the press to contact the spokesperson before he or she has been properly prepared.

Headline – Just as in a newspaper or magazine, the release should contain a headline that grabs the editors' attention and spurs them to continue reading. Moreover, because the release will live on long after the story appears on your website, the headline should also draw in the average reader. Headlines are typically printed in bold type, sometimes in a larger font than the rest of the release.

Subhead – The subhead gives you a chance to flesh out your angle and further hook the reader. It may offer additional details, substantiate a claim, or underscore an achievement. Subheads should be printed in a smaller font than the headline, and they are sometimes italicized to distinguish them from the headline.

Dateline – In the United States, the dateline should include the city, state, and date of the press release, followed by either two dashes or an em dash. For example, a release would start "San Francisco, CA, October 31, 2013 –." If an announcement is made at an industry event, it is common practice to include the city and state where the event is taking place. Outside of the United States, common practice is to use city and country, and sometimes simply the city if it is well-known.

The lead – The first paragraph is known as the lead paragraph, or simply the lead. In the United States it is sometimes spelled "lede," supposedly to distinguish it from the heavy metal lead type used by typesetters, though there is much debate about the reason for this spelling. The lead should capture the entire story as if the rest of the press release were not there. It essentially serves two key purposes. First, it draws the editor, reporter, or reader further into the story. Second, in the case of what is known as a *news lead*, it provides journalists with the five Ws and the H: who, what, when, where, why, and how. Journalists are trained to include this information in the leads to their news stories, so you will be giving them exactly what they need. The press release is, after all, packaged news and a tool you use to inform editors and reporters. A *feature lead* is written in a similar style to the lead of a feature article in a magazine or newspaper, and it may set the scene or tug on emotions. It serves to draw the editor in, but it does not need to contain the hard news elements of the news lead.

Here are two fashion industry examples pulled from PR Newswire, one a news lead and one a feature lead:

BURLINGTON, Vt., Nov. 15, 2012 /PRNewswire/ – Burton Snowboards and Mountain Dew today announce the arrival of the new 2013 Green Mountain Project outerwear collection, which utilizes sustainable fabric made from recycled plastic bottles, now available in stores worldwide.

In this news lead, Burton Snowboards and Mountain Dew (who) are announcing that their new product, 2013 Green Mountain Project outerwear (what), is today (when) available in stores worldwide (where), and that the line is made from sustainable fabric (why).

> BEVERLY HILLS, Calif., Nov. 27, 2012 /PRNewswire/ – At 24, many young women are just starting to figure out where they're going in life. But 24-year-old Evelyn Fox has never been one to follow the crowd. Instead, the trendsetter is helming her own successful high-end fashion company, Crystal Heels™ (http://crystalheels.com) – and it all started with a pair of Louboutins, a couple thousand Swarovski crystals, and a heady mix of creativity and passion.

This feature lead is written in the style of a feature article and is very different from the news lead above. There is no hard news, but it does draw you into Evelyn Fox's story.

The body – The body is the continuation of the story. After you have provided the details for hard news or set the stage with a feature lead, you should continue with additional details or explanations. The body should also contain quotes from an executive at your organization, a partner if you are announcing a joint venture or project, a customer, and/or an industry expert. It can also include headings if they make the press release easier to read. A common section in product announcement press releases is the "Pricing and Availability" heading, followed by details of when a product will actually ship, where it can be bought, and how much it costs.

Boilerplate – The *boilerplate* is a description of your company or organization that is designed to be used over and over without change.[*] It

---

[*] "Boiler plate" originally referred to the small metal plate that identified the builder of a steam boiler. The term was borrowed by the printing industry, where plates of text for widespread reproduction, such as advertisements or syndicated columns, were cast or stamped in steel (instead of the much softer and less durable lead alloys used otherwise) ready for the printing press and distributed to newspapers around the United States. They came to be known as "boilerplates."

supplies the editor with additional information about the newsmaker. The boilerplate should be preceded by the words "About [your company name]," and it should be limited to a single paragraph of no more than roughly a hundred words. The boilerplate should also include the URL for your organization's website. Twitter handles are becoming increasingly common in boilerplates.

Ending – To indicate the end of the release, type "END" or "###," centered below the boilerplate.

Figure 2: Standard press release format

PRESS RELEASE

For Immediate Release or For Release on [Date]

Contact(s):
Contact(s) Name
Contact(s) Company
Contact(s) Phone
Contact(s) E-mail

Headline
Subhead

CITY, State – Month Day, Year – Lead sentence. One or two more sentences in first paragraph.

Second paragraph

Quote

Additional paragraph(s)

Additional Information
Links to product or service information for readers
Links to social media pages or share feature

About Organization Name
Boilerplate paragraph. Organization website URL.

#

Press Kit
Links to additional information—photos, B-roll, supporting studies

Photos, images, videos, B-roll – Because the press release is meant to be a packaged news story, don't forget to include all of the elements that a magazine, website, newspaper, or television reporter might need to complete the story. These elements include photographs of the new executive whose appointment you just announced, images or technical diagrams of the new product you just announced, and videos that illustrate how the product works. You can even consider a *B-roll*—supplemental or alternate footage intercut with the main shot in a televised interview or news segment. B-roll can be anything pertinent to your organization, such as footage of your manufacturing assembly line, your automobiles on the test track, consumers using your smartphone or computer, your bond trading floor, or any number of other examples. The easiest way to supply these elements is to provide a URL to a web page containing all of the relevant materials.

Social media links – If you want readers of your online press release—on your website, for example—to share it with others and generally promote it, you can include links in the release that let them do so. A number of social media companies provide tools that enable you to embed these capabilities directly into your press release.

Although a press release should include all of these elements, it should never exceed five hundred words. Like a news story, the release should place most of the news up top, supported by the details in the paragraphs following the headline and lead. It should be composed in a basic font, double-spaced with wide margins and page numbers. Using company letterhead is a nice touch, but it is not required.

In terms of style, pick a news style guide, such as the *Associated Press Stylebook* or *The New York Times Manual of Style and Usage*. Use plainspoken language. Most importantly, avoid hyperbole and puffery, because they detract from the legitimacy of your news.

It is possible that you will obtain coverage if you don't use this structure, but your odds are greater if you present your news in a format that is familiar to editors and reporters. In addition, adopting the preferred format will make your organization appear more professional and worthy of attention.

Distributing the Press Release

Most organizations want to get their press release "on the wire." The term dates from the mid-1800s, when news agencies would transmit their stories via teletype over the telegraph wires. The term stuck. Even today, when news is transmitted in all kinds of ways, the term "newswire" is still used to refer to well-known news services like the Associated Press (AP), Reuters, and others. Likewise, a press release news service is commonly referred to as a "press release newswire." The grandfather of all press release newswires is PR Newswire, which distributes thousands of press releases each year.

The value of using a press release newswire is that journalists subscribe to them. Reporters can subscribe to certain companies, topics, or regions. In addition, newswires like PR Newswire also distribute your press releases to Google News, Yahoo! News, and other news websites, making them immediately available to customers who are searching for them.

Sending your release directly to reporters and editors is a proven and recommended tactic. In addition, many reporters subscribe directly to news feeds using the Really Simple Syndication (RSS) protocol. They may subscribe via your website, if they follow your industry, or via a news aggregator that groups news by topic, thereby functioning as a sort of press release news service. Many companies also post their press releases, or a modified version, to their company blog, hoping to attract a slightly different set of writer—the blogger—to pick up their story and write about it. Finally, with the advent of Twitter, some editors and reporters "follow" a company's handle, or identifier, and will be alerted via a tweet from that identifier. We will examine Twitter in greater detail in the chapter on social media.

Dealing with the Media

Media Selection

Although adopting an accepted format will improve your chances of securing news coverage, you also need to implement a productive media strategy. One approach is simply to issue your press release and hope some editor finds it and assigns a reporter to write about it. As you might imagine, we do not recommend this strategy. The best method for obtaining coverage is to identify the individuals who write about your industry, your market, and your customers, and send the press release directly to them.

You can perform this task yourself by looking through newspapers, magazines, and trade publications. Find the reporters who have written stories about your industry, market, or customers. You can also find the names and contact information of the editors in the masthead of a print publication or on the website of an online publication. If your company is not new, chances are you have interacted with the media before. In such cases, you can search online for articles about your company.

If you are working with a PR agency, they will help you build a list of editors and reporters to target. Agencies have the advantage of having worked with the media over the years, so they know the types of stories editors will be interested in. As discussed in the previous chapter, they also have relationships with editors and reporters. These relationships help the e-mail with your press release stand out from the others in a reporter's inbox. None of this assures coverage, of course, but it gives you a much better chance of being noticed.

Press Briefings

You or your PR agency should set up a number of live or phone meetings, known as *press briefings*, before your release date. Press briefings give the media a chance to ask questions and gain details about your news. Send the reporters or editors a press release anywhere from a day or two to a week in advance, depending on how "hot" the news is. Make sure the journalists know that the press release is embargoed, meaning they agree not to release your news before the listed release date. Embargoes are gentlemen's agreements, but are rarely broken. Today most briefings take place over the phone, primarily because many reporters now work from home.

To build a relationship with the media, your agency may set up a *press tour*, though these are becoming less common as reporters increasingly work from home. Your spokesperson, internal PR person, and agency representative will travel to one or more cities to brief the editors and reporters in person. This can be a good strategy, especially if you can convince your CEO or another high-level executive to act as the spokesperson. Reporters often appreciate the effort.

Timing is important. If there are key analysts that the media will turn to, they should be briefed first, before the media. This way analysts are familiar with your news and prepared to comment. Likewise, if there are customers or partners the press will want to speak with, they should be prepared in advance. Your PR manager or agency should schedule all of this for you, with customers briefed first, then industry analysts, and finally the media. Writers for publications or programs that come out weekly, with earlier submission deadlines, should be briefed earlier to accommodate their schedules.

Press Conferences

A *press conference* is a staged public relations event in which an organization or individual presents information to members of the mass media. Along with the press release, public relations professionals use press conferences to draw media attention to a potential story. Press conferences are typically used for political campaigns, sporting events, emergencies, and promotional purposes, such as the launch of a new product. There is no hard-and-fast rule to determine which stories merit a press conference and which ones where a simple press release will suffice. Nevertheless, there are some obvious criteria, including access to spokespeople—especially celebrities—reaction to a recent or current event, and the ability to visit or experience a setting, such as a new factory or a space launch.

Promotional press conferences offer several advantages, such as the ability to reach all media outlets at the same time while controlling the message.

A press conference also can build excitement or anticipation about an event. A setting that offers great visuals—for example, a celebrity in a local setting, the stadium where a game just concluded, a dramatic vista that looks good on television, up-close access to a new product—will greatly enhance a press conference.

Logistics and organization are essential to staging an effective press conference. The media should be informed in advance, and a media advisory with details of the press conference should be sent out. The location should offer easy access for the media and easy parking for broadcast trucks if they are expected. The flow of the press conference should be scripted, with prepared statements from key spokespeople followed by questions from the assembled media. Additional background information, in the form of press kits (discussed below), should be available at the event and then afterward online.

Media Alerts

Earlier in this chapter we distinguished between press releases and media alerts. A *media alert* informs the media of an upcoming event, activity, or press conference. In contrast to a press release, which provides information about your event as well as background information on news items, a media alert includes only basic information—who, what, where, and when—and leaves out the why and other details in order to draw the media to the event.

When writing a media alert, use the following guidelines to make it easy for the media to understand what you are contacting them about. Many of these guidelines are similar to the press release format.

- Use company letterhead, or include your organization's logo at the top.
- Always include a contact name, phone number, and e-mail address so the media can follow up with questions.
- Keep it brief, ideally to a single page.
- Conclude it with three #s (###). This indicates the end of the document.

- At the top of document, write "MEDIA ALERT" in a large font.

- Keep the headline short, but include location, time, and date.

Media alerts include the what, who, when, where of an event.

- What: What kind of event is this, and what is its purpose?

- Who: Will any notable figures (fire chief, local officials, celebrities) be present?

- When: What arethe date and time of your event?

- Where: Where is it? Make certain to include the exact location of your event. Provide nearby cross streets and a phone number.

Press Kits

If you want to provide additional information to the media, then a standard strategy is to build a press kit. A press kit is simply background information about a person or organization. In the case of a company, press kits typically contain a fact sheet about the organization, product literature, biographies and photos of executives, a few previous press releases, and sample news stories. They are especially useful when your company or organization is new or is introducing itself to a new editor. Traditionally, press kits were printed and placed in a folder. In today's digital age, however, they increasingly are available online. Press kits should also contain versions of your logo in various online and print formats, product pictures, screenshots—whatever reporters might need. Better they get it from you than run with whatever they find in a Google search.

Selecting and Training Spokespeople

Another important element in creating an effective media strategy is choosing an effective spokesperson. In most cases, the selection is obvious. He or she is the expert on the topic, or the company CEO. These are the individuals the press typically wants to communicate with. However, you can use other criteria to select a spokesperson. Many companies, for example, decide that certain stories, while newsworthy, are too low-level for senior executives, so they delegate someone else in the organization. Also, if you are dealing with the media in a foreign country, then you might select a regional representative who is familiar with the languages and culture. Finally, some executives are simply not good with the media. For example, CEOs who get testy or argumentative can generate negative publicity for their organization and create headaches for their PR team.

Regardless of whom you select as your spokesperson, media training will always make him or her more effective. Even if someone is articulate, a terrific public speaker, and a charismatic presence, mastering the nuances of communicating with the media in the context of an interview is very important. Most good PR agencies provide crash courses in interacting successfully with the media. In addition, there are many firms that specialize in media training. In general, a good spokesperson should be skilled in the following areas:

- Staying on message – The job of a good spokesperson is to get the story out there, not to make friends with the reporter. Make certain to iterate the main points—and then reiterate them.

- Not getting trapped or goaded – Most reporters did not just fall off the turnip truck. They are savvy and will employ several techniques to obtain a juicy quote or a nugget of information. A good spokesperson will not get goaded into saying things he or she shouldn't. Beware the seemingly dumb reporter who keeps asking the same question over and over again. He or she may be "dumb like a fox" and asking the same question over and over to get a rise out of you or to get you to answer the question a certain way.

- Not answering a question that was not asked – In trying to be helpful, you answer a question that you think the reporter *might* ask but has not. This can get you into trouble. At this point, you are off message, or "off-road," as some jokingly call it, and the reporter will likely raise all kinds of new questions you are not prepared for.

- Learning to "bridge" – This is a PR technique for getting back to—bridging to—your message. Bring things back around to your way of thinking. Bridging is an especially useful technique when you are asked a negative or leading question on the air.

- Knowing when to go off the record or not to comment – Sometimes you want to give information that you don't want to be attributed to you or your organization. Everything you say in a briefing is on the record. You can ask the reporter if you can go off the record or "on background." This should be done carefully and only on occasion.

- Wrapping up – Ask the reporters if you have provided them with the information they needed. They will appreciate your asking. If they say no, try to get them what they need.

The PR team should also prepare a frequently asked questions (FAQ) document that provides answers to common queries concerning the news item. The FAQ ensures that the entire organization understands the news and is "on message" when speaking with customers, partners, and other influencers.

Case Study – Holding a Press Conference at a Needy Landmark

There are times when a setting can make the press conference. There are also times when the setting *is* the press conference. This was the case for Bletchley Park, located in the town of Milton Keynes, England. Bletchley Park was the home of the code breakers who helped decrypt the German codes during WWII, an accomplishment that contributed significantly to the Allied victory.

The plight of Bletchley Park came to my attention while I was serving as the head of marketing for PGP Corporation, a major producer of encryption software. Despite the historical importance of the site, it had fallen into disrepair, and it lacked the funds to make critical repairs. Emphatic requests to the British government for funds, bordering on outrage, went ignored, as did an open letter to the government from leading academics in the United Kingdom. Bletchley Park, and the work performed there, were ancestors of sorts to the security software my company developed and sold. Thus, there was a strong historical interest among our technical customers and the analysts who covered our industry.

PGP decided to help a good cause and burnish our brand at the same time. Along with IBM, we kicked off a fund-raising drive to raise money for the repairs at Bletchley Park. PGP and IBM each contributed $50,000 to the cause, and we set up a website that enabled concerned individuals to contribute directly. We announced the fund-raising drive at a press conference staged on the historic grounds of Bletchley Park. The reporters could see for themselves the buildings where the code breakers had worked (the "huts") and the ancient (but first) computers that the code breakers used for the job. They could also see for themselves the extensive repairs needed to restore the site.

The daylong event was a major success, with journalists, prominent members of the academic community, and members of industry attending. The attendees heard speeches from representatives from PGP Corporation, IBM, and the Bletchley Park Trust.

In the week following the press launch, the campaign received more than one hundred pieces of coverage—broadcast, national, corporate IT press, and blogs—including major British media BBC Online, TV and radio; ITV; the *Times of London*; and the *Independent*. It became the most widely read news via social media in PGP's history, and it was frequently mentioned by analysts and customers in the United Kingdom. Best of all, it generated major fund-raising momentum, and Bletchley Park finally got the funds it needed.

Learning More

- Catherine V. McIntyre, *Writing Effective News Releases: How To Get Free Publicity For Yourself, Your Business, Or Your Organization* (London: Piccadilly Books, 2008).

- David Merman Scott, *The New Rules of Marketing & PR*, 4th ed (Hoboken: Wiley, 2013).

Chapter 7

Social Media and Word-of-Mouth Marketing

Every year businesses in the United States pay billions of dollars to agencies to create colorful, clever, attention-grabbing marketing and advertising campaigns.[24] Although these expenditures are essential to success in the modern business environment, the most trusted forms of advertising are far less elaborate—namely, recommendations from personal acquaintances and opinions posted by customers online. According to the 2012 Nielsen Global Online Consumer Survey, 92 percent of consumers surveyed reported that they trust recommendations from people they know. Going further, a slightly lower but still impressive 70 percent trusted consumer opinions posted online.

With numbers like that, it's no wonder that word of mouth is a hot marketing topic. As consumer trust in conventional forms of advertising continues to decline, there has been increased attention in marketing circles toward marketing tactics that can address this tendency to trust opinions of acquaintances, peers, and other consumers. The trend has been inspired in no small part by the emergence of new social media technologies that enable marketers to engage with these potential recommenders and to monitor and measure their sentiments. This chapter will examine these new social media tools, the opportunities they create for marketers, and the connections between social media and word-of-mouth (WOM) marketing.

Social Media

The term *social media* refers to a broad array of tools and technologies that turn online communications into interactive dialogues. These tools fall into multiple categories. The most popular are:

Blogs – A blog (a portmanteau of the words "web" and "log") is an online journal that is frequently updated and intended for public consumption. Blogs are defined by their format: a series of entries posted to a single web page in reverse chronological order. A key social aspect of blogs is that they include the option to allow readers to leave comments. In addition, bloggers frequently include links that enable readers to connect to other blogs. Blogs exist on just about every topic under the sun. By the end of 2011, there were over 181 million blogs around the world, up from 36 million only five years earlier in 2006.[25]

Social networks – Social networks are services, platforms, and sites that focus on building online relationships and communities. This usage is an online extension of the social networks that exist among humans, a concept that was popularized by twentieth-century sociologists. Social networking services enable people to share recent activities, opinions on popular culture, photos, dating or job status, and many of life's other myriad details with their friends and colleagues. Facebook and LinkedIn are currently two of the more popular social networks out of hundreds in existence.

Microblogs – Microblogs are posts of very short entries or updates on a blog or social networking site. The short format fits well with the use of smartphones, where longer entries are tedious to type, and users can post on location. Most microblogs have tags and identifiers that make it easy for users to subscribe to a particular microblog—known as "following"—based on author or topic. Twitter is far and away today's most popular microblog.

Photo and video sharing – These are services that enable users to post photos and videos with relative ease. These services give the posters control over whom they share the photos or videos with while enabling the viewers to comment on the photos and videos. YouTube is the leading video sharing service in the world today and catalyzed all sorts of short videos "going viral"—reaching millions of viewers.

These four categories of social media are only scratching the surface. There have been literally hundreds of sites and technologies that classified themselves as social media. Some are merely on the periphery, rebranding themselves to take advantage of the social media craze. Others are hybrids—or *mash-ups*, to borrow an in-vogue term from social's Web 2.0 cousin—that combine two or more social services, such as Pinstagram, which combines the web photo sharing site Pinterest with the mobile photo sharing site Instagram.

In today's intensely competitive and ever-evolving business environment, it is essential that we consider how to leverage these technologies as marketing tools. How can we utilize these new media forms to learn about our existing customers, reach new ones, and engage with them? Blogs are where people speak about their interests, beliefs, and opinions on the products they buy—a no-brainer opportunity for market research. Many bloggers become influential through their writing. As such, they are influencers we need to target in both PR and word-of-mouth marketing efforts.

Social networks are communities where people socialize with friends and connect with other people to share common interests. In these networks, people demonstrate who they are by whom they associate with. They express their interests in order to attract others. Marketers can leverage this information, either by observing these people's behaviors or by participating in the community. Warning: If your company or brand is looking to participate in a social network, it is very important that the participation be well thought out and appropriate, lest your brand be shunned for crashing the party. Many CEOs of business-to-business product companies, for example, have insisted that their companies create a presence on Facebook, which is not a business-oriented social network. This can be the equivalent of your parents crashing the party. Everyone wonders what they are doing there. Consumer brands, on the other hand, are learning how to use Facebook to promote their products.

Moving on to microblogging, the word that comes to mind is broadcasting. Twitter (which, let's face it, owns microblogging) allows companies or employees to broadcast anything from opinions and comments on other users' posts to promotions and alerts about significant events—press releases, product launches, upcoming webcasts, event appearances, almost anything. Clearly, then, microblogging represents yet another medium for companies to broadcast themselves. Of course, Twitter brings you additional capabilities, such as the ability to gain followers and keep a count of their numbers. You can monitor Twitter for people who praise or condemn your product by "tweeting" to your identifier—either your "handle" or a tag called a "hashtag" that is associated with your product or company. ("Tweets" are individual comments; they are limited to a maximum of 140 characters.*) Tweets can be quite useful for finding and mollifying unhappy customers or influencers. PR agencies use Twitter to follow reporters they are interested in influencing, monitoring their Tweets to stay on top of what they are researching or writing, or simply to flatter them and curry favor by sending private messages or rebroadcasting their articles.

Many companies have also taken advantage of YouTube to promote their products or services. The simplest way to use YouTube is to post useful videos, typically informative or buzz-worthy, with descriptive titles containing relevant keywords. Videos posted to YouTube have high search ranking, which accomplishes YouTube's original mission—the easy sharing of video content. Thus, as with microblogging, this medium lends itself to word-of-mouth marketing. In fact, some companies have created their own channels, treating YouTube like a community and trying to garner a following. Others have created full-blown advertising campaigns specifically designed for YouTube and intended to create a following. My favorite example is Blendtec's "Will It Blend?" series on YouTube, where CEO Tom Dickson demonstrates the power of his company's blenders by "blending" skis, hockey sticks, two-by-two lumber, and even an iPad, among other things. The series has been viewed over one hundred million times, landed Dickson on *The Tonight Show* with Jay Leno, and according to Dickson, drove a significant increase in sales.

As existing media forms are improved and new forms are created, the social media landscape inevitably will change. Facebook is dominant today, but who knows who will be the dominant provider in ten years? It doesn't seem that long ago that MySpace and Friendster were the places to be. Just as these tools were supplanted by Facebook, some novel technology may come along to make Twitter look tired. Marketers, therefore, must adopt a two-pronged approach to social networking media. On the one hand, they need to appreciate the capabilities that these media offer and look to leverage them in the

---

* Why 140 and not a round number like 125 or 150? Twitter was designed to be compatible with short messaging service (SMS), which had a limit of 160 characters imposed by the telcos. Twitter's 140-character limit leaves room for a (shortened) URL and Twitter handle in the remaining 20 characters.

marketing mix. On the other hand, they constantly need to be on the lookout for "the next big thing."

Word-of-Mouth (WOM) Marketing

Word of mouth essentially refers to consumers providing information to other consumers. Word of mouth is a preexisting phenomenon that marketers are only now learning how to harness, amplify, and improve. As Nielsen and numerous others have demonstrated, having customers and consumers promote your products and services is highly effective. *WOM marketing* isn't about creating word of mouth—it's learning how to make it work within a marketing objective.

To spark this process and then manage it as part of your marketing mix, there are four common WOM marketing techniques you can consider.

Buzz marketing – Using high-profile news or other programming to get people to talk about your product or brand.

Viral marketing – Creating entertaining, informative, or sender/recipient-beneficial messages designed to be passed along, typically via e-mail. The Blendtec videos "went viral" because people had to share them with their friends.

Community marketing – Forming or supporting specialized communities (such as user groups and online forums) where consumers can discuss or promote your products or brand. You can use social networking platforms to cultivate community marketing.

Influencer marketing – Identifying key influencers who are likely to help form other people's opinions. This strategy may also include "product seeding"—giving products to key influencers so they talk about them, review them, or are photographed wearing or using them. We discussed this strategy in chapter 5 on public relations.

In his book *The Tipping Point*, Malcolm Gladwell effectively blends social networks and word-of-mouth marketing by looking at the types of people important to WOM. He characterizes three types of people: connectors, mavens, and salesmen. As the name suggests, connectors are linked with lots and lots of people. They typically have social networks (the original kind) that exceed a hundred people. Whereas connectors link us up with people, mavens link us up with ideas. Mavens have deep knowledge of a subject (the word stems from Yiddish and means "one who accumulates knowledge") and look to share it with others. Mavens are the people you know whose opinion you trust, whom you might consult about purchases such as the best wine to buy, where to go on vacation, or whether to buy a Mac or a PC. Finally, there are the salesmen, who have the persuasive skills to convince someone of an idea.

All three types are critical in what Gladwell calls "word-of-mouth epidemics." In a word-of-mouth epidemic, mavens are data banks. They provide the message. Connectors are the social glue—they spread it. But there is also a select group of people—salesmen—with the skills to persuade us when we are unconvinced of what we are hearing, and they are as critical to the tipping of word-of-mouth epidemics as the other two groups.

Creating buzz marketing is a little different from the viral marketing, community marketing, and influencer marketing WOM marketing techniques above. Mark Hughes's *Buzzmarketing* describes buzz as "Captur[ing] the attention of consumers and the media to the point where talking about your brand or company becomes entertaining, fascinating, and newsworthy."

Hughes should know. While serving as the head of marketing at the online marketplace Half.com, he convinced a small town in Oregon to change its name to…Half.com. The press ate it up. It was outrageous—which just happens to be one of Hughes's "six buttons of buzz." The other five are:

- taboo;
- the unusual;
- the hilarious;
- the remarkable;
- secrets.

In its day, Procter & Gamble's "Don't Squeeze the Charmin" commercial featuring Mr. Whipple was taboo enough to spark conversation. In 2012, energy drink producer Red Bull sponsored a skydive from the edge of the stratosphere—twenty-three miles above Earth. Pilot Felix Baumgartner broke the jump height and speed record, and Red Bull got worldwide media buzz. If you can craft a story that pushes one of the six buttons and feed it to the media, then you are on your way.

Getting a Handle on Customer Sentiment

Net Promoter

Net Promoter is a customer loyalty metric created by Fred Reichheld and publicized in his 2003 *Harvard Business Review* article "The One Number You Need to Grow." It measures the likelihood that customers will recommend—that is, promote—a given company or product.

The connection between WOM and Net Promoter Score is encapsulated in the question NPS surveys ask: "How likely is it that you would recommend our company (or product) to a friend or colleague?" Recall that consumers frequently purchase products based on the recommendations of other consumers. From a marketing perspective, then, if your NPS indicates that customers would recommend your product to others, the question becomes "What can I do to activate this sentiment?" Are you employing WOM techniques to get the word out, using these positive sentiments to your advantage?

The Net Promoter Score is calculated by asking customers a single question: "How likely is it that you would recommend our company (or product) to a friend or colleague?" Responses are scored on a scale of 0 (zero) to 10, where 0 is "Not at all likely" and 10 is "Extremely likely." Based on their responses, customers are categorized into one of three groups: promoters (9–10 rating), passives (7–8 rating), and detractors (0–6 rating). The percentage of detractors is then subtracted from the percentage of promoters to obtain the NPS. For example, if out of 100 customers, 20 are promoters, 10 are passives, and 70 are detractors, then the NPS is -50 (20–70). Note that passives are ignored because they neither promote nor detract. NPS can be as low as -100 (everybody is a detractor) or as high as +100 (everybody is a promoter).

Figure 1: Net Promoter Score (NPS)

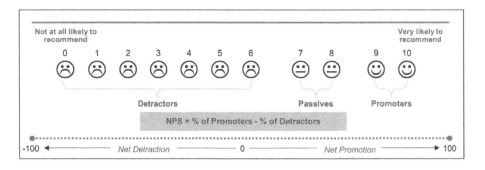

An important element of NPS is that detractors carry a lot more weight (0–6, or 64 percent) than promoters (9–10, or 18 percent). Why is this? The reason is quite simple. People who are unhappy are much more likely to express their displeasure. This is simply human nature, and customers can get really angry about bad service or a shoddy product. In contrast, people have to be really pleased with a product to feel confident enough to recommend it to friends or colleagues.

NPS was a significant departure from typical satisfaction surveys that simply use an average score from 1 to 10. These surveys fail to take into account two factors: (1) detractors exert substantial negative power, and (2) people who weren't extremely satisfied (delighted, some would say) really have no effect. An NPS above 0 (a higher percentage of promoters than detractors) is considered good, and anything over +50 (showing a wide margin between promoters and detractors) is thought to be excellent. If you are in negative territory, then you have work to do.

Social media is a great place for detractors to vent. Many bloggers write product reviews. Others rant in tweets. For marketers, then, staying tuned in to all communications channels and responding appropriately is critical. In his book *The Anatomy of Buzz Revisited*, Emanuel Rosen stresses the importance of listening to detractors and working to solve their problems. Rosen also tackles the problem of what he calls "secondhand detractors"—people who have never used your product but spread the negative views of others. Valid complaints, even spread secondhand, should be considered, of course. But Rosen suggests this is where an organization's reputation, built over the years with the aid of PR and advertising, can be the "immune system" against this kind of negativity.

Monitoring NPS is straightforward. A company sends out the NPS survey to its existing customers so they will see the results. Many companies monitor NPS on an annual basis and use it to drive strategy, product direction, and budget allocation. I believe that the marketing department should own the NPS process, because marketing ideally represents the customer's voice to the company. I will come back to this in chapter 21 on metrics.

Social Sentiment

The way to track WOM is to monitor social media. Fortunately, marketers have several reliable tools to assist them in this task. Most monitoring tools work by searching social networks for mention of a particular product, company, or person and then reporting out on the number of mentions and their tonality, sometimes called *social sentiment*. Some companies actively monitor and triage social media mentions. Product complaints are handled first and get routed to customer service or customer support. Remember, turning around detractors has a disproportionate effect on NPS. Questions on how to use the product get routed to customer support or product management. People looking for product recommendations may get routed to sales or sent toward a known influencer outside the company. Rants or unhappy influencers may be forwarded to the PR team for special handling. Over time, by being connected to what customers are saying, working to address their issues, and activating the social network using WOM techniques, companies can influence social sentiment and NPS.

Social sentiment can be measured by comparing positive mentions to negative ones. One widely used formula for performing this calculation is Net Social Sentiment (NSS). NSS measures the "temperature" of the social conversation concerning your product, service, or company. It uses *actionable Internet mentions (AIM)*, which are mentions of your products, services, or company on social networks, forums, and blogs that you deem to have value to your organization. You may choose not to include, for example, forums that discuss the history of your product or company and tweets that only marginally concern your product. You also need to decide whether to include dedicated "hate" or "rant" sites.

Consider the case of Dell. In June 2005, new media blogger Jeff Jarvis used the catchy phrase "Dell Hell" in his blog, *The Buzz Machine*, and Dell's customer support issues were publicized two days later in the *New York Times*. Rather than try to spin the news or brush it off as a PR black eye, Dell, to its credit, responded by implementing an entire social media program to listen to its customers and use social media to turn "ranters into ravers."[26]

The formula employed by NSS is:

$$NSS = \frac{(Positive\ AIM - Negative\ AIMs)}{Total\ AIMs}$$

The result is expressed as a percentage. Figure 2 below provides an example of NSS monitoring from a high-tech company in Silicon Valley. Notice that NSS plunges into negative territory on June 8, the day with the highest AIM volume for the period. Why did this occur? The reason is that the company released a product that contained numerous bugs that caused extensive customer problems. In response, the customers took to social media to express their anger. The company had to work hard, both to fix the product and to communicate with customers via social media, to eventually restore their NSS to positive territory. Remember, these efforts involve influencing customer sentiment, and may take time before you see results.

Figure 2: Monitoring Net Social Sentiment (NSS)

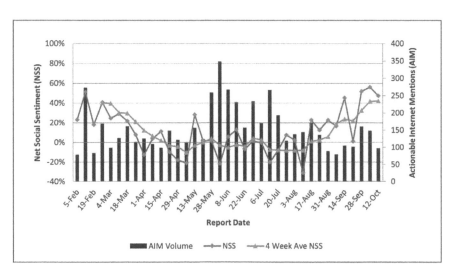

Case Study

One of the best examples of WOM marketing comes not from this century or last century, but from the nineteenth century. And, it happened in neither the United States nor Western Europe, but in Russia. As retold in Linda Himelstein's fascinating *The King of Vodka*, Pyotr Smirnov, father of the now-worldwide Smirnoff vodka brand (rebranded using the more popular French spelling), faced the imposing challenge of making his product stand out among the competition. At the time, Moscow had hundreds of distillers, and vodka was available at almost all taverns. Each tavern had its favorite distiller, and customers were used to drinking whatever brand they were served. Although Smirnov was convinced that his revolutionary charcoal-filtered vodka was a superior product, he realized that he was going to have a hard time convincing people of that himself, tavern by tavern.

To address this challenge, in 1872, Smirnov crafted a highly unorthodox marketing strategy. His efforts began in the Khitrov market, a grimy section of Moscow frequented by those newly arrived from the countryside who were looking for work. It was a busy part of the city, with as many as ten thousand people a day moving through it and all of its pubs. Smirnov went there to recruit a group of men who would become his representatives.

Smirnov took his small band of recruits back to his house, where he fed them and gave them vodka to drink. The group was a collection of men from a broad range of neighborhoods in and around Moscow. Smirnov informed them he would pay them to eat and drink vodka, on one condition—they demand Smirnov vodka everywhere they went. If Smirnov vodka were not available—which at the time was true more often than not—they were to complain loudly and refuse any other brand of vodka that was offered. When the manager came over, they were to ask him, "How is it possible that your respected establishment does not have such a vodka? It is absolutely the most remarkable vodka there is!" They would then leave the pub in a huff and start the performance all over again in the next tavern.

As the story goes, Smirnov began getting inquiries from tavern managers the very first day. Smirnov kept it up, having his word-of-mouth crew fan out all over the city until they had visited every drinking establishment in Moscow. Once Smirnov had saturated the city limits, he sent his representatives on the rail lines, stopping at every station along the way. It was said that news of Smirnov's vodka "traveled like a virus," spreading his vodka throughout Russia. Smirnov's campaign was undoubtedly one of the earliest examples of viral marketing.

Smirnov did not limit his marketing efforts to his WOM methods. He was, by most accounts, a marketing genius. Indeed, he was an early practitioner/advocate of newspaper advertising, charitable donations in the company's name, and award gathering for prestige—all tried-and-true tools of today's marketers.

Learning More

♦ Malcolm Gladwell, *The Tipping Point: How Little Things Can Make a Big Difference* (New York:Back Bay Books, 2002).

♦ Linda Himelstein, *The King of Vodka* (New York:HarperCollins, 2010).

♦ Mark Hughes, *Buzzmarketing* (New York:Portfolio, 2005).

♦ Fred Reichheld, *The Ultimate Question 2.0: How Net Promoter Companies Thrive in a Customer-Driven World* (Boston:Harvard Business Review Press, 2011).

♦ Emanuel Rosen, *The Anatomy of Buzz Revisited* (New York:Doubleday, 2009).

♦ "WOM 101," Word of Mouth Marketing Association, 2007

Chapter 8

Beyond the Press Release – Product Reviews, Awards, Surveys, and Studies

C ustomers and prospects are often suspicious of material that was obviously created by marketing. Today's marketers are paying the price accrued from decades of marketing—customers have become jaded. This may come as a rude awakening to marketing professionals, but loss of credibility can be an occupational hazard.

How can marketers address this problem? As we discussed in the previous chapter, one remedy is to have other people promote your product, service, or organization for you through social media and word-of-mouth advertising. If a WOM campaign is not feasible, however, what other options does a marketer have? The answer is to leverage the opinions of product reviewers, editors, industry experts, and customers themselves via product reviews, awards, surveys, and studies. All of these have more credibility and engender more trust than marketing-generated assets.

This chapter focuses on various methods that marketers and organizations can utilize to promote their products and themselves, both to key influencers and to prospective customers. Specifically, it examines the following marketing tools:

- Product reviews

- Awards

- Surveys

- Studies

Marketers can use any or all of these tools in their marketing mix, depending on their goals.

Product Reviews

A review can make or break a product. For example, the opinion of Walter Mossberg, who reviewed technology products for the *Wall Street Journal* for over twenty years, would significantly affect a product's market performance.[*] In general, a great review will attract interest and pave the way for your salespeople. Conversely, a negative review can make prospective buyers shun you and create yet another obstacle for your sales team. Regardless of whether you are selling a consumer device, a car, or enterprise software, buyers trust third-party reviews, so you need to obtain them. All effective marketers appreciate—or should appreciate—this simple reality. Nevertheless, it's amazing how little time and effort many organizations devote to maximizing their chances of obtaining positive reviews.

In order to attract positive reviews, it is important first to understand the life of a product reviewer. Quite often, reviewers are freelancers who were assigned to your product. They may not be paid a great deal of money to write the review, and they probably have a tight deadline. Understandably, then, a product that is hard to obtain, hard to understand, and difficult to install and use is not likely to elicit a glowing review. A good rule of thumb, then, is to

---

[*] Based in Washington, DC, Mossberg is nonetheless the most important critic of technology and consumer electronics products. *Wired* magazine called him "The Kingmaker" in a profile. He was reportedly the highest paid columnist at the *Wall Street Journal*. Mossberg left the *Journal* in 2014 to start his own media site Re/code.

place yourself in the position of the reviewer and ask, how would I feel about this product?

In the case where your product is being reviewed by a publication or an organization with a paid review staff in their labs, don't forget that although the staff may be experienced reviewers with a bit more job security, they are not necessarily experts in your product or market area. Therefore, you need to help them understand whom the product is designed for and how to install and use it.

One widely used strategy for assisting reviewers is to prepare an informative reviewer's guide. As its name suggests, the *reviewer's guide* is a document created specifically to help product reviewers do their job. Not providing a guide forces the reviewer to rely only on the user's manual, online support, and the product itself. You can decide not to create a reviewer's guide, but you do so at your own risk. Even if your documentation, product, and support team are great, you would be missing out on the opportunity to paint your product in the best light. Fortunately, the process of creating a reviewer's guide is straightforward, and it is well worth the effort. Below are key elements of the reviewer's guide:

> Product and market overview – Make certain the reviewers understand who the product is intended for. You don't want them citing a lack of enterprise-grade features in a product intended for consumers, or comparing your ecowagon's acceleration to that of an imported sports car. Context is important.

> What's new – Try not to list every feature in your product. Instead, focus on what's new and interesting. This is the information that will grab the reviewers'—and hopefully the consumers'—attention.

> Competitive positioning – Tell the reviewers why your product is superior to the competition. This is your chance to set the agenda, so be certain to take maximum advantage of it.

> How to install/use the product – If you have a "quick start" or a simplified instruction manual, then it's easy to create this section of the reviewer's guide. You can also highlight key features in this section explaining why they are interesting or unique. I also like to highlight

any cautions so that the reviewers don't erase their hard drives or set themselves on fire when trying to use the product.

Key contacts – Provide reviewers with the contact information for the following individuals: (a) a product expert who can help them install and use the product, (b) a spokesperson who can give them additional background on the market and your product's distinctive features, and (c) a PR contact to whom they can direct logistical questions. Make sure to provide direct-dial and, ideally, mobile phone numbers as well as e-mail addresses for all of the contacts. Dealing with reviewers should be a top priority for the contacts, so make certain they have time to perform this role and they understand its importance. They don't need to be oleaginous, just helpful and responsive.

Pricing – The preferred policy is simply to list the suggested retail price of the basic configuration or package. For a head-to-head review, where your competitors' products will be listed alongside yours, you should think about how your product's price will look in comparison. If the way you package your product—for example, as part of a bundle with other products—will make your product look significantly more expensive by comparison, make sure to explain this clearly so the reviewer can put the price in context.

Company overview – The overview can be your standard corporate boilerplate, plus any other information you think is relevant.

Graphics, photos, box shots – Provide print- and web-ready graphics that the reviewers can use in their articles. You don't want the reviewers to have to do their own screen captures if they are not set up for it. Make certain the reviewers have access to high-resolution versions of your logo so they don't have to use whatever they happen to find on a Google image search. A box shot is what your product looks like in its package, or box, and is appropriate for some consumer products.

Additional research and benchmarks – You may want to provide the reviewers with additional proof points that you know they will not be able to reproduce in their environment. You may have performance benchmarks for your enterprise software, for example, or the results of leaving your new smartphone in a frozen tundra for thirty days.

Your reviewer's guide should be well organized, well written, and easy to use. You should provide it in electronic form to make it easy to cut and paste from. Remember, reviewers are on a deadline, and providing text they can cut, paste, and edit helps them as well as you. Avoid marketing hype, because it may turn off a jaded writer. A good reviewer's guide is comprehensive yet to the point, and it should not exceed ten to fifteen pages.

You should consider tweaking the reviewer's guide for each reviewer, perhaps highlighting things you think they may be interested in, or even organizing the details to match the way they write their stories. Your PR agency can assist with this task. Make certain that someone is assigned to check in with the reviewers periodically (without bugging them) to see if they need anything. Quite often reviewers are writing other reviews—or articles, if they are reporters—and they are too busy to ask for help. Therefore, adopting a proactive strategy can make their job easier.

As vital as product reviews are to your organization, there may be times when it's in your interest to *decline* a review. For example, your product could have problems, or your company could have a bad history with the reviewer. Perhaps your better-than-ever new version is just around the corner. In circumstances such as these, it is okay to decline. If you do so, however, you should find out whether the reviewer plans to publicize the fact that you declined to participate—for example, in a multi-product review. If so, then you need to provide a reason for declining that you would be comfortable seeing in the media.

Awards

Many publications hand out awards. These awards can take all forms. In some cases, they are the result of a successful head-to-head review against your competition. Your product may win an "Editor's Choice" or a "Best Buy" designation that you can highlight in your marketing. Other awards are bestowed via annual roundups, like "Product of the Year." Sometimes publications work in conjunction with trade shows or conferences on "Best of Show" awards.

Whatever the award, you should make certain your product or company enters as many contests and competitions as it possibly can. As the great New York Lottery marketing slogan proclaims, "You gotta be in it to win it." Your PR agency should assist you by monitoring the editorial calendar of the publications on your media list, both for review opportunities and for annual awards. In addition, you should inquire as to whether the trade shows and conferences you attend have awards. In most cases, to be considered for an award, you simply have to fill out an entry form.

One basic, yet effective, strategy to enhance your chances of winning is to review past winners to determine how and why the judges selected these products and what characteristics they valued the most. Then, make certain to emphasize the same elements in your submission. If the award is being handed out during a trade show, creating buzz around your product can help. You might brief a select group of influencers who will be at the show, like bloggers and analysts, and try to get them to talk and blog about your product while at the event. Or you could stage some kind of stunt involving your product to get the buzz going. Finally, some publications confer "Reader's Choice" awards where the readers decide the winners by popular vote. Mobilizing your customers via direct mail and social media outreach will improve your chances of winning these awards.

While you are pursuing all of these product awards, don't overlook awards for your executives or your company. There are many "Fastest Growing Companies," "Top Companies," and "Most Influential Companies" types of awards sponsored by the business media. You may even want to enter a "Best Companies to Work For" contest if you are looking to recruit or retain talented employees. Your CEO or founder may be a good entrant in a "Most Influential" or "Top Executives" award. No matter what the type, winning an award adds luster to your products *and* your company. Put every award you win on your website and your company overview and in your press kit. Even the media like to back a winner, and awards can influence them to view your organization in a more positive light.

Surveys

Although some people consider surveys boring or mundane, they are great public relations tools. Surveys encourage direct interaction with your customers, and they provide you with a snapshot of what your customers or your market are thinking. Moreover, if they are managed properly, they can generate news that you can then promote to the media.

Marketers usually employ surveys to sample attitudes or to solicit feedback on a product, service, or experience. In addition, if marketing teams want to understand how prospective customers perceive your company, then surveys are extremely useful.

But these examples are all "outside-in" uses of the survey—ways to capture how the market is viewing your company or products. Although this is valuable information, none of these uses really has a news angle. To achieve this objective, you need to design a survey specifically to generate newsworthy nuggets. If you do this successfully, then the survey can also educate your executive team about the market, and it can inform your product development team about what they should be working on.

To create a newsworthy survey, you need to determine what your customers are wondering about. How can you do this? The most effective strategies are to talk to your salespeople, review your online forums, and communicate with some of your customers. First, figure out what *they* want to know. Then, figure out what *you* want to know about their habits, purchasing plans, fears, or anything else. Finally, construct a survey that will elicit answers to these questions in a way that is quantifiable.

The media love to write stories that focus on customer attitudes and trends. Readers love to find out what other people like them are doing or thinking. Don't assume the press will not publish survey findings from a company with a vested interest in the results. The media are too busy to create their own surveys, and they prefer to utilize a third-party source that is authoritative. Although there are lots of research firms that specialize in polling and surveys, there are thousands of things they do not cover. Creating a survey that yields interesting findings not currently covered by existing surveys is how you get the media's attention.

Packaging the findings for the press is essential. After you have conducted your survey and analyzed the responses, write up the results clearly in a press release, and call out the key findings, ideally in bulleted form. Provide an expert opinion concerning the reasons for certain trends and beliefs, both in the release and via a spokesperson who was involved in the survey process. You may also want to incorporate selected quotes or excerpts from responses that illustrate or strengthen some of the key findings.

In addition to issuing a press release, you should provide a copy of the results to the media. We recommend that you furnish a summary version of the results in the form of a report, and that you create a longer, more detailed version that you make available to prospects as part of a lead-generation offer. You can offer the prospects a "deeper look" or "exclusive content" to drive their interest.

Finally, many companies create *infographics*, visual representations of information, to augment their surveys. Infographics are prevalent in modern media, so why not create your own? At the very least they will help convey your results to the media, even if the reviewers don't actually use them. Some journalists, and especially bloggers, will include them in their write-ups. Plus, the infographics might go viral via social media. Below is an example of an infographic created by the PR team at Symantec, based on a survey comparing attitudes of users and IT staff.

Figure 1: Infographic showing results of 2012 Symantec survey of IT staff and users

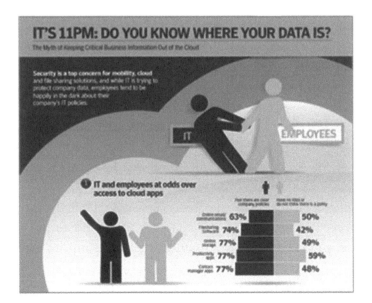

Studies

In some cases, a survey will identify a particular topic that your customers need to better understand. Perhaps there are important legal or regulatory developments that would cause customers to become interested in your product or service. As another example, the safety improvements in your latest version might make it attractive to a market segment that is currently paying hefty insurance premiums. If teens in Peoria knew what teens in New York or Los Angeles were wearing, would it change their buying habits? The possibilities are limitless.

Suppose, however, that no one is studying the topic that your customers need to know about. Industry analysts typically have their own research calendars, and you may not be able to influence them. How do you resolve this problem? The answer is actually rather simple: Create your own study. You can conduct your own study if you have expertise and cannot afford a third party. Just as with surveys, if your organization has expertise and no one else is offering a current study on the topic, you should exploit the opportunity. If the study is interesting, of good quality, and not overtly biased, the media will be interested. Figure 2 below is an infographic from an annual security study conducted by Symantec's internal research team. This infographic was viewed thousands of times, and the study itself generated hundreds of articles and blog posts.

Figure 2: An infographic for Symantec's 2011
Internet Security Threat Report

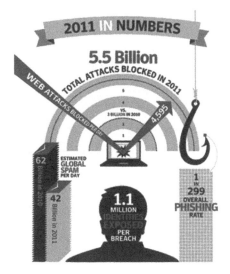

If you prefer to use a third-party expert, finding one to conduct a study is not difficult. You just need to look a little harder and dig a little deeper. Locate a professor at a university who has researched and written about the topic. Search for a consultant who has years of experience in a particular industry or with a certain kind of product. Think tanks, research institutes, and advocacy groups that focus on certain issues are also fertile ground.

The best arrangement is for your organization to sponsor the research. You pay an honorarium to the researchers to conduct research on the topic you are interested in. Most researchers will agree to pursue the project and publish the study if (1) the topic is of interest to them and (2) the results are based exclusively on the research and are not biased or modified by the sponsoring organization. Many researchers actually view these types of studies as opportunities to publicize themselves. You can assist them with these efforts by having your PR team arrange press interviews for them. Just as with surveys above, draft a press release summarizing the results and highlight the key findings, but use the researcher as the spokesperson.

Regardless of whether you do your own study or hire a third party, the research results are great fodder for all of your marketing materials. You can train your salespeople to utilize the research while they are prospecting. Various studies over the years have revealed that customers prefer to deal with salespeople who bring them useful information. You should package the actual study in a document and use it to generate demand for your product, either by uploading it to your website or by e-mailing it to prospective customers. If you plan to mail the study to the customers, we recommend a two-step process in which you send them a summary and then offer them the full version in exchange for a meeting or a phone call.

Ultimately, studies will bring credibility to your organization. Customers and prospective customers appreciate quality research. If industry analysts are not publishing research on the topic, then your organization should step in to fill that void. The longer you employ this strategy—whether publishing an annual study or a series of related studies—the more trust you will accrue.

Case Study – The Ponemon Cost of a Data Breach Report

In 2004, this author's former employer, PGP Corporation, faced a big challenge. Several state governments in the United States had passed legislation requiring companies that lost sensitive customer information—such as credit card numbers or social security numbers—to publicly disclose the facts in a press release in order to inform consumers. PGP Corporation sold software that protected against these types of data breaches. The software would encrypt details like credit card numbers stored in spreadsheets on hard drives, so that even if this information were inadvertently lost or exposed, it would be unreadable. The software, of course, cost money. The question confronting prospective customers was, which was more expensive—the cost of the software or the costs associated with a data breach? No one knew the answer.

So, in 2005, PGP searched for an expert who could help assess the costs of a data breach. We eventually found Dr. Larry Ponemon and his recently formed Ponemon Institute, then a small but well-regarded research organization based in Traverse City, Michigan, that focused on privacy, data protection, and information security policy.

Dr. Ponemon possessed three key qualifications. First, he was dedicated to the study of privacy and the impacts of breaches of privacy. Second, he possessed both the reputation and the ability to conduct sensitive research with companies that had suffered breaches. Finally, he had the financial and accounting background to create the risk models—a skill well beyond what anyone on our staff possessed.

Dr. Ponemon published his initial study in 2006. His research involved interviews with fourteen companies that had suffered data breaches. These were sensitive conversations that Dr. Ponemon handled confidentially. The research was beneficial to our prospective customers—another key to creating a successful study—because they could use the results to quantify the risk of future breaches for their management. The study broke down the costs into four main categories:

- Legal and PR costs
- Staff time spent investigating and fixing the breach

- Miscellaneous expenses, such as software and credit protection services offered to mollify angry customers

- Lost revenues from enraged customers who took their business elsewhere

The study calculated the cost to be $138 per customer record lost. At first glance, this number might not seem particularly severe. Consider, however, that if a company lost a thousand records, then the costs would total $138,000. In general, the more records a company lost, the greater the cost. The average costs to the fourteen companies studied were a staggering $4.5 million. Significantly, the greatest costs were not technology or legal fees. Rather, they were the lost revenues of upset customers taking their business elsewhere—something any business executive could relate to. With the business impact and the potential costs in the millions, and the PGP software costing about $200 per user, the sales reps could present a straightforward return on investment, supported by real data.

Since 2006, PGP (now Symantec, which acquired PGP and continued the research) and the Ponemon Institute have collaborated on a research study every year. Over this time, the studies have attracted greater publicity and a substantially larger audience. The initial study generated only a handful of articles. By 2011, Symantec was conducting the study in eight countries, measuring the costs specific to different customer bases and regulatory environments. More than two hundred articles, hundreds of blog posts, and thousands of clicks, tweets, and downloads have made the study a killer thought-leadership piece that helps drive the business.

Chapter 9

Direct Marketing

What might seem commonplace today was actually revolutionary not too long ago. In a famous speech delivered at the Hundred Million Club of New York in 1961, Lester Wunderman drew an important distinction between how most of Madison Avenue marketed and how he and a handful of other upstarts did it. As he explained:

> The din of advertising becomes louder and louder, and it costs more to make a consumer remember the advertising he saw, heard, or read when he makes a buying decision. Isn't it logical to sell him at the point of his greatest conviction, when he has just absorbed the sales message?

While most of Madison Avenue was using mass media to conduct mass marketing, Wunderman and a few others were using mass media to target individual buyers and elicit responses from them. Wunderman defined this policy of focusing on individual buyers as *direct marketing*. Over the ensuing fifty-plus years, direct marketing has evolved from a groundbreaking strategy to a critical tool in almost every marketer's toolbox. Although direct marketing has undergone a number of major technological changes, it is as relevant today as it ever was.

This chapter covers the basics of direct marketing—the tools and terminology—as well as how to measure its effectiveness. We will start by tracing the roots of direct marketing to the time-tested practice of direct mail.

Direct Mail – The Start of Direct Marketing

Before there was direct marketing, there was direct mail. Richard Sears sent out his first printed mailer selling jewelry and watches in 1888, followed six years later by what would become the iconic Sears & Roebuck catalog.[27] However, despite its history, and the success of the Sears & Roebuck catalog, many practitioners of direct mail, also known as mail-order marketing, felt like second-class citizens, and they were treated as such by their advertising agency brethren. As print advertising grew, and as radio and television advertising came on the scene in the middle of the twentieth century, the contempt of ad men for mail-order marketing men grew.

Perhaps it was the medium. Today, the term "mail order" conjures up cheap, even tawdry, images. But it was Wunderman who realized that it was not the medium but the direct connection to buyers that was important. A few years after addressing the Hundred Million Club, he was invited to explain the *theory* behind direct marketing. As he argued in his landmark 1967 speech at MIT titled "Direct Marketing—The New Revolution in Selling":

> Mail-order and mail-order advertising are bigger, healthier, and more vital today than ever before—even though much of it is no longer done by mail…The very term itself has lost validity, and it will be less applicable in the future. In a strict sense, mail-order means that the customer's order is sent by mail and that his merchandise is, in turn, delivered to him by mail. Already this is not true. Phones are easier, faster, and more personal. But it will not stop there. More sophisticated and better methods of ordering and delivering will surely come, whether they be orders geared directly to computers, video phones, closed-circuit television, or some newer technology.

Thus, whereas direct mail was restricted to printed materials, direct marketing meant reaching the customer directly, no matter the medium. With the proliferation of the telephone, for example, telemarketing became a standard practice in many operations. Years later, as the nation entered the digital age, computers and the Internet emerged as a foundational marketing and sales medium. (Significantly, Wunderman presciently predicted the impact the web would have on commerce with his predictions that computers would play an important future role in ordering and delivering goods.)

In sum, then, *direct marketing* involves selling via direct contact with the customer or prospective customer. In contrast, advertising makes prospective customers broadly aware of a product, but the selling happens later and not directly. Importantly, direct marketing seeks to elicit a behavioral response, or action, such as a call or click, to drive a business outcome, such as an appointment, visit, donation, subscription, or ultimately, a purchase. As we'll discuss next, direct marketing utilizes an array of delivery mechanisms, ranging from traditional mail to the Internet.

Direct Marketing Methods

Today, marketers have a number of direct marketing methods at their disposal. The six primary methods are:

Catalogs – Catalogs still fill mailboxes of consumers and businesses around the world, decades after critics predicted the web would kill them off. One of the oldest forms of direct marketing is alive and well—and thriving. Almost ninety million Americans bought products from catalogs in 2011.[28] The reason? For consumer catalogs, the number of women working outside the home, with less time to shop, combined with increased comfort with telephone and web ordering, have combined to drive revenues to all-time highs. In the case of B2B catalogs, the increased cost of salespeople compared to catalog mailing, combined with the same telephone and web ordering, are the drivers. Catalogs can be expensive to produce and mail, but the results are worthwhile for the right type of business. According to the *Direct Marketing Association 2010 Annual Response Rate Report*, catalogs had the lowest cost per lead/order at $47.61, just ahead of inserts at $47.69, e-mail at $53.85, and postcards at $75.32.[29]

Direct mail – As we've already discussed, *direct mail* is a marketing effort that uses a mail service to deliver a promotional printed piece to your target audience. Typical direct mail pieces include postcards, letters, brochures, and catalogs. In addition, some marketers send packages or specially designed three-dimensional mailers—commonly known as "dimensional pieces"—to increase both customer interest and open rates. Because all forms of direct mail involve both printing and mailing costs, this delivery mechanism can be expensive.

Direct e-mail – As the name suggests, *direct e-mail*, or *electronic direct mail (eDM)*, delivers a promotion to your target audience via e-mail. An eDM can be plain text e-mail, or it can use HTML to make it more visually appealing and to identify it more explicitly with your brand. Compared with traditional direct mail, eDM is less expensive, and it allows customers to respond directly via reply or hyperlink (eDM's instantaneous delivery also reduces anxiety among direct marketers who would otherwise be waiting on tenterhooks for their mail drop to arrive in prospect mailboxes). One major disadvantage is that eDM is subject to anti-spam regulations (and anti-spam filters on e-mail servers that reduce delivery rates).

Direct-response advertising – Another widely used mechanism is *direct-response advertising*. In this strategy, the marketer urges a viewer to respond to an offer using a direct-response mechanism, such as a coupon, a business reply card, a toll-free number, or a web link. We'll consider these mechanisms in more detail below. Direct-response advertising differs from advertising designed for awareness in that it requires the audience to *do* something. There is some debate in the case of ads that do not contain a strong offer or *call to action (CTA)*, but list a toll-free number or a company website URL, as to whether this is truly direct-response advertising.

Online advertising – Depending on its format, *online advertising* can be a form of direct-response advertising. Some online ads are geared toward awareness or brand building and do not seek to elicit an immediate action. The appeal of online advertising is that the marketer can target a buyer more accurately than with print advertising. (We will cover this in more detail in chapter 13 on advertising.) In addition, it is simple to put a CTA in an online ad, such as "Click Here." Not all online ads have explicit or strong offers, which is critical to the success of direct marketing.

Telemarketing – Telemarketing involves the use of telephone calls to market goods or services directly to prospective customers. Compared with direct mail and direct-response advertising, telemarketing is a more active form of marketing, because it provides a real human being to present your message and respond to customers' questions.

In addition to targeting prospective customers much more carefully, direct marketing offers another advantage over traditional general marketing or advertising efforts; namely, the results of a direct marketing promotion can be measured—often very precisely—in terms of customer responses.

Direct Marketing Terminology

Practitioners boil down direct marketing to four key elements: the list, the copy, the offer, and the call to action. Each element has to be right for a direct marketing campaign to be effective. The *list*, or the database, is the set of people who will be contacted. In the case of direct-response advertising, demographics are substituted for a list of explicit names. How the offer is written—the *copy*—is critical to grabbing the readers', the listeners', or the viewers' attention and convincing them that the product addresses a need or fulfills a wish.*

The *offer* is the hook. What are you offering prospective customers in return for their response? The offer can be a discount, a free gift (an unfortunate marketing redundancy that has stuck), educational material like a white paper or study, or whatever you think will motivate the buyer. The call to action is a directive that urges the reader, listener, or viewer to take an immediate action, such as "Write Now," "Call Now," or (on the Internet) "Click Here." Be careful

---

* David Ogilvy had a lot to say about writing copy. Here's one that's especially appropriate for cost-conscious direct marketers: "On the average, five times as many people read the headline as read the body copy. When you have written your headline, you have spent eighty cents out of your dollar."

not to mix up the offer and the CTA, as some marketers do. Both are critical. Asking someone to "Call Now" will not work without an effective offer. But wait, there's more. (Just kidding.)

As was mentioned above, measurement is a key advantage of direct marketing over advertising. Direct marketing has a discrete set of *actions*. Each can be thought of as moving the prospective customer, subscriber, or donor closer to the desired *outcome*. Below are the most common measurements of actions.

> Open rate – The measurement of how often letters, packages, or pieces of electronic mail direct marketing are opened or viewed. You want to know if they at least looked at the copy, as opposed to throwing the mailer in the trash or deleting the e-mail unread, because it can give you clues about the effectiveness of the envelope, package, or subject line of an e-mail, for example. In the case of physical mail, the open rate is measured by surveys conducted by direct marketing organizations. Online, with e-mail, the rate can be measured automatically.

> Click-through rate – The measurement of how often customers click on links or CTA buttons after they open an eDM message.

> Callback rate – The measurement of how many customers call a toll-free number. For television or radio advertising, measuring during the period just after the ad is broadcast is best. Marketers can also use multiple toll-free numbers to track by media type and/or ad variant.

> Conversion rate – The measurement of *conversions*, that is, the number of prospective customers who reach the desired outcome. The conversion rate is typically expressed as a percentage.

Response Mechanisms

Not only does direct marketing allow marketers to utilize several delivery methods, it also provides prospective customers with a number of options for responding to the marketing messages (i.e., ways to take action). In fact, as technology has evolved over time, marketers have invented new and innovative ways for their targeted customers to heed their call to action. Each strategy is designed to make it as convenient as possible for the consumer to act, or "convert." Interestingly, all of these strategies are still in use today. This section covers the following response mechanisms:

- Business reply cards
- Business reply envelopes
- Toll-free numbers
- E-mail
- Links
- Promotional codes
- Quick response codes
- Text messaging

A *business reply card (BRC)* is a preaddressed postcard that is bound, glued, or inserted into a magazine, or included with direct mail. These cards often fall in your lap when you open or read a magazine. They are specially designed so that prospective customers can fill them out quickly and return them. To make this practice more affordable, the post office charges marketers a lower business reply mail (BRM) postage rate.

Similar to the BRC, the *business reply envelope (BRE)* is a preaddressed envelope that is included in a direct mail envelope. Customers can easily return BREs at the reduced "business rate mail" postage rate. Another benefit of BREs is that customers can pay by check. In addition, if they choose to pay by credit card, they can keep their credit card number or other personal information private.

The 1-800 *toll-free number* was introduced in 1967 by AT&T to reduce the number of operators needed to handle collect calls to businesses. Direct marketers quickly seized on this innovation. Lester Wunderman is often credited with fueling the use of toll-free numbers by direct marketers.

Although *e-mail* is not as widely used as other, more efficient digital response mechanisms, such as links to a landing page, a number of companies allow customers to respond via e-mail, typically via a custom e-mail address that is tailored to a specific advertising campaign or product line. You might, for example, create the special e-mail address donations@foundation.org for a fund-raising campaign.

Links are a major form of online direct marketing. Shortly after the web became popular in the mid-1990s, some companies began to include their company URL in print advertising. This strategy was particularly popular with companies that appealed to younger, tech-savvy demographics. It has evolved into so-called "vanity URLs" that are tied to specific print or television advertising campaigns, such as company.com/vacation. These URLs usually point to a web landing page—sometimes called a *microsite*that is tailored to capture information from the user and turn it into a lead, for example, www.companyname.com/offername.

A *promotional code* is a short alphanumeric code used to track an offer. The code typically appears in a direct mail, eDM, or an advertisement. A customer enters the promo code into a web form to receive the offer, typically a discount on a purchase. Strictly speaking, promo codes are not response mechanisms in the same way links or toll-free numbers are, but they do compel a prospective customer to take action, because promo codes typically offer a discount. They also allow the marketer to track the effectiveness of a particular direct marketing program, since a unique promo code can be used for each one.

Originally created by a Toyota subsidiary for tracking cars on the assembly line, the *quick response (QR) code* really gained popularity with the adoption of camera-enabled smartphones. Readers of ads, in-store product displays, and transit shelter signs can take a picture of the code with the cameras on their phones and then be directed to a website that allows them to move to the conversion step.

Figure 1 below shows the first QR code used by Coca-Cola in 2011. It was printed on cups at convenience store 7-Eleven. The code was part of a clever, interactive cause marketing campaign to help the World Wildlife Fund protect polar bears—an animal Coca-Cola used widely in its advertising at the time.

Scanning the QR code downloaded a fun smartphone game called *Snowball Effect* that encouraged users to donate one dollar to the World Wildlife Fund efforts, which Coca-Cola would match.[30]

Figure 1: Coca-Cola's first use of a QR code on convenience store 7-Eleven's cups in their "Arctic Home" campaign

Finally, *text messaging*, more commonly known as "texting," enables users to send short messages via their mobile phones. Advertisers have taken advantage of texting, allowing users who view a television program, a television advertisement, a print ad, or an out-of-home advertisement to respond using their phones by sending a short message to a special shortened phone number. Texting has the advantage of enabling prospective customers to instantly download applications and add-ons for mobile phones, as well as coupons. Texting also enables marketers to conduct quick surveys or polls. One major limitation of text messaging is that it doesn't allow marketers to capture additional information about the user, in contrast to web links, e-mail, and postal mail response mechanisms.

Selecting the Right Direct Marketing Method

Figure 2, below, lays out the complete direct marketing taxonomy, including methods, outcomes, response mechanisms, and measurements.

Figure 2: Direct marketing taxonomy

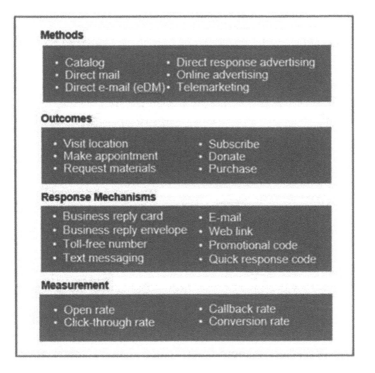

You are the best judge of which methods and response mechanisms will work for your prospects. If you have a mass market product and a small budget, for example, then direct mail might be too expensive to even consider. In contrast, sending an eDM and having your inside salespeople follow up would be cheaper and can generate the desired outcome.

Knowing your prospective customers and their behaviors is critical to an effective direct marketing effort. Marketers who study and know their buyers are worth their weight in gold. Some sets of buyers get so many offers via e-mail they don't even look at them anymore, so while eDM would be cheaper overall, it would not be effective.

A good way to approach a direct marketing effort is to think about how many outcomes (whether leads or actual purchases) you need and how much you are willing to pay for each. *Cost per acquisition*, or CPA, is how much it costs per prospective customer to get him or her to convert to the desired outcome. CPA is your total cost for a particular direct marketing effort—including any costs associated with the offer—divided by the number of conversions. The math is part of what makes direct marketing fun—learning to tweak tactics and lists to get the best possible return at a cost that makes sense. Not surprisingly, it also makes direct marketing more palatable than other types of marketing to CEOs, CFOs, and other numbers-driven executives.

Importantly, many experts believe that the best way to send an offer to a prospect with whom your company has already made contact is by using the same delivery mechanism that worked the first time.[31] So, keeping track of the offer and response medium in your database is critical for retargeting prospects or customers in your database.

Always make sure you have a good offer, one that will appeal to your target audience. Even if you can afford to reach a sufficient number of your prospective buyers to justify the costs of the marketing effort, a bad or uninteresting offer will decrease your conversion rates, thus driving up your CPA.

Finally, understand what a reasonable return looks like. Conversion rates are usually very low. Table 1 provides an example of the average response to eDM. Two lessons to learn from these numbers. First, percentages are low, and you need to get used to single digits. Second, use house lists (which we will cover in the next chapter) whenever possible, as they almost always perform better. As table 1, below, shows, marketers get several times more conversions from house lists for eDM.

Table 1: Average eDM response rates for house and third-party lists

Action	House List	Third-Party List
Open Rate	22.05%	11.43%
Conversion Rate	1.5%	0.4%

Source: *Direct Marketing Association 2012 Annual Response Rate Report*[32]

Testing and Measurement

Two hallmarks of direct marketing are testing, and measuring the results of the campaign.

As we would expect, direct marketers spend a lot of time testing their copy, their delivery mechanisms, their response mechanisms, and their offer. They tweak each of these elements until the conversion rate meets the objective. Direct marketers usually have a target conversion rate and CPA in mind when they are developing a direct mail piece.

Very often, direct marketers will send out two variants of a direct marketing piece simultaneously, known as "A" and "B." These variants might contain two different offers, different copy, or a different layout. Alternatively, they might send the same copy to two different lists—perhaps different age groups or cities—using a tracking mechanism to ascertain which copy generates more responses. This strategy is commonly referred to as split testing, bucket testing, or A/B testing. The marketer then adopts the "winner" of the A/B test as the preferred direct mail piece.

Going further, many direct marketers do not send out, publish, or broadcast their entire message all at once. Instead, they send out smaller batches. This approach enables them to refine their campaign along the way. For online campaigns, marketers will often change the subject line of an e-mail, or the placement of the call to action on the HTML e-mail, and then send out revised versions to try to gain incrementally better results. The idea is to change just one thing in each A/B test, send it out to a limited subset of your list, pick the winner, and then continue tweaking.

Measuring success is all about conversions. You can measure the open rate, but that will really only help you refine your delivery mechanism. What you really want to know is (1) what percentage of people responded to your offer and (2) how much each response costs per customer—your CPA. Marketers can decide that they are willing to pay up to a certain amount for a new prospect or customer, and they measure success based on whether they were able to come in at or under that amount. Costs include all variable expenses—list acquisition, production, and delivery.

A caution: As mentioned, great response rates can often be very low numbers, in some cases less than 1 percent. Make certain to educate management on what success looks like before showing them the results, or they might mis-interpret a successful campaign to have been a disaster.

Below is a simple example that illustrates the costs and return on a direct marketing effort. Let's assume sales has asked for ten leads for next quarter. We will use eDM and assume our only variable costs are renting a list and paying a creative agency to design our e-mail and landing page. We will further assume that anyone who downloads the technical white paper on our freeze ray gun is diabolical enough to become a lead. We will use numbers close to the typical response rates in table 1, rounded to make the math a little easier to follow.

In the example below, one thousand e-mails were sent, and 10 percent, or one hundred, were opened. Again, since this is a third-party list, we should expect an open rate in this range. Of the one hundred people who opened, ten clicked on the link and then filled out the form (our desired outcome) to receive the brochure. So sales will be happy with their ten leads, and the eDM achieved a 1 percent conversion rate. If our total cost for the eDM effort is $500, and we paid the creative agency $500 (fifty cents a name) to rent the list, then our CPA is $1,000 ÷ 10, or $100.

TABLE 2: Opens and conversions for a simple eDM program

Action	Rate (%)	Total
eDMs Sent	--	1,000
Opens	10%	100
Conversions	1%	10

Case Study

It seems fitting to use an example from Wunderman's career in a chapter on direct marketing. To demonstrate the broader meaning of direct marketing, I have chosen one of his more successful campaigns that did not use direct mail. Back in the days before music was bought and sold online as digital files, "record clubs" were big business. These clubs advertised in newspapers and magazines, and their ads encouraged readers to sign up for the club, which would typically send them one record every month.

Wunderman had worked with a number of mail order clubs in his career, from rosebushes (yes, rosebushes) to books to art to records. His biggest opportunity came when he landed the Columbia Record Club direct marketing business in 1955 for his agency Wunderman, Ricotta & Kline. Fast-forward almost twenty years, and the Columbia Record Club had over three million members and was a substantial business. However, it also had an annual attrition rate of 50 percent. Clearly, the club needed to develop strategies to acquire new customers. In his book *Being Direct: Making Advertising Pay*, Wunderman describes how around that time, he conceived of an idea to help drive the business, which he presented at a client meeting in Aspen. It was the "Gold Box of Colorado"—an idea so simple, it was brilliant.

Wunderman instructed his creative team to put a small gold box on the bottom of the ad, underneath the registration coupon on newspaper ads and on the business reply card for mailings. Significantly, the ad contained no explanation of what the box was for. Wunderman called this the "buried treasure" in the ad. Wuderman then created television ads for the record club that explained what the gold box was for—letting them in on the secret that they could get an extra record for free. People who had not seen the ad would have no idea what it was for. Those who did would fill it in, and Columbia House would count the number of coupons with gold boxes filled in to determine how many people had responded to the offer.

Figure 3: The "buried treasure" gold box in an advertisement for the Columbia Record Club

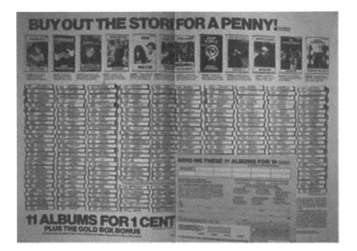

It took Wunderman two years to convince Columbia Records to run with the concept. Part of the delay was due to Columbia's internal conflict between Wunderman's direct marketing agency and its incumbent ad agency, McCann Erickson. Wunderman finally convinced Columbia to allow him to test his ads against McCann's, which had no direct-response mechanism. He ran the ads in thirteen test markets around the country. Rather than purchasing television advertising during prime time, as McCann did, he bought cheaper ads in "fringe time." The results? Wunderman's television support ads increased print ad response rates by 80 percent. He also drove down the cost per new customer acquisition from $18.60 to $4.00. In contrast, the McCann ads actually added to the cost of customer acquisition. Not surprisingly, Wunderman got all of the direct marketing business after that.

Wunderman called the television support advertising "the fuse that could ignite the ads in all media." The little yellow box made the viewer, in his words, part of "an interactive marketing system." Wunderman proved that even with all of the modern technology and mainstream ideas that might tempt a marketer, thinking creatively and measuring relentlessly are far more important.

Learning More

+ Lester Wunderman, *Being Direct: Making Advertising Pay* (New York: Random House, 1996).

Chapter 10

Marketing Lists and Databases

The previous chapter discussed how marketers increasingly rely on carefully targeted direct marketing to reach, and, ideally, elicit some type of response from, prospective customers. Let's assume you have used your segmentation exercise to identify the appropriate demographic targets for your campaign, and you want to contact them via direct mail or telemarketing. The question you now face is, where do you get the names and contact information for these individuals? And at a price you can afford?

Two of the less glamorous, but critically important, tasks in marketing are acquiring and maintaining the names and contact information for the people you want to sell to. The very best marketers know that data is gold. Lists of customer names and contact information allow marketers to make phone calls, send postcards, and transmit e-mail and text messages. Databases store these lists so they can be reused or mined for new insights.

This is not a fad, either. Some of the earliest practitioners of direct marketing invested in technology to help them get better results. Lester Wunderman, the father direct marketing, was directly involved in the creation of a European computer data center for Ford. This chapter will cover the tasks involved in building, using, and maintaining lists and databases.

Data Strategy

A *data strategy* is simply your plan for collecting, purchasing, maintaining, and using data for marketing purposes. Some marketers use the term, in a limited sense, to mean the list names they select, as in "What's our data strategy for the holiday sweater promotion?" This use of the term is too narrow, in my experience, and it fails to take into account the ongoing work of building and maintaining a good database.

Sophisticated organizations have full-time staff whose entire job is data strategy. Even small organizations, however, can execute an effective data strategy by using marketing automation tools, such as Act-On, Eloqua, HubSpot, and Marketo, and the services of marketing database service providers like Harte Hanks or Epsilon.

Although the specifics of data strategies can vary from company to company, all effective strategies include certain key components, listed below.

> Data collection – Defining the types of data to be collected about prospective and existing customers, including demographic, psychographic, and contact information; sales and service call records; purchase history; and even analysis of their web clickstreams. Deciding what information you need and how to collect and organize it is a lot of work.

> Data maintenance – Maintaining data quality, creating processes for sharing data, integrating the data with marketing and sales applications, maintaining customer privacy and complying with privacy regulations, and defining ownership or governance of data.

> Data selection – Deciding who to target for a new program or campaign. Data selection is probably the most fun part of the data strategy. It ranges in complexity from pulling basic contact information from the marketing automation tools to analyzing data, such as past marketing performance and purchase history, to generate optimal results. Some data strategists try to predict results based on past performance.

Don't confuse data strategy with *database marketing*, which is simply direct marketing using databases of customers or potential customers to generate personalized communications.

Creating and Obtaining Marketing Lists

For the purposes of this chapter, a *list* will be defined as a subset of a *database*. Both contain prospective or existing customer names, contact information, and a range of demographic and behavioral *attributes* that were discussed in chapter 3. Lists are created by pulling a set of customer records that match a certain set of attributes from a database—for example, all women between the ages of twenty-five and thirty-five with a median income over $100,000.

An organization can collect names for its database one by one from its marketing activities, or it can purchase a list from a third party. In some cases, organizations share lists if they are co-marketing products or services, or if one company is a reseller for a larger company's products.

Buying and Renting Marketing Lists

Lists, also referred to as *marketing lists*, can be purchased from a number of sources. Selecting where to buy a list is an important decision, with cost, quality, and even legal ramifications. (The legal aspects of the use of lists and databases is discussed at the end of the chapter.)

Although companies employ myriad strategies to acquire customer information, most companies need to rent or buy lists at some point. Collecting names one by one may not yield enough data to work with. Remember, most marketing programs generate response rates of 5 percent or less. So, unless you need only a handful of leads, your database will need thousands of names, at least. B2C direct marketing campaigns in particular may need tens, even hundreds of thousands, of names to hit their target. Going further, purchasing lists of names is often a necessity when a company is entering a new geographic area or is selling a new product. Finally, as databases age and contact information becomes less reliable over time, companies typically purchase new names to keep their database current.

There are a number of well-known and legitimate marketing database service providers, such as InfoUSA, Harte Hanks, and Epsilon. Many of these companies also provide additional services, such as direct mail fulfillment (producing, addressing, and sending out mailers or catalogs for you) and managing e-mail marketing campaigns. Another valuable source of lists is magazines, which commonly offer lists for purchase. In fact, selling lists is an important component of their revenue model. Magazines can be particularly valuable because they target a certain demographic or specialty, which increases the likelihood that the prospect is interested in what you are selling. A final source of lists is self-service online databases that are designed for easy access via a web browser. Prominent examples are Hoover's on Demand and Jigsaw. Marketing and sales people can use these databases to create their own lists.

Most list owners allow you to customize your list based on specified attributes that are commonly called "selects." What the selects are and how many you can choose from depend on the database owner. Common selects are usually drill-downs* on typical marketing segmentation criteria: geographic, demographic, and industry related. Some database owners also keep track of psychographic and behavioral elements, as well as areas that prospects have expressed interested in learning more about from vendors.

Another option is to utilize the services of a *list broker* to secure the best lists at the best price. List brokers act as intermediaries between the marketer and the list or database owner. List brokers know which database owners are legitimate, they have a feel for how good the owners' data are, and they can usually negotiate a better price. Moreover, if the list has problems—for example, an unusually high number of e-mail bounce backs—then the broker can act as your advocate and attempt to acquire additional names or obtain a refund. List brokers buy at a "broker's discount," typically around 20 percent off of the full price of what is called the "base cost" of the list (there are various other setup, select, and transmission fees charged). Overall, using a broker may be slightly more expensive than going to the list owner directly, but their experience and knowledge will save a marketing team time and probably improve results by dint of a better quality or more suitable list.

In most cases, you have the option to either buy or rent a list. When you rent a list, the database owner works with a trusted third party known as a

---

* This is technology-speak for moving from summary to more detailed information by focusing on a specific element. The term equates clicking a mouse pointer on an item on the screen with "drilling" deeper into the content. Yes, I spent many years working in high-tech marketing…

bonded mail house. Bonding is a special form of insurance that holds aside funds in case of theft. Therefore, a bonded mail house is contractually bound to the list owner to treat the list with care and, obviously, not give the list to the list renter. Otherwise, its insurance company would forfeit funds, and the mail house would likely lose its bonded status. The mail house receives the list from the database owner and the physical mailer or e-mail file from the list renter. Some of the larger database owners sidestep the bonded mail house and provide these kinds of fulfillment services themselves.

Which strategy is preferable, renting or buying? The answer depends on your circumstances. Renting a list has the advantage of being cheaper. In addition, although you don't actually receive the list you rented to put into your database, you do get to collect and store the names of the people who respond to your direct marketing. However, if you have a finite set of buyers and you can purchase a list that contains all of their information, then it may be worth the price.

Building House Lists

Clearly, marketers have numerous options for acquiring lists. Nevertheless, your in-house marketing database, sometimes called a *house list* for short, remains one of your most valuable marketing assets. The house list is the names you have collected over time through your marketing activities. In practice, marketers create sublists as required. Some are long-standing, such as your list of customers. Others are created for a specific need, such as a direct marketing effort targeting a certain type of customer or prospect. Perhaps you want to sell a new product, C, only to those existing customers who own both product A and product B. The act of creating a sublist based on a set of criteria is known as "pulling a list," or sometimes just a "pull."

Marketers commonly acquire names using "lead capture" forms on their websites. Because the respondents have taken the time and trouble to reply, the marketers assume they are at least somewhat interested in the company, the product, or the service.

Permission marketing is a best practice popularized by marketing guru Seth Godin. The idea is simple: you ask prospective or existing customers for permission to send them additional information. You may ask them if they would like to subscribe to your newsletter when they fill out the lead capture form the first time. Or you may ask if they would like to receive special offers, product updates, or other information. The fact that you ask them and they accept indicates they are receptive to your marketing and are better prospects in the long run. Godin terms the practice of those who don't ask permission "interruption marketing." Lists built using the permission marketing approach will undoubtedly be better.

In addition, marketers of all kinds collect names at events like trade shows and conferences. Another common strategy is to encourage consumers to fill out warranty cards when they make a purchase. Many consumers don't realize that the main purpose of these cards is to continue to build the manufacturer's database.

Although creating and maintaining a marketing database can entail more time and expenses than renting a list, house lists consistently outperform third-party lists. The people contained in your database have already expressed some level of interest in your products or demonstrated an affinity for your brand. Thus, creating and maintaining a marketing database not only will spare you the expense of renting new lists, but the returns you get on your direct marketing will be higher.

Maintaining Marketing Databases

Nurturing Databases

It is very likely that only a small percentage of the individuals on your house list will be ready to buy in a given month or quarter. That does not mean, however, that you should continue to market only to new names from rented lists. Customers in your database who are not yet ready to buy need to be "nurtured" until they are ready to buy. Creating a nurturing database first requires that you segment your marketing database by those who are ready to buy, those who may eventually buy, and those who will never buy.

Segmenting your in-house database into logical subsets will make your marketing efforts more productive. The best policy is to divide your list into three categories—active sales pipeline, nurture, and deadwood. The *deadwood* includes bad or wrong information, people who have requested to opt out of your mailings, and accounts that don't fit your target market segments. These data should either be ignored or deleted.

The *sales pipeline* segment consists of qualified opportunities. Your sales team, partners, or customer service team will deal with these customers. We will discuss what constitutes a qualified opportunity in the next chapter.

The middle segment is your *nurturing database*. These are people who fit whatever buyer profile you have defined, and have some interest, but are not ready to buy for whatever reason. You should keep them warm, nurturing them until they are ready, with direct mail or eDM pieces that they will find useful and that will move them toward a purchase decision. Although this may seem obvious, many companies waste revenue opportunity by ignoring this critical segment, as well as overspend by constantly buying or renting more expensive third-party lists.

Figure 1, below, shows the basic structure of the marketing database and how customer names flow in from acquisition. Once customer names are acquired, invalid ones are moved to the deadwood segment. Active opportunities are routed to the sales pipeline segment. Prospects not ready to buy are routed to the "Nurture 1" segment. Existing customers are kept in the "Nurture 2" segment. Lists are pulled as needed for subsequent direct marketing.

Figure 1: Basic structure of the marketing database

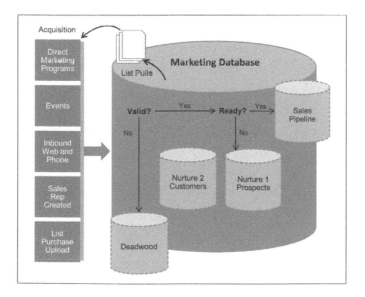

Nurturing, as we discuss in the next chapter, is a sustained program designed to move leads into the active pipeline. Nurturing is also referred to as "drip marketing" or "remarketing." The idea is to market to these leads slowly, over time. For example, if a prospect was not ready to buy because your price was too high, sending them an e-mail when you run a holiday price promotion is a form of nurturing that gets to their issue. Some prospects may be waiting for a certain product feature to become available, so you would want to send them the announcement when you release a new version that contains that feature. For big-ticket, complex products, you may send them material over a period of time to help educate them so they are ready to buy. How you nurture depends on your buyers and their issues.

Another important aspect of the nurturing database is economic. You have either paid money for the contact information, spent money on marketing programs, or both. Not leveraging this prospect is a waste of existing resources, because purchasing new contacts is expensive.

A company's existing customers, known in technology marketing as its *installed base*,[†] should also be nurtured. Good marketing teams look to entice existing customers to buy more, and nurturing is one way to do it, whether organizations are focused on the lifetime value of a customer—how much product they can sell to the customer over the length of a relationship—or the "share of wallet" they can gain from a customer in a given year. Nurturing, or drip marketing, can be effective in increasing the lifetime value or share of wallet of existing customers. Rather than simply mailing bills and holiday greetings to existing customers, you should send them offers to entice them to make additional purchases. Keeping the existing customer, or installed base, database segment current and using it to generate a new pipeline is a good marketing approach. This is shown in figure 1, above, as the "Nurture 2 Customers" segment.

---

† We will see if this term holds up with the advent of software that is hosted on the Internet and never truly installed. *Customer base* or *subscriber base* seem likely successors.

Progressive Profiling

The process of collecting information about contacts over a period of time is called *progressive profiling*. The more information your company has for a contact, the better you will be able to target that individual.

One cardinal sin marketers commit is asking prospects too many questions at one time. Doing so will cause them to get annoyed with a telemarketing or sales rep on the phone, and it will likely discourage them from filling out a lead capture form, known as "form abandonment." In fact, research conducted by MarketingSherpa has consistently revealed that prospective customers fail to complete 60 percent of registration forms, with form length being a major factor.

So, how should you approach progressive profiling? To begin with, in the first interaction, you should request only the essential pieces of information—somewhere between three and five. If you are capturing leads via the web, then you should ask for only the information you need for your next step. For example, name and e-mail address should be sufficient to add these leads to an e-mail nurturing program. Alternatively, you would request a phone number if the next step is to have a telemarketing rep call them.

After you have established contact with prospective customers and elicited their basic information, you can get additional information with subsequent marketing activities. When you send prospects a nurturing e-mail, make certain to add a few additional fields for them to complete—for example, information about their titles, roles, and responsibilities could be useful to a B2B salesperson. Really good marketers make the answers relevant to the offer, in effect customizing the offer based on their responses. In this way, the contacts see value in providing additional information. As an example, you might ask prospects how big their company is and which industry it operates in so that you can send them a customized version of a report your team produced. Creating this type of customizable asset requires a bit more effort, but the continued contact engagement and the reduction in abandonment this extra step generates are worth the effort.

Most modern marketing automation systems include built-in tools for progressive profiling. They automate the request for additional information based on the information that is already contained in the database record for that prospect, or what particular offer is being made to the contact. Progressive profiling still requires up-front planning about the lead flow, a bit more work on automation, and potentially consideration during asset creation.

Maintaining Database Quality

Thus far, I've described a number of strategies for effectively utilizing lists and databases. Even the most carefully crafted and executed strategies, however, will generate few positive results if the information contained in those lists isn't accurate and current. For all kinds of reasons, the quality of your data may not be what you need it to be. Prospects and salespeople may not be great typists, thus introducing spelling and other mistakes into your database. Lead collection forms may not have been created with all the same fields—or names of fields—over the life of the company. Prospects move on and don't send you their new contact information. For these and myriad other reasons, you need to periodically clean up your database. If not, then your data, and not your campaign, creative, or offer, will drive down the effectiveness of your marketing efforts. Marketers often refer to the process of cleaning up your database as "list hygiene" or "database hygiene."

There are five common steps to improving the quality of your database:

- ◆ Standardize

- ◆ Cleanse

- ◆ Deduplicate

- ◆ Enrich/Augment

- ◆ Validate

The first step is to *standardize* the format in which your data are represented in your CRM or marketing automation system. In some cases, you need to begin this process by resolving differences between your sales automation and marketing automation systems. How you represent country names (e.g., USA or United States), company names (e.g., IBM or International Business Machines), and telephone numbers (e.g., dashes or parentheses) will make a big difference in the ensuing cleansing and deduplication steps.

The next step is to detect and correct (or remove) corrupt or inaccurate records from your database. This process is known as *cleansing*. Inaccurate records can range from bad or bogus e-mail addresses or phone numbers for companies that have gone out of business. *Deduplication* is similar to cleansing. The "dedupe" step is designed to remove duplicate records from your database. Deciding which of two duplicate records overrides the other, or whether information in the two records should be merged, is an important decision.

Just as your database can contain inaccurate or duplicate information, it can also be missing key information. This information can range from simple things like the prospect's company address and website, to the purchase history of the contact's company or organization, to pertinent industry or demographic information. Progressive profiling, mentioned above, is one way to *enrich* your database over time. You can also purchase additional information from sources like Hoover's and append it to individual records.

After you have completed the first four processes, the final step is to review all of the changes to your records to *validate* that they are correct. There are a number of ways to do this, but the most common approach is to compare the updated records to known correct "master data" sources, such as valid zip code lists, company names from sources like Hoover's, product or part lists, and so on.

Figure 2: Maintaining the marketing database

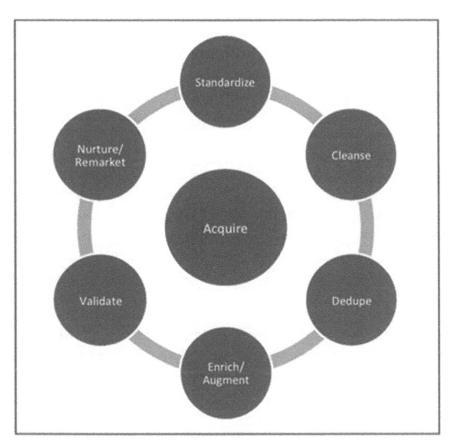

There are a number of data-cleansing tools and services on the market that will fix common formatting issues, match zip and postal codes to state and province codes, and change the status of a contact based on an e-mail bounce back. Some list renters and database owners offer data cleansing and augmentation for an additional fee, or as a value add of their service.

Privacy and Legal Aspects

As stated at the beginning of the chapter, how you obtain and manage lists has important legal aspects. To complicate matters, laws and attitudes vary from country to country. Moreover, these laws are changing rapidly as consumers realize how much of their information is out there, and governments respond with regulations to protect their citizens.

Rule number one: if you are purchasing a list, make certain the list owner is legitimate. Inquire as to how they acquired the names and whether they have secured the permission of the individuals to sell their information. Avoid fly-by-night list providers that own names of shady provenance. Although these lists are often cheap, they are probably not well vetted, and the providers might have obtained the names in violation of state or national privacy or consumer protection laws. You want to make certain you are working with a reputable provider of "permission-based" marketing data, meaning data that customers have given permission to the database owner to share their information with other vendors.

Obtaining the permission of individual consumers is necessary to be in compliance with anti-spam and privacy laws. In the United States, the major law governing the use of customer information is the Controlling the Assault of Non-Solicited Pornography and Marketing (CAN-SPAM) Act. Signed into law in 2003, the CAN-SPAM Act recognizes consumers' right not to be marketed to, and it establishes penalties for companies that violate consumers' wishes. The name of the act is also a play on the usual term for unsolicited e-mail of this type, spam.

Two other widely known laws are the German Federal Data Protection Act, which, among other things, lays out specific criteria on how a name and contact information can be legally obtained; and the UK Data Protection Act, which states that data can be used only for the purposes for which it was collected, and only within the European Community. The International Association of Privacy Professionals is a good place to begin if you are looking for a deeper understanding of privacy laws worldwide.

A second reason why a company needs to exercise caution in its use of databases is customer sentiment. Even if you have legitimately obtained contact information and permission to market to people—whether you bought the list or collected the name yourself—they can get annoyed if they feel their information has been abused by marketers. For this reason, it is important to allow for quick and easy unsubscribing—which is required by most laws—and to always allow a customer to "opt out" from further communication.

The most common methods of opting out are to unsubscribe to e-mail communications and to ask a telemarketing rep not to call anymore. If you contact customers after they have opted out, not only will you be annoying them and wasting your time, but you may run afoul of laws like the CAN-SPAM Act. If you are nurturing a customer, then you should consider how often you send him or her information. One effective standard for making this decision is to ask yourself, "Would I be okay with the volume of communications?"

Case Study – Barack Obama and Big Data

Behind the election of Barack Obama to his second term as president of the United States was another story: the Obama 2012 campaign team had revolutionized electioneering using data. No matter what your politics, the Democratic National Committee's approach holds an important lesson. Big data, when understood and analyzed, is incredibly powerful. Big data equals better marketing and can be used in any field.

Big data is a technology term of art for a very large amount of data (terabytes and above) from multiple sources and in varying formats. The term was coined to describe the massive amounts of data Internet and web companies were collecting. User clickstreams were captured and told companies all kinds of things about where users went, how long they spent there, their viewing and reading habits, who their friends were, and many other things. Inexpensive storage made retaining this data affordable. Since big data comes from many sources, it is usually uncorrelated. Finding that correlation is the goal.

The Obama campaign first started using big data during candidate Obama's first run, in the 2008 presidential election. Starting with an analysis done by Dan Wagner, the DNC's targeting director, the Obama team was building a new way to predict the outcomes of elections using big data.[33] Wagner's team had assigned every voter a pair of scores based on the likelihood they would perform two distinct actions: cast a ballot and support Obama. These scores were calculated using big data collected from a massive volume of phone surveys. Using these scores, the campaign specifically targeted—*microtargeted*—individual voters. Microtargeting allowed the campaign to target specific individuals rather than demographic groups or neighborhoods, as had been the common practice in previous elections. Field workers could knock on doors of voters they knew they could convince or activate, and not waste time on die-hard Republicans or entrenched John McCain supporters.

Though incumbent, Obama's reelection in 2012 was far from guaranteed. The midterm election losses showed the average American's dissatisfaction with the direction of the country under Obama's leadership. For all that the Obama team knew about voter tendencies in 2008, there was more data to be had. So, the first thing Wagner did after the 2008 victory was to create a "constituent relationship management system" that combined the phone survey data and scores with all of the other information known about voters, including their social media profiles and online interactions with the campaign. By the time campaign season was in full swing in 2011, the DNC had grown and enriched its big data set with even more voter information it could use for microtargeting.

The Obama team then began an advanced form of message testing known as "experiment-informed programs," or EIPs. Here, the campaign moved beyond typical message testing in focus groups that had been used by campaigns for decades, to more typical direct marketing approaches. The team went beyond A/B testing and would test as many as four direct mail variants to understand which was most successful. The campaign found, for example, that a direct mail piece focusing on women's issues was most likely to persuade conservative women voters to vote for President Obama than a piece about education or foreign policy. This was a refinement of the microtargeting used in the 2008 campaign, enabled by more data about each voter and more sophisticated means of reaching them.

The Obama campaign also used social media extensively during the 2012 election. Social media was both a means to collect more data about voters, and a channel by which to microtarget them. In 2012, adult use of social media in the United States was 69 percent, nearly double the 37 percent in 2008. More importantly, according to Pew Research, 66 percent engaged in political activism online.[34] Obama dominated the social media space, because his team understood social networking. The real power of social media is user engagement. As evidence of Obama's superior user engagement, he logged twice as many Facebook "Likes" and nearly twenty times as many retweets as Republican challenger Mitt Romney.

The Obama team's most ambitious project of the 2012 campaign, however, was to combine big data and microtargeting and apply them to a familiar campaign medium—television. By its nature, television is mass media. The campaign wanted to do something that had never been done—microtarget persuadable voters with an appropriate message on television. Doing so meant the campaign needed to know the viewing habits of targeted voters.

In a deal worked out with research firm Rentrak, the campaign provided a list of persuadable voters' profiles to the firm, and Rentrak provided back a list of cable subscribers that fit the profile. Households were assigned a household ID that protected the voter's privacy but could be used in the campaign's analysis. Working with a custom-made software application dubbed "The Optimizer," the campaign was able to target advertising in markets by maximum "persuadable targets by hour." Not only was this technique highly effective, it also served to confuse Romney's campaign team, who could not figure why Obama was running ads during reruns on obscure channels like TV Land, which showed decades-old shows like *The Andy Griffith Show* and *Charlie's Angels*.

Obama was reelected and by a much wider margin than many had expected. Obama himself lauded his big data team as his secret weapon and credited them with helping win what was a very tight election. Several of the Obama big data staff went on to form Analytics Media Group (AMG), which now is taking the techniques they perfected in the campaign to other businesses, like casinos and consumer packaged goods. In an unusual turnaround, campaign marketing was now informing consumer marketing—another first for Obama.

Learning More

- Sasha Issenberg, "A More Perfect Union," *MIT Technology Review*, December 2012.

Chapter 11

Leads, Opportunities, and the Funnel

Peter Drucker's measure of successful marketing is the point at which the act of selling becomes unnecessary. Some companies have reached the point where their product is so essential or desirable that no one needs to "sell" to their customers, or to consumers in general. They are already sold.

In most cases, however, a salesperson from your company or one of your partners is essential for answering questions, alleviating consumer fears, ensuring that your product's advantages are understood, and closing the deal. This process can take a couple of minutes on a store floor, fifteen minutes during a test drive, or, for more complex products and services, several months.

Regardless of the scenario, however, the role of marketing is the same: to generate *demand* for the organization's products or services. It is essential for marketers to differentiate demand from awareness. As the name suggests, the goal of awareness is to make certain that prospective customers know about your product or company. Although under ideal circumstances awareness ultimately leads to a sale, by itself it does not compel customers to take any specific action. In contrast, demand generation does mean compelling prospective customers to take action to achieve a desired outcome, whether visiting a store, calling a toll-free number, or requesting additional product information. Some people go so far as to define marketing's mission as "making the phones ring."

In this chapter, we will discuss the process and terminology of demand generation. Specifically, I focus on strategies for transforming prospective customers—known in the trade as leads—into satisfied customers. I also cover the automated systems that today's marketers utilize to accomplish this goal. To begin, let's explore the all-important concept of the funnel.

What Is the Funnel?

The *funnel* is a shorthand term for describing the route by which prospective customers, or *prospects*, become customers. The visualization of the process looks like a funnel. A larger number of prospects go in the top and are reduced to a smaller number of customers who come out the bottom.

Who came up with the funnel? Interestingly, the idea for the funnel visualization was a refinement of a previous visualization, also derived from a piece of kitchen equipment—the pot. In 1904, Frank Hutchinson Dukesmith, editor of *Salesmanship* magazine, created a mnemonic to help salespeople remember the critical stages of the sales cycle. The key stages were attention, interest, desire, and conviction. Dukesmith later changed *conviction* to *action*, and the popular sales mnemonic AIDA was born.

Dukesmith explained that the number of prospects decreased with each stage—more potential customers will be interested than will finally take action. He represented each stage as an iron pot, with the size of each pot diminishing from A to I to D to A. If you stacked the pots, with the smallest on the bottom and the others balanced on top, it resembled a funnel.[35]

Perhaps this is what inspired Arthur Peterson, a marketing and sales executive in the pharmaceutical industry. Nearly fifty years later, he connected the idea of a "customer funnel" with Dukesmith's AIDA mnemonic in his book *Pharmaceutical Selling, Detailing, and Sales Training*: "The progression through the four primary steps in a sale, i.e., attention, interest, desire and action, may be compared to that of a substance moving through a funnel."[36] Rather than envisioning a separate pot for each stage, Peterson's funnel was dissected horizontally into four sections: A-I-D-A. The concept has stuck, and nearly every sales executive learns it early on in his or her career. Peterson's funnel is shown in figure 1 below.*

Figure 1: The original sales funnel, from a 1949 pharmaceutical sales manual.

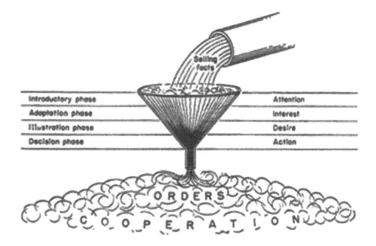

Although some marketers still use the AIDA system, the majority employ a more modern evolution of the funnel that involves five stages: awareness, research, consideration, purchase, and customer. We discuss this model below, and we illustrate it in figure 2.

> Awareness – As we previously explained, this is the process by which prospective buyers become aware of your brand, company, or product. Organizations can promote awareness through advertising, public re-

---

* To "detail" a doctor is to give that doctor information about a company's new drugs, with the aim of persuading the doctor to prescribe them. Long the only avenue for marketing drugs, pharmaceutical companies are now evaluating the cost and effectiveness of detailing versus advertising direct to consumers.

lations, word of mouth, or other means. Recall that this process can occur long before the prospective buyer intends to make a purchase.

Research – Once prospective buyers intend to make a purchase, they enter the research stage. At this point, they want to learn more about your product, particularly its features and its price, as well as about similar products on the market. They can conduct this research in a number of ways—reading your website, examining product reviews, talking to a friend or colleague, or seeking the opinion of an industry analyst.

Consideration – At this stage, buyers are choosing between the most likely purchases, having eliminated any products that did not meet their criteria. They may seek additional information, look to take a test drive, or want to witness a demonstration. They also might want to talk to existing customers.

Figure 2: The funnel: customer journey view

Purchase – This is the point in the process when the prospective customer actually makes the purchase. At this point, the prospective buyer transitions to a customer.

Customer – Even after a customer has made the purchase, he or she is still part of the funnel. Why? Happy customers—the net promoters we covered in chapter 7—will buy additional products, renew subscriptions, and recommend your products to other potential buyers who are in the research or consideration stage. Really happy customers even help at the awareness stage, talking up their new purchase as well as recommending it to friends and colleagues. From the opposite perspective, unhappy customers may malign your product, refuse to purchase any of your other products, and even defect to your competition.

The funnel is sometimes referred to in marketing departments as the *customer journey*. The length of the journey will depend on the type of product, how expensive it is, and whether it is a consumer product or one sold to businesses. For an inexpensive consumer product, this journey can occur in minutes. Consider, for example, a thirsty shopper who recognizes the logo of a popular soft drink on a refrigerated display case (awareness); quickly scans the package, nutrition facts, and ingredients (research); compares it to the labels and prices of other drinks (consideration); buys it (purchase); and then tells her friend how good it tastes (net-promoting customer). In this example, marketing has supplied everything the consumer needs to make an on-the-spot decision, including weeks or months of advertising that contributed to awareness.

For more expensive goods, such as cars, or complex business-to-business products, like software, the journey will usually take longer. Prospective buyers frequently search for specific information as they descend through the funnel. Marketing's job is to ensure that the right information is available when prospective buyers need it, either by sending it directly to them or by providing it via the sales team. The best marketing teams use the funnel visualization to illustrate their customer's journey, and work with sales to determine what materials marketing needs to create for prospects and salespeople at each stage.

Leads and Opportunities

A *lead* is the name and contact information of a potential buyer—someone who has the interest and authority to purchase a product or service. Leads are the lifeblood of a sales organization, and providing leads to sales is a vital function of the marketing organization.

In previous chapters, I have used the term "lead" fairly loosely, but marketers employ specific terms to describe the "state" of the lead. As a lead progresses down the funnel, it becomes more "qualified," meaning there is a higher likelihood of a purchase. Sales and marketing need to understand the number of leads in each state to know whether they will reach their ultimate revenue target.

Importantly, both the sales and marketing departments are part of the sales process. The degree to which each is involved depends on the type of sale and the organization. In our soft drink example, marketing was responsible for the awareness, research, and consideration stages, through advertising, display, packaging and pricing.

Generally speaking, in B2B sales, the marketing organization is responsible for a lead through the awareness and research stages of the funnel. A lead at this stage may not be ready to speak to a salesperson, or they may not be qualified enough to warrant a salesperson spending his or her time working on it. B2B sales organizations will certainly get involved during the consideration and purchase phases, and may be involved with leads during the research stage. Since there is variability depending on their business, organizations need an agreed-upon process by which marketing turns over the customer to the sales team. This is known as the *hand-off*. Leads can be e-mailed, uploaded, or their status can be changed in an organization that is using a marketing or sales automation system, which we discuss later in the chapter. In the case of some consumer goods, there may be a hand-off at the point at which a prospective customer calls, e-mails, or walks into the store in response to a marketing offer.

But one question remains: How can a marketing team track what stage a lead is in? Most customers don't think of what they are doing the same way a sales and marketing team do. This is why marketing and sales need to track the *state* of the lead. The *lead state* describes its status in terms of fit with the desired buyer profile and activity of that lead. Below are the definitions of the states of a lead, and figure 3 illustrates a view of the funnel based on lead state.

> Name – As its generic nature suggests, this is just a name on a list or in a database. At this point, marketing has performed little, if any, qualification, except perhaps that the person matches the desired demographic or buyer profile.
>
> Inquiry – At this stage, a prospective customer has responded to a marketing offer. He or she has expressed some level of interest in your product or service.
>
> Marketing-qualified lead (MQL) – An MQL is a lead that marketing has qualified to some level and is ready to turn over to sales. The qualification process will vary from company to company, but it typically comprises a combination of profile (demographics, role) and activity (inquiry). For example, a software company may decide an MQL is a director-level person who works in the information technology department at a company of over a thousand employees, who has viewed an online demo of its product.
>
> Sales-accepted lead (SAL) – At the SAL stage, sales acknowledges that an MQL meets the agreed-upon criteria and agrees to work with this individual. Just as the criteria being met are important to sales, an agreement to follow up within a proscribed time frame is important to marketing so that a qualified lead does not "go cold."
>
> Sales-qualified lead (SQL) – An SQL involves a decision by sales, after additional qualification via discussions with the potential buyer, that there is a sales opportunity with a time frame and a budget. Leads at this point are commonly converted to *opportunities*. Leads

that are not converted should be sent back to marketing, preferably with some explanation as to why they did not make it to the opportunity stage.

Customer – Once a deal is closed, the lead has become *closed business*, better known as a *customer*. Existing customers can, of course, become leads again for the purchase of additional products or services. Many companies track repeat sales to existing customers, and some track their "share of wallet," which is covered in chapter 21.

Figure 3: The funnel: demand generation view

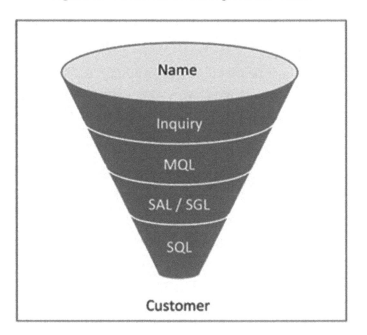

You may hear a few other terms used to describe leads. One such term—*raw lead*—is not well defined. As its name suggests, it refers to a lead that has not been qualified. It may be either a name or an inquiry. *Suspects* are names that fit the profile, but have neither inquired about your product or service nor been further qualified. Attendees at a trade show who buy products like yours, for example, are suspects. Finally, a *prospect* is somewhere between a marketing-qualified lead (MQL) and a sales-accepted lead (SAL). Disagreements as to whether the leads that marketing hands over to sales tend to be good or bad prospects are frequently the cause of friction between the departments, but can be overcome with frequent communication and refinement of the criteria.

Two additional terms that salespeople typically use are *pipeline* and *forecast*. A pipeline is the collection of opportunities, typically expressed in dollars by multiplying the number of opportunities by the average expected sales price. A forecast is the subset of opportunities that the sales rep expects to close within a given time period. When a sales leader says his pipeline is low, the marketing team should think about how to increase the number of MQLs. If the forecast is low and the pipeline is okay, it may point to a product or sales effectiveness issue. In other words, sales is talking to enough qualified leads, but something else is causing those opportunities to fall through.

Lastly, consider using the two views of the funnel in your demand generation efforts. The customer-journey view is most useful in planning what types of customer collateral and sales training a marketing team needs to produce to move prospects to customers. The demand generation view helps sales and marketing teams communicate specifically about the state of their efforts, and ultimately, the health of their business. To align the two, marketers need to know their customers and sales process well.

Calculating the Number of Leads You Need

To effectively drive demand for a business, the marketing organization must have a concrete target number of leads *in each state*. The easiest way to calculate these numbers is to start with your revenue target and then work backward up the funnel. Using known or estimated conversion rates and the average sale size, you will *reverse calculate* how many SALs and SQLs you need to produce the required number of customers. Likewise, you will calculate how many MQLs you need to generate the required number of

SQLs, and how many inquiries you need to produce your target number of MQLs.

There is an additional important consideration. Make certain you understand how much new revenue marketing is responsible for generating. Marketing is often not responsible for generating 100 percent of qualified leads. For example, if an organization's revenue includes recurring annual fees, such as support and maintenance for software, or subscription renewals for telecommunications services, then sales or customer service may be responsible for handling this, and they probably will not require marketing assistance for demand generation (unless there is an attrition problem, in which case a marketing program aimed at retention will be needed).

If you work with a dedicated direct sales force, sales management typically will assume responsibility for generating 15 to 50 percent of the pipeline. These leads are sometimes referred to as sales-generated leads, or SGLs. This pipeline comes from repeat business from existing customers, pipeline carried over from previous quarters, or a desire on the part of sales leadership to make their salespeople prospect for new business. If you don't have a dedicated sales force, then you may be expected to generate 100 percent of the pipeline.

After you have established your revenue target and percentage of qualified leads marketing needs to generate, you can start your calculations. If you do not have historical conversion data to rely on, you can obtain conversion rates from a number of marketing research firms, including SiriusDecisions and Forrester Research.

Let's say you have a new revenue target of $10 million. Sales will take responsibility for half of this amount from the existing pipeline and by prospecting from their own contacts. So, marketing needs to generate the other half, or $5 million. To keep the math simple, our product will sell for the nonnegotiable price of $100,000. Figure 4 illustrates our process. I've flipped the funnel upside down to emphasize the reverse process I use.

Figure 4: Demand generation planning

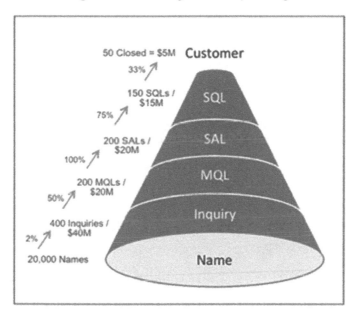

There are six steps to demand generation planning:

- Step 1: Start with our target of $5 million.

- Step 2: Divide this total by the price of an individual product ($100,000) to determine the number of customers we need. 5,000,000 ÷ 100,000 = 50 closed opportunities.

- Step 3: Calculate the total number of opportunities, or SQLs, we need to generate fifty closed opportunities. Our reps believe they can close one out of every three deals. Thus, 50 × 3 = 150 SQLs.

- Step 4: Calculate the number of MQLs needed to provide sales with 150 SQLs. Having worked with this team for a while, we know that sales accepts all of our MQLs. So, the number of SALs and MQLs will be the same. We also know that sales qualifies approximately three in every four MQLs (75 percent). 150 ÷ 0.75 = 200. So, we need 200 MQLs to generate 150 SQLs.

- Step 5: We have to determine how many inquiries we need to produce two hundred MQLs. We know that about 50 percent of our inquiries convert to MQLs. 200 ÷ 0.50 = 400. So, we need four hundred inquiries.

- Step 6: Our final step—and potentially the most discouraging—is to factor in the response rate for direct e-mail. In our case, this rate is 2 percent. 400 ÷ 0.02 = 20,000. Thus, to obtain four hundred inquiries, we need twenty thousand names.

The best sources for data on conversion percentages are your market nous, results from prior activities, your sales team, and firms that track these statistics by surveying sales and marketing teams, such as SiriusDecisions and MarketingSherpa. Make sure to be a realist and not a Pollyanna. Your sales price should be your average sales price—reflecting typical discounts, not your suggested list price. When in doubt, be conservative by picking lower conversion rates. Keep in mind that conversion rates are usually much higher for existing customers, so treat them well and market new products to them whenever you can. If your CFO wants to know why marketing needs so much money, show him or her the funnel, and explain the costs associated with buying or acquiring twenty thousand names.

Finally, make certain you have enough opportunities to achieve your revenue number. Marketers refer to the required ratio of opportunities to target revenue as *pipeline coverage*. A coverage ratio of 3:1 is typical (this is why we multiplied closed opportunities by three in step 3 above). Consequently, when you run a "pipeline coverage report," which you should pull from your marketing automation system on a regular basis, a ratio of 2:1 would not provide sufficient coverage to achieve your number, whereas 4:1 would provide more than you need. When the coverage is too low, you should invest additional money to raise the number until you achieve your target. Conversely, when the coverage is too high, then you should consider allocating a greater share of your budget to other marketing activities (or, you can suggest raising the revenue forecast).

Lead Scoring

Lead scoring is a technique for quantifying the value of a lead based on profile and activity. Points are given to leads based on certain attributes of their profiles and activities they engage in. The total of these points is the score.

The purpose of lead scoring is to segment leads based on a score and then pass over only truly qualified leads to the sales team. In a manner of speaking, lead scoring takes the qualitative out of lead qualification and replaces it with a quantitative measure. Not only does lead scoring make automation possible, it also makes the process more effective and should boost the number of MQLs that become SALs.

The profile attributes used in lead scoring include the prospect's name, title, company, location, and similar data. This information can be supplemented with data concerning the prospect's budget, purchase authority, and purchase timeline, if collected. Activity takes into account both online and off-line activities, such as seminar attendance, website visits, and views of marketing assets. A marketing team might decide to give attendees of a seminar more points than attendees of a webinar, for example, since taking the time to travel to a seminar, park, and sit through the presentation demonstrate more interest and purchase intent.

Most marketers perform lead scoring using a marketing automation system (I discuss automation software later in the chapter). Each of these will have its own proprietary method for implementing lead scoring—there is no universal scale used. So there is no absolute score at which the lead state changes from inquiry to MQL. It is the relative score, not the absolute score, that is important. What score must a lead achieve to be worth handing over to sales? The answer varies and is determined by two factors: (1) your business and (2) the hand-off negotiated between sales and marketing.

Refining lead scoring requires trial and error. Companies start with some assumptions concerning the target buyer profile, based on the target market and persona, and then they try to map the customer journey and associated activities to lead states. So, for example, a lead that is a good profile fit, has downloaded a few white papers (likely researching your product), and has examined pricing information (to determine whether he or she should consider your product), will probably accrue a lot of points, achieve a high score, and get passed along as an MQL. In contrast, is a lead that is an average profile fit but has proceeded directly to a free download of your product in the consideration stage or just a hobbyist with no real need or budget? Understanding these patterns and tweaking the scoring calculation to better map to your ideal lead can take time. Figure 5 below is an example of lead scoring where both profile and activity scores have thresholds for sales hand-off. In this example, sales will only accept leads with activity and profile scores over twenty-six (shown as shaded boxes), and prefers leads with profile scores over fifty, which are the "A" leads.

Figure 5: Lead scoring

			Activity Score			
			50+	26–49	1–25	0
Profile Score	50+	A				
	26–49	B				
	1–25	C				
	0	D				

Just because a lead has a low score does not mean that it should be thrown away. Perhaps the prospective buyer's budget was taken away, but he or she will be back next year when a new budget is created. Or, perhaps an event in the consumer's personal life has made it impossible to purchase that new flat-screen television. If conditions improve and these leads return, you can continue scoring and then pass them on to sales when they are ready.

From the opposite perspective, you can downgrade a score over time. Maybe you find out that certain leads inflated their titles, are perennial tire kickers, have published negative comments about your product in online forums, or any other number of factors. You should reduce their scores accordingly.

Lead Nurturing

So what happens when a prospective buyer fits the profile and has expressed some interest, but is not ready to buy? Maybe he or she made an inquiry or two, looked at some of your collateral, but doesn't have the money or budget to make the purchase and is not sure when he or she will. If you are using lead scoring, perhaps the score did not meet the MQL hand-off threshold. Or, maybe sales accepted the lead, but when they qualified further and realized the buyer was not ready, did not convert to an SQL.

Since you have already paid money for the lead—the total cost of acquiring the name, any asset printing and mailing costs, and the time of your telemarketer and salesperson—doing nothing would be a waste. Yet many companies do just this. They go out and buy a whole new set of names and start the process all over again. This approach is both inefficient and very expensive.

This is where *lead nurturing* comes in. Lead nurturing, which we touched on briefly in the last chapter, is a systematic process for moving leads to the next state. Nurturing is typically aimed at moving names or one-time inquirers to the MQL stage, but can also be used to drive interest in additional purchases with your installed base of customers.

What distinguishes nurturing from other marketing programs is that it is sustained. Nurturing has been around for decades in an informal fashion. Salespeople making periodic calls to prospective customers they have met but not sold to is very common. More modern nurturing uses marketing automation software to systematize the process, and better target leads with offers designed to appeal specifically to them.

In his book *The Leaky Funnel*, Hugh Macfarlane adds to the funnel metaphor and describes a more realistic version. At each stage of the funnel, customers drop, or "leak," out. Imagine the funnel with multiple holes in the side, with leads leaking out all over the place, but for different reasons. Some customers do not have the budget. Others were looking for a particular feature that you do not have. Maybe your price was too high. There are any number of reasons a buyer would leak out and not move down to the next stage.

Highly effective marketing departments segment the leads that fall out by reason and aim their nurturing at those reasons. Prospects who fell out because they were looking for a certain feature, for example, should be sent an e-mail when your product adds that feature. If a new price promotion or pricing scheme becomes available, prospects who fit the profile but fell out for budget or affordability reasons should be targeted. You might send a glowing product review to prospects that researched but did not seriously consider your product.

Creating a lead-nurturing database, as we discussed in the last chapter, can be facilitated by lead scoring. Leads with scores below the MQL hand-off threshold can automatically be added. Leads that drop or leak from the funnel should also be added, along with a code or label that indicates the reason.

Marketing Automation

As we discussed above, marketers increasingly employ marketing automation tools to assist them in transforming prospects to customers. Before these tools became widely available, managing the marketing database and leads was time-consuming and tedious. Automated nurturing and lead scoring were extremely difficult. Targeted nurturing, based on the leaky funnel concept above, was virtually impossible. All of this has changed with the emergence of marketing automation systems.

When evaluating marketing automation systems, consider the following baseline capabilities:

> Marketing database management – You should keep your marketing database separate from the customer relationship management (CRM), or sales force automation (SFA), database to keep the CRM database clean and free from the deadwood we discussed in the last chapter. The marketing automation system should enable you to cleanse your data and segment multiple databases.
>
> Landing page and lead capture management – The most common method of capturing a lead is via a form on a web landing page (I discuss landing pages further in chapter 14). Creating and managing landing pages and lead capture forms can be tedious, but automation

can help a marketing team focus on content rather than development and tracking. These tools should also include webpage content optimization via automated A/B testing, smart forms that recognize return visitors, and other valuable features.

E-mail management – Sending out direct e-mail, eDMs, requires a great deal of effort, including coding HTML e-mail, dealing with unsubscribe requests and bounces, automating e-mail delivery preferences such as form factor, and enabling sales reps to personalize the e-mail they send to prospective customers. Your system should provide tools to automate all of these.

Multichannel management – Marketing programs may span multiple media, including e-mail, direct mail, social media, and online advertising. Any system you choose should help track and manage efficacy across those channels.

Lead scoring and nurturing – Scoring leads is almost impossible to do at a large scale without marketing automation. Marketing automation enables marketers to create rules that score leads based on demographic characteristics, purchase readiness, and online activity. These systems can also automate multistep nurturing programs and the ability to automatically trigger offers based on user behavior.

Lead routing and SFA integration – Routing leads to the SFA system is, of course, a critical linkage, and this process should be included with marketing automation to ensure timely delivery so leads don't get cold. These systems should also automate the acceptance process of MQLs and the reintegration of rejected leads into the marketing database.

Reporting – Marketing automation systems should assist the marketing team in achieving visibility across the range of marketing activities. In addition, it should help them justify expenditures and demonstrate return on investment to the organization's executives.

Marketing automation systems can also include other functions, such as website tracking, social media monitoring, marketing asset management, and others. Marketing teams should decide whether buying specific tools for these ancillary functions makes sense or if the convenience of an integrated solution outweighs buying best-of-breed point solutions.

Learning More

◆ Hugh Macfarlane, *The Leaky Funnel* (Toorak:Bookman Media, 2003).

Chapter 12

Events – From Trade Shows to Webinars

arketers stage events for one overriding reason: to put sellers in direct contact with buyers. This practice has been around for hundreds—some experts claim thousands—of years. The direct ancestor of today's trade show first emerged in medieval Europe, where produce and craft vendors visited towns to participate in trading fairs, where they would sell and showcase their products and services. In 1851, intent on expanding into new overseas markets to assure its status as a leading industrialized nation, Great Britain staged the first international trade fair at the massive Crystal Palace—1,000,000 square feet of exhibit space covered by 293,655 panes of glass. Over six million people attended. Even today's mega exhibitions pale in comparison.

Commercial exhibitions as we know them today stemmed from the growth of trade groups in the twentieth century. In the early 1900s, there were about one hundred trade associations in the United States. By 2004, there were over eighty thousand. Trade associations used trade shows—and their close cousin, conventions—to grow their notoriety and expand their memberships. They thereby also created an opportunity for their members to market their products, and trade shows became important marketing events. Over twenty-one million people attended trade shows in 2004.[37]

Today, conferences, conventions, exhibitions, and trade shows are ingrained in the marketing landscape. They are often the most expensive items in the marketing mix Thus, understanding how—and how often—to use the various event types is critical to marketing success. This chapter will cover the range of events available to marketers today, discuss strategies for selecting the type of event, cover some best practices for maximizing return on investment, and end with an amusing case study on creating buzz even when you are not attending an event.

Types of Events

Understanding the landscape of events is the first step in leveraging them effectively. Marketers have a broad range of events to choose from, so they need to select a type that will attract their prospective customers. Traditionally, marketers held events in a large space where all interested parties would attend in person. In today's digital age, however, marketers increasingly are conducting events online. Let's take a closer look at both.

In-Person Events

In-person events have the benefit of enabling sellers to interact face-to-face with customers, partners, and even competitors. There is no substitute for directly interacting in person with potential buyers, letting them see and touch products, and watching their body language. The most common types of in-person events are seminars, conferences and conventions, and trade shows and exhibitions.

A *seminar* is a lecture or presentation delivered to an audience on a particular topic, or set of topics, that is educational in nature. A pharmaceutical manufacturer, for example, might hold a seminar to educate physicians on medical developments and practices related to its drugs. A seminar is typically held at a hotel meeting space or within an office conference room. Seminars are typically paid for by the sponsoring company or organization and are, therefore, free for participants. Audience size ranges from ten to a hundred. Seminars are an effective medium for educating prospective customers and converting "suspects" into qualified leads.

Conferences are usually organized around a topic or an area of interest and put on by media or event companies. *Conventions*, while also organized this way, are sponsored by a specific trade association or industry group. Both formats are aimed at education and feature talks by topic experts, and may also include exhibitions, depending on the size of the event. Most conferences arrange talks by topic areas called "tracks," which run concurrently. Attendees pick the track that best suits their area of interest (e.g., a legal track versus a technical track at a conference on online privacy), or they can pick and choose talks from multiple tracks. In contrast to seminars, customers normally pay a fee to attend. Size can vary greatly, from one hundred to ten thousand and up. Conferences and conventions are an effective strategy for interacting with likely customers, influencing their opinions, and have the added benefit of seeing what the competition is up to.

Technically speaking, trade shows and exhibitions are separate entities. *Trade shows* are held for people in the same industry or trade. For example, the Consumer Electronics Association's Consumer Electronics Show is the largest in the United States. In contrast, *exhibitions*—for example, automobile shows—are aimed at the general public. In modern marketing, however, this distinction has been largely forgotten, and most people use the two terms interchangeably.

A trade show or an exhibition is designed specifically to showcase products. Trade shows and exhibitions sometimes feature keynote speeches and tracks with speakers on various topics, blurring the distinction with conferences and conventions. When a trade show or exhibition involves both talks and exhibits, quite often a smaller number of attendees pay to listen to the talks, while the exhibits, which are either free or accessible for a nominal charge, attract a larger audience. Although trade shows and exhibitions can vary in size, large exhibitions regularly attract hundreds of thousands of visitors. Trade shows and exhibitions enable marketers to expose their company and products to a large number of prospective buyers while also keeping an eye on their competition.

Online Events

Advances in Internet connectivity and bandwidth have made online events increasingly popular alternatives to live events. They are less expensive, and they offer flexibility for all involved parties. The most widely used types of online events are webinars, virtual trade shows, and webcast and video channels.

The term *webinar*—short for "web-based seminar"— refers to a presentation, lecture, workshop, or seminar that is transmitted over the web. The term *webcast*, a similar portmanteau created by combining "web" with "broadcast," is sometimes used. Like a seminar, webinars are produced by the sponsoring organization and are free to participants. Webinars gained popularity in the late 1990s when companies like WebEx began to offer easy-to-use and inexpensive webcasting software. A major advantage of webinars is that they are inexpensive for vendors and convenient for attendees. In addition, they are recorded, so interested parties can view them after the fact. Audiences usually range from tens to hundreds.

What a webinar is to a seminar, a *virtual trade show* is to a real-world trade show. Virtual trade shows utilize special software that enables prospective buyers to interact with virtual vendor "booths" over the Internet. Virtual trade shows are produced by event or media companies that charge vendors to participate. They are more expensive than webinars, but they still cost less than the fees and travel involved in hosting and attending live events. Virtual trade shows usually last for a limited time—typically a day— and audience sizes range from hundreds to thousands. They are still something of a novelty.

One of the newest forms of online events is the *webcast and video channel*. Similar to the idea of a television channel, these services allow you to collect the webcasts and videos you produce in one place. Webcast and video channels are owned by third parties that charge organizations to post their content. The advantage of these services is that they provide simple registration for users, promotion of webcasts and video beyond your company's house list of known contacts, and social media tie-ins to drive more people to your content. Some third-party channel owners also stage "virtual seminars" where speakers from a number of companies speak on a topic during a full- or half-day event. Audience sizes are similar to webinars, though over time, subscribers to the channel can grow into the hundreds or thousands.

Selecting the Right Events

The hardest thing about events, no matter the industry, is picking the right ones. Aggressive event salespeople will tell you all about how many of your competitors will be there. Your regional salespeople will tell you how great a show has been for them in the past. Partners and customers may expect your company to be at a particular trade show or conference. Usually, unless you have exhibited at a show before yourself, it is hard to know for sure if an event will be a good use of marketing money—and live events are always among the most expensive items in a marketing mix. A perspicacious marketer should always analyze an event new to his or her company before investing.

So, first, define your goals for events overall. This should be part of your annual marketing plan. Is your goal to gain awareness—part of your reputation program? Or to get prospects for your sales team—part of your demand generation program? It is fine to answer "both," but be sure to have a way to objectively measure both. For example, you might deem a conference a successful tactic in your reputation program if you meet a certain number of industry analysts and potential partners, even if you do not get many leads for your sales team.

Table 1: Event cost work sheet

Cost	Components
Exhibit space	Space and sponsorship
Exhibit-related	Exhibit cost
	Exhibit storage (per show)
Promotions	Preshow promo
	At-show promo
	Post-show promo
At-show services	Freight
	Drayage
	Electric

	AV & technology at show
	Exhibit installation and dismantling
	Carpet or flooring
	Booth cleaning
	Lead capture
	Floral
	Furniture rental
Staff costs	Travel
	Hotel
	Meals
	Booth staff attire
	Taxi, ground transport, parking
	Staffer show registration
Miscellaneous	

If your goal is demand generation, then set a target number of leads and cost per acquisition and view an event through that lens. Ask the show organizer for the estimated attendance and demographics, and then take a swag* at how many prospects might stop by your booth or tabletop. Divide the total cost for the show by the estimated number of leads, and you will have an estimated CPA. At this point, you can decide if the show is a fit. If you choose not to attend, use the estimates to explain your decision to your salespeople. You can also use these numbers with the event salespeople and see if you can negotiate a lower price that would reduce your CPA and might make the show a fit. You should do these same calculations if you are putting on your own seminar or online webinar.

---

* Not to be confused with the trade show giveaway meaning of the word, *swag* is an acronym for "scientific wild-ass guess." Another acronym courtesy of the US Army. *Guesstimate* is the more polite synonym.

In-person events can be quite expensive. The cost to exhibit is just one line item of many. Every show is different, but table 1 below lists costs common to most and can be used to calculate total cost.

In the case of live events, you should "scout" them if possible. Get a free pass, or ask the event organizer for one (tell them you are scouting their show for future consideration) and go see for yourself. Look at companies like yours and see how much foot traffic they are getting at their booth. Attend a few of the talks, if you can, to judge their quality and suitability for your prospective customer. Approach a handful of attendees, tell them why you are there, and ask them why they came to the show and what they think of it. This firsthand experience and information will be much more useful to you than the organizer's event brochure.

Event Best Practices

Once you have determined an event is a fit, then you need to make sure to maximize your return on investment. Below are some best practices to help you get the most out of your investment, broken down by event type.

Conferences

Speaking – The best formula for achieving publicity for your organization is to be a speaker at a conference. Conference organizers need good speakers with relevant experience or knowledge to share. If you are fortunate enough to have the industry, or the world's, expert working at your company, or as a customer, then he or she should be the one speaking. Two effective strategies to secure a speaking invitation are to (1) encourage your PR team to submit an attractive proposal to the conference organizers and (2) purchase an event sponsorship package that includes a speaking slot.

Sales meetings – If your customers or prospective customers will be attending a conference, then you should send salespeople and executives to meet privately with these individuals, preferably in a hotel suite or a meeting room. Make sure to reserve a room that is conveniently located and work directly with your sales team to schedule meetings.

Trade Shows, Exhibitions, and Conferences with Exhibits

Demand generation – Decide before you show up if you are looking for a name, an inquiry, or an MQL. Knowing this will help you in your CPA calculation and how your staff behaves at the event. There are two seemingly opposite approaches when it comes to demand generation at live events. Some organizations are quite pushy, their staff standing in the aisles looking to buttonhole every passerby. Organizations that behave this way are looking for names and inquiries to add to their marketing database. The other approach is to have your staff standing patiently in the booth, answering attendee questions when asked, and only scanning their badges or taking cards when attendees ask for more information or a meeting. Organizations that behave this way are looking for MQLs. Make sure your staff is clear on the type of lead you are looking for.

Exhibits – Pick a size of booth (or "stand" if you are in London) you can afford and try to get a position on the show floor where there will be enough foot traffic to achieve your demand generation target. Sometimes rows in the back or on the edges of an exhibit floor can be "slow." Make sure it's clear from your booth signage what you are selling; filling your signage with jargon will confuse people. Build in a presentation area and hold live presentations or demos every hour to stop passersby and draw them in. Be careful with giveaways, aka *tsotchke*[†] or *swag*. Attendees are often only interested in what you are giving away and not your company or product. So, unless you are looking to collect names or trying to generate buzz in support of your reputation program, don't invest in giveaways. If you want to draw people in to start conversations, a bowl of candy is cheap and will do the trick.

---

† From the Yiddish word for "toy" or "trinket," and commonly pronounced "chach-ka," no one in marketing is ever sure how to say this word. Or spell it. Here are just some of the accepted spellings: tshotshke, tshatshke, tchachke, tchotchka, tchatchka, tchachke, tsotchke, chotski, and chochke.

News – Reporters usually attend major shows and cover news at them, so timing news around an event is often an effective way to attract press attention and to create buzz about your organization on the show floor. Issuing a press release at major industry conferences is often expected, though some companies choose not to announce if they feel there will be too much competition for news coverage among all the vendors fighting for media attention.

Sales meetings – Because your prospective buyers attend trade shows and exhibitions, you should proactively be planning to meet them. Use the same approach as mentioned above for conferences. Since some trade shows and exhibitions are so large (the Consumer Electronics Show takes up over 1.4 million square feet) you may want to design a meeting room into your booth so you can meet customers as they come by, or set up a breakfast for a group of your customers so you catch them before they hit the expo floor.

Analyst meetings – If the analysts who cover your industry or market are at an event, your PR or analyst relations (AR) team should schedule a meeting with them, especially if you have news. Even a quick update meeting or a drink in the hotel bar can help your cause.

News from the show – Not all of your customers will be in attendance at any given event, but they are probably interested in what's happening. Therefore, why not summarize the news and report it to them yourself? This is also a great opportunity to use social media tools like Twitter.

Parties – Many companies throw parties in the evenings during conferences and trade shows. These events provide an opportunity to wine and dine existing and prospective customers. They also offer a chance for executive interaction while creating a little bit of buzz on the show floor. In fact, there can be something of an unofficial competition regarding which company throws the best party.

Sponsorship – Conferences, trade shows, and exhibitions usually solicit additional funds from companies to become sponsors. Sometimes these offers are part of a package that might also include a prime booth position and a speaking slot. Premium sponsorships often include keynote speech slots. The actual benefits of sponsorship are hard to quantify. Large companies are often sponsors because they have the money and it helps reassert their industry standing at the event annually. For smaller companies, sponsorships can represent a valuable opportunity to attract notice and appear larger. Sponsor logos are usually highlighted on the floor banners and the show's website, as well as in the show guide.

Webinars

Invitations – E-mail invitations are the norm. Always use direct marketing best practices: compelling content, an offer, a clear call to action, and A/B testing.

Registration – Use best practices for web landing pages and registration forms to boost registration. Do not include sales qualifying questions, because they will make the recipients feel more like sales targets than participants. To increase the targets' commitment, you should allow them to submit questions or topics in advance when they register. Anticipate that roughly 50 percent of registrants will not attend, but be happy they registered. Filling out the registration form was an inquiry, and the registrants are a step closer to becoming a marketing qualified lead.

Reminders – You should always send a confirmation e-mail to the registrants after they sign up, preferably in the form of an invite they can import directly into their online calendars. Send these reminders twice: once on the day before the webcast and then again a few hours before the event.

Length – With few exceptions, webinars should not last longer than one hour. Increasingly, with people feeling overscheduled, shorter thirty-minute, and even fifteen-minute, webcasts are becoming popular. People may be more willing to give you fifteen minutes of their time, thereby increasing your total leads captured.

Logistics – Anticipate that something will go wrong during a webcast, whether it's your computer, your phone, the webcasting service, or your participants' connections. Have someone other than the presenter standing by to help with these issues while the presenter carries on. Make certain you have a backup computer, a phone or headset, and even the ability to e-mail the presentation to the participants if all else fails.

Interaction – Insert a survey or poll question into the webinar to encourage participation. You can also publicize the results via social media if they are interesting.

Questions – Allow participants to submit questions either during registration, via text or chat functions, or live at the end of the webinar. The person responsible for logistics should prioritize questions and manage those that deal with logistical issues, like problems with the webcasting tool or getting copies of the presentation. Prepare a few canned questions in the event the audience doesn't ask any.

Recording – Always record the webcast, and make it available to interested parties who missed the live version. Remarket the recording, and use it to capture additional leads.

Driving Attendance at Live Events

Driving attendance to your booth or your speaking sessions at a conference, trade show, or exhibition is important. There is nothing more demoralizing than standing at a booth where no one bothers to stop by.

Promoting your participation in an event is not that different from other marketing your company performs. Here are a few suggestions:

Invitations – Invite customers and prospects who might be interested in the event topic or would like to network with their peers. Inviting contacts from your house list is easy to do. Invitations should be regional, unless there is an important industry show that will interest all of your contacts and prospects.

Free passes – Many conferences offer a certain number of complimentary passes to each participating vendor. These passes are valuable—they usually have a face value of twenty to a hundred dollars—so you should market them to hot prospects. Alternatively, your sales team can hand them out to their most promising prospects.

Contests – Simple contests for small prizes will attract a lot of attention and traffic. Of course, participants whose only motivation is to win your prize might not be a well-qualified lead. Even in these cases, however, using a contest to add names to your database may be a good economic decision.

Talent – You can hire models, actors, and performers to work in your booth. How effective they will be depends on the show and industry. Models, sometimes called "booth babes," are common at auto shows and any show that is male dominated (female attendees may be turned off, however). You can hire performers—magicians, mentalists, even sumo wrestlers—to create a bit of a spectacle, if you think that will draw people in. If no one in your company is a good presenter, you can hire a professional actor to do it for you. You should take into account your demand generation target and CPA when deciding what, if any, talent to hire.

Publicity Stunts – Doing something zany or interesting can get you noticed at a show. People will talk about it and stop by your booth to meet the people responsible. Make certain, however, to run it by show organizers so you don't tick them off. Some companies have been known to get kicked out of shows for going too far.

Case Study

Marc Benioff, founder and CEO of Salesforce.com, did something unconventional at a trade show to gain attention for his then-fledgling company. In his book *Behind the Cloud*, he describes the stunt he used to kick off his now-famous "No Software" campaign. As part of a planned attack on the Goliath in the customer relationship management market, Siebel Systems, Benioff decided to carry out his plan at the 2000 Siebel User Group conference at the

Moscone Center in San Francisco. Well, not exactly at the event, but rather *outside* it.

Salesforce.com had staked out a unique position in the CRM market. Its application was delivered over the Internet. In contrast, Siebel sold software to run on a customer's computer servers, in the customer's data center. The "No Software" campaign was designed to drive home that distinction. Though we take it for granted today, running CRM over the Internet was still in its infancy in 2000.

Benioff decided to stage a fake protest outside the convention center during the Siebel event. On the morning of February 22, 2000, he sent a bunch of paid actors down to Moscone. They waved "No Software" protest signs and chanted, "The Internet is really neat...Software is obsolete." Benioff also hired actors to pose as a news crew from KNMS—a bogus local TV station whose call letters stood for "no more software." The reporters "covering" the story asked passersby their opinions concerning the Internet and the protesters' position.

Siebel executives were not pleased. According to Benioff, they came pouring out of Moscone. Enraged, they called the police. However, the actor protesters were there legally. So, what did the police do? They protected the protesters! The police action drew even more attention to the protest—exactly what Benioff and his marketing team wanted.

In addition to attracting attention, Benioff's marketing team took the opportunity to invite passersby to their Salesforce.com launch party that evening. Many of them actually showed up. In the end, the mock protest, though controversial, kicked off the campaign that would garner *PR Week*'s High-Tech Campaign of the Year award.

Staging a mock protest may or may not work for your company. It certainly fit with Benioff's bombastic style, and it set the revolutionary tone for the company and its employees. Since 2000, Salesforce has expanded into a multibillion-dollar juggernaut. Meanwhile, Siebel has become a shadow of its former self, and it was acquired by Oracle in 2006.

Chapter 13

Advertising

Advertising is the most romantic marketing discipline. The popularity of the television drama *Mad Men*, set in the nascent days of Madison Avenue, has helped to cement that image. So, who better than Don Draper, the handsome albeit moody creative director from the series, to define advertising in its series premiere, "Smoke Gets in Your Eyes":

> Advertising is based on one thing, happiness. And you know what happiness is? Happiness is the smell of a new car. It's freedom from fear. It's a billboard on the side of the road that screams whatever you are doing is okay. You are okay.

Moving from fiction to the real world (if advertising *is* the real world), advertising great David Ogilvy expressed it this way in *Ogilvy on Advertising*:

> I do not regard advertising as an art form, but as a medium of information. When I write an advertisement, I don't want you to tell me you find it "creative." I want you to find it so interesting you *buy the product.*

Romantic or not, advertising plays the key role of making potential customers aware of a product and, if it is done well, predisposing them to buy it. Advertising is too vast to cover in great detail here. For the purposes of the professional marketer, this chapter discusses advertising strategy in general and summarizes the key advertising concepts and methods. It also examines how to purchase advertising, select an agency, and measure results. A fair amount of time is spent on online advertising best practices, as this is something many internal marketing teams manage themselves.

Advertising Strategy

In 1962, *Time* called David Ogilvy "the most sought-after wizard in today's advertising industry." His advice on advertising is as important today as it was then. In his book *Ogilvy on Advertising*, he starts with a chapter on how to create advertising that sells product, which he believed was the only "good" advertising. Below is a digest of his thinking:

> Do your homework – The big idea, the "aha moment," will come only from a deep understanding of the product. Many advertising executives skip the research, and their ideas fall flat, and their copy fails to convince. Ogilvy recounts spending three weeks engaging in background research before he came upon his big idea for the Rolls-Royce account. An editor at car magazine *The Motor* had written "at 60 miles an hour, the loudest noise comes from the electric clock." That became the headline of his very successful campaign.

> Positioning – Knowing what a product does and who it is intended for is essential to creating a great ad. Ogilvy was among the visionaries who moved advertising from the image era to the positioning era, as discussed in chapter 2. For example, he positioned Dove soap for women with dry skin, feeling its scent and name would not appeal to men with dirty hands. That position is still in use today. Similarly, lacking any measurable profile, Ogilvy positioned Saab as "the car for the Norwegian winter."

Figure 1: Ogilvy's Rolls-Royce ad

Brand image – After you position your product, you need to determine an appropriate image for it. As we discussed in chapter 2, products are like people: they have personalities, and they need one that appeals to the buyer. Importantly, a product needs both a position and a brand image to be successful. Ogilvy's realization was that image alone had become insufficient.

What's the big idea? – Big ideas are the product of a lot of homework and a bit of inspiration. Discovering them is part of the magic of Madison Avenue. Big ideas can come from anywhere. Ogilvy maintained that *recognizing* a big idea is one of the most important traits of an ad man. As for what characterizes a big idea, Ogilvy encouraged advertisers to ask themselves the following questions: Did the big idea make you gasp when you first saw or heard it? Is it unique? Did you wish you had thought of it? Does it fit your strategy perfectly? Will it last for over forty years like the Marlboro Man did?

Make the product the hero – Always make certain that the product, and not a gimmick or the ad itself, is the center of the campaign. When a product seems too dull or undifferentiated, dig deeper into the product itself rather than resort to gimmickry.

Repeat your winners – If something works, stick with it. Don't change for the sake of change. Many marketing organizations become bored with an idea that is still fresh and resonates with buyers.

An important part of any advertising strategy is knowing the buyer. Insights into the buyer's preferences and attitudes will help you discover the big idea, inform the creative and the language of an ad, and inform you where you should be running it. I suggest you revisit chapter 3 on market segmentation to ensure you have done your homework on the buyer.

Types of Advertising

After you have finalized your advertising strategy, your next step is to communicate it to the prospective customer. Fortunately for advertisers, there is no shortage of outlets they can utilize: print, radio, television, online, and outdoor advertising. We examine these options below.

Print – Printed advertisements appear in newspapers and magazines. *Display ads* are large-format ads that are created by combing photographs, images, and typography, and are the dominant ad format in newspapers and magazines. Newspapers also offer *classified ads* and *supplements*—those full-color inserts that typically comprise the bulk of your Sunday paper. Print advertising has two major advantages over other types of advertising: (1) consumers spend more time paying attention to print ads, and (2) these ads can convey more detail than television, radio, or outdoor ads. Historically, organizations have invested more money in newspaper and magazine advertising than in television and radio.[38]

Radio – Commercials or program sponsorships that are broadcast on the radio. Commercials are typically ten, fifteen, twenty, thirty, or sixty seconds long. They are sold nationally as *participations* or locally as *spot announcements*. Radio is still a widely popular media format and is the most effective way to reach prospects while they are in the car.

Television – Commercials or program sponsorships that are broadcast on television. Commercials are typically ten, fifteen, twenty, thirty, or sixty seconds long. They are sold nationally as *participations* or locally as *spot announcements*.

Online – These range from banner advertisements to electronic newsletter sponsorships to sponsored search engine advertisements. Online ads are becoming increasingly popular as consumers perform more and more activities online. At this time, however, online is still a small market relative to print and television advertising.[39] One major benefit of online ads is that it is easier to measure their effectiveness than that of other types. (We discuss measurement later in the chapter.)

Outdoor, also referred to as out of home (OOH) – These include signs or billboards that appear either outside or indoors in public spaces such as airports. OOH includes ads in or on taxis, buses, trains, transit shelters, news racks, and stadiums.

Choosing the right ad media will depend on a number of factors. First, what is the goal of the advertising campaign—awareness, brand building, or direct response? Second, who is the target customer? And last, what is the budget? Not everyone can afford a Super Bowl ad. The types of media used in an ad campaign is known as the *media mix*. A *media plan* is a document that reflects the strategy, goals, audience, budget, and media mix for an ad campaign.

Again, an organization's media mix will be determined by an ad campaign's goal, prospective customer, and budget. Most marketers use some form of online advertising, because it is flexible enough to achieve multiple goals, reaches both business and consumer buyers, and is relatively inexpensive. Television and radio advertising are used primarily by B2C companies. (IBM is a notable exception in using television advertising to reach business buyers of its computers and software.) Print advertising is used heavily by B2C marketers. B2B marketers in larger companies use print for brand building in the mainstream business press. B2B marketers of all sizes should consider print ads in specialized *trade publications*, which are both cheaper and more narrowly targeted than the mainstream press.

Like television and radio, OOH advertising is utilized largely by B2C marketing. B2B marketers should consider OOH ads around trade shows and in airports and train stations their buyers pass through.

One innovative and exclusive form of OOH advertising is the blimp. Blimps are effective mobile billboards due to their slow speed, extremely long "loiter time," and inexpensive fuel costs. In 1925 Goodyear Tire and Rubber Company became the first company to use aerial advertising when it created its in-house blimp series, the Goodyear Type AD. Today Goodyear and other companies use blimps to promote themselves at sporting events, where they provide broadcasters with aerial television coverage in exchange for television exposure. Current models of blimps that display aerial advertisements often have sophisticated LED billboards for night-time exposure.

Using Online Advertising

Many marketing teams handle their online advertising in-house, without engaging an advertising agency. A company may primarily use textual pay-per-click ads, for example, and not require the creativity or copywriting an agency brings. Some companies can produce suitable banner ads with their graphic design team or creative agency. Online advertising is covered in detail here because it is the one type of advertising almost all marketers will be involved with directly.

Online Ad Formats

Banner Ads

Display advertising that appears on the web is known as *banner advertising*. This name derives from the fact that the ads were originally available as rectangular "banners" across the top of a web page. Today banner ads are available in a number of standard sizes called "ad units," which are defined by the Interactive Advertising Bureau (IAB). Among the most commonly used are tiles, skyscrapers, leaderboards, and pop-overs. Banner ads can be static, animated, or contain video. Most banner ads contain a call to action that links to the advertiser's website or landing page.

Figure 2: IAB's display advertising portfolio

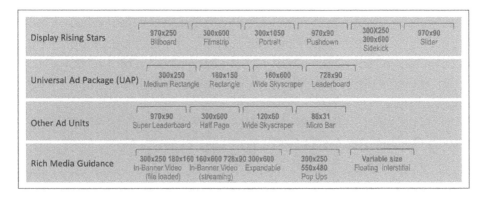

Figure 2 shows the banner advertising portfolio defined by the IAB. The width and height in pixels is shown along with the name of the ad unit. The Universal Ad Package is a set of four ad units offered by publishers as a "package" where ads in these four formats are used collectively across the publisher's site. Rising Star Display Ad Units are designed to be the only ad on a page.

The first known online display ads appeared on Prodigy, an online service owned by the unlikely partnership of CBS, IBM, and Sears, starting in the 1980s. America Online joined in later. The first true web banners—those actually on the World Wide Web and not on a proprietary online service—were introduced by HotWired, the online division of *Wired*.[40] AT&T's 468x60 pixel ad with the unoriginal teaser "Have You Ever Clicked Your Mouse Right Here? You Will" received a stunning 78 percent click-through rate—a percentage never again achieved in banner advertising.

Figure 3: The first banner ad displayed on HotWired on October 22, 1994

Banner ads are most often measured in *impressions*—the number of times they are available for view. Advertisers purchase them in lots of one thousand

impressions, and pricing is given in *cost per thousand*, commonly called CPM.*
Cost per thousand was originally a method of comparing the cost effectiveness of two or more alternative media vehicles with different pricing schemes,
but is now most commonly associated with banner advertising. Conversion
rates for banner ads can be very low, often a fraction of 1 percent. Therefore,
banner ads should be used when the primary goal of a campaign is awareness.

Pay-Per-Click Ads

Pay-per-click (PPC) ads, also known as cost-per-click ads, were introduced
in 1998 by GoTo.com. As the name suggests, advertisers pay the site owner or
ad network when a PPC ad is clicked, not simply when it is displayed, in contrast to banner ads, which are purchased in lots of one thousand impressions.

Pay-per-click ads are almost always displayed on search engine results
pages (SERPs), usually on top and to the right. Advertisers select a list of keywords that, when used in a search, will trigger the display of the ad. These
ads are usually text based, further distinguishing them from display ads. This
system is known also known as "paid search" advertising. Working to have
your products or company shown in the unpaid "natural" or "organic" search
results on a SERP is done via search engine optimization (SEO), a topic covered in the next chapter.

Google is by far the largest provider of PPC ads. Although not the creator
of PPC—and for many years a harsh critic—Google is credited with creating
the auction system for ad purchase. Advertisers bid what they are willing to
pay for a certain keyword or phrase. The amount they bid influences their
position on the page, with the top positions being most desirable.

The term *search engine marketing (SEM)* was introduced in the early
2000s to describe the practice of using search engines to promote a web page
or website. SEM includes both SEO and PPC, though many people mean just
PPC when they say SEM.

---

* The CPM abbreviation is a little confusing. In a strange confluence, the English words
"cost" and "per" were combined with the Latin "mille" for thousand, represented by the
Roman numeral *M*.

Affiliate Marketing

Affiliate marketing is the placement of an ad by an online retailer on a number of other websites, called *affiliates*. Typically, these affiliate sites have something in common with the retailer, such as online travel guides working with airlines or hotels, or they cater to an audience the retailer seeks to reach. Affiliates are paid upon conversion, for example, when a customer purchases a product or signs up for a service. Payment is usually calculated as a percentage of the total sales generated directly by the referral. This model differs markedly from the banner ad CPM and PPC pricing models.

Affiliate marketing was created by CDNow in 1994, and it became popular following the success of the Amazon.com affiliate program, launched in 1996. The Amazon program generated low-cost brand exposure, and it provided small websites with a way to earn supplemental income by displaying ads for books relevant to their visitors and sold by Amazon. Affiliate marketing remains popular in bookselling, and it is used extensively in the travel industry. Orbitz Worldwide is a popular online travel company that pays commissions to travel guide and other qualified websites through its affiliate program.

Retargeting

Targeting ads at people who have previously visited your website is known as *retargeting*. Your banner ads are shown on other websites via a display network that uses cookies to track the users you want to retarget.

Retargeting is a strategy to boost your conversion rate. The goal is to increase the number of people who click on your ads by reminding them of you or your product after they have moved on to another site. Some marketers find them to be very effective, but results can vary. Imagine a husband who finds ads for his wife's hand cream showing up repeatedly on the home computer. Some consumers get turned off—or "creeped out"—by ads that "follow" them around. Some are concerned about their privacy and consider retargeting a form of online surveillance. Advertisers need to closely monitor the sentiment of the customers they are targeting. Limiting retargeting to display only on sites relevant to the product is a good idea. Having a clear privacy policy and heeding consumer complaints are also essential.

Social or Viral Advertising

Despite the size and continued growth of the global advertising market, there is concern that consumers are increasingly tuning out the incessant cacophony of advertising messages. Significantly for marketers, modern technologies have made it easier for consumers to avoid advertisements. For example, digital video recorders (DVRs) enable television viewers to speed past commercials. Apple's iTunes lets people listen to whatever music they want, whenever they want—without commercials. And conversion rates on banner ads are tiny. To increase consumer attention, advertisers have introduced a new type of advertising that engages viewers and in some cases actually recruits them to pass the ad along. It is known as *social advertising*, or *viral advertising*, and it can be very effective.

The majority of social advertising relies on two fundamental tactics—the pass-along video and "gamification." The pass-along video is one that is so unbelievable, funny, interesting, or some other superlative that viewers pass it along to their friends or share it with their social networks. Pass-along videos can be used for brand building and product awareness. YouTube is an easy outlet for distributing pass-along videos, and this is one type of media that is okay to produce in-house. The Blendtec videos mentioned in chapter 7 are a great example. Slick production that resembles a television commercial can have a negative impact, as the viewer may sniff an advertisement. You can also use pass-along videos for direct-response advertising. One way is to produce a teaser video with an offer of seeing the conclusion on registration.

Gamification is the creation of a game that involves the brand. As an example, Green Giant placed peel-off stickers on their frozen vegetables that could be redeemed for "cash" in the online game FarmVille. (Note the obvious connection between their products and the fresh produce of farming.) Similarly, Nike created a game of "tag" for users of its Nike+ running band, where users can share their running stats online. Players tried not to be "it" by running more than people in their game group—a natural motivator for people who find it difficult to psych themselves up for running. Other examples are photo scavenger hunts where users are given a list of objects to take a picture of with their phones, joke contests, and companies that have created original online or mobile games that feature their products.

Mobile

Smartphone and tablet use is exploding. According to the IAB, 46 percent of American adults own a smartphone or tablet.[41] Where users go, advertisers will follow. By 2016, it is estimated that US mobile ad spending will grow to over $6 billion.[42]

In the face of such large numbers, marketers should consider mobile advertising as part of their strategy. Banner and pay-per-click are still the dominant forms of advertising on smartphones and tablets. The most important consideration for mobile advertising is the difference in user expectations on a mobile device. Space is at a premium, so the ads are smaller, and there are fewer of them. The landing page an ad link leads to needs to be a mobile-ready site that is easy to navigate. (Mobile websites are discussed in the next chapter.)

Mobile brings additional opportunities. Some companies are creating mobile applications—"apps"—to extend their brand experience. The practice of "geofencing," or establishing a virtual fence around a geographic area, allows advertisers to target ads based on location, such as near a retail location. Increased bandwidth and reduced rates for data download may bring more television-style commercials to our phones. Marketers need to monitor their target customer or demographic to decide when and what kind of mobile advertising makes sense.

Online Advertising Best Practices

Many elements go into creating a successful online ad campaign. Just as in print and television advertising, no single format will work for every company. All of Ogilvy's rules apply to online campaigns. In addition, a few other practices will maximize your results:

- Targeting – Though it sounds obvious, it is essential that your ads are displayed in the right places and to the right people. Because online ads are so easy to set up, and the reach of the Internet so vast, you need to pay attention to where your ads are being displayed, lest you suffer "spill" or "leakage"—money wasted on displaying ads to the wrong demographic or in the wrong geography.

◆ Format and size – Research by the ad network DoubleClick has revealed that larger ad units generate higher click-through rates. These ads are more expensive, but they can be worth the money if they motivate consumers to take your desired action more often.

◆ Keyword matching and context – Make sure your textual PPC ads make sense in context. These ads are much more effective if the ad text fits in with the search a user is performing. Most ad networks allow for multiple variants of an ad, and text substitution, based on the keyword.

◆ Strong offer and clear CTA – As we discussed in chapter 9, a strong offer and call to action are essential to any direct marketing effort. The prize, discount, report, or whatever you are offering must be compelling, and the CTA should be clear.

◆ Landing page optimization – A *landing page* is the web page prospective customers see when they click on your ad. Bad landing pages hurt conversion. Your landing page should match your ad—same offer, same look and feel, same language. Otherwise, potential customers may get confused, turned off, pissed off, diverted, or any number of things you don't want. A pervasive bad habit of online marketers is to send users to their home page regardless of the product or service being advertised.

◆ Continual testing – Everything matters online: the creative, the offer, the CTA, the placement, the frequency, and share of voice (which we discuss below). To maximize the ad's effectiveness, it is essential that you test and tune everything. A/B testing, as we discussed in chapter 9, is a must. And, the unfortunate news is that you will never be done, so make sure you have the staff to keep on top of it.

Measuring Advertising Effectiveness

Advertising is expensive, so you need to measure its effectiveness to ensure you can justify the spend. Measuring also helps you allocate your budget to the most successful properties and ad types. You should express the goals of your ad campaigns in terms of

- reach, the number of buyers in the target market who view or hear the ad;
- frequency, the number of times a target buyer should view or hear the ad; desired outcome, the action a buyer should take after being exposed to the ad.

Marketers employ a number of metrics to measure reach, frequency, and desired outcome. The most widely used ones are

- impressions;
- share of voice;
- click-through rate;
- conversion rate;cost per acquisition.

Let's examine each of these.

Impressions, also known as *ad views*, are simply the total number of times an ad unit is available for view. Impressions can be measured for any type of advertising but is most accurate for online ads. Ad networks can tell an advertiser exactly how many times an ad was shown. While broadcasters may know how many times a radio or television advertisement aired, they have to rely on viewership estimates to calculate impressions. Publishers estimate print ad impressions based on circulation. OOH ad network owners estimate based on foot or vehicle traffic.

In advertising, *share of voice* is the percentage of ad impressions for one brand in a particular product category as compared to other brands in the same category. SOV is also sometimes referred to as *advertising weight*. Measuring SOV in print, radio, television, and OOH relies on third-party reports that calculate total available advertising inventory. The amount of money spent on advertising is sometimes used as an estimate when reliable impression data is not available. Measuring SOV online, sometimes called *impression share*, is easier. The percentage of times an online ad unit appears compared to the number of times it could have been shown, based on the total available ad space inventory, is its SOV. Google AdWords calculates impression share automatically. In some cases, an advertiser or agency may have to request total inventory numbers from the ad network or web property owner.

The *click-through rate* is the measure of the number of ad impressions that convinced a user to respond to the call to action, measured as a percentage. Click-through rates are typically low, less than 1 percent of impressions (nowhere near the 78 percent the first banner ad produced). Though this may seem low, it is typical for direct marketing efforts, as we discussed in chapter 9. Remember, banner and PPC ads are two types of direct-response advertising, which is a form of direct marketing.

Whereas the click-through rate measures how many visitors accessed your landing page or offer page, the *conversion rate* calculates the percentage of visitors who were compelled to take a desired action to achieve a business outcome. Desired outcomes can range from downloading software to buying a product to subscribing to a newsletter to completing a registration form. Conversion rate is an essential measurement in any form of direct-response advertising. Conversions can be measured for any print, radio, television, or OOH ad that contains a response mechanism, such as a unique URL, phone number, or QR code.

Cost per acquisition is how much it costs per prospective customer to get him or her to convert to the desired outcome. CPA is your total cost of the direct-response advertising campaign—including any costs associated with the offer—divided by the number of conversions.

Which of these measures you should employ depends on your organization's business goals. Some companies aim to create buzz by achieving maximum SOV. Others—for example, e-commerce companies—are more focused on maximizing conversions. The failure to tie the measurement to a business objective—which is simply accounting for how money was spent—is a common failing of marketers. Leaders of your organization do not really care about clicks or impressions. They care about a particular business objective, whether a purchase, a meeting, a lead, or something else. Your conversions should align with these objectives, and this is what you should be reporting. The marketing team, on the other hand, should absolutely dig into the details and try to maximize outcomes for as little money as possible.

Purchasing Ad Space

Online

The major mechanisms for purchasing online ad space are keyword auctions, advertising networks, and major web properties and publications. Let's take a closer look at each one, beginning with keyword auctions.

PPC ads are usually sold on the basis of a keyword auction. A *keyword auction* is a process by which advertisers bid on keywords used in searches for the right to have their ads displayed on the SERP. The position of the ad on the page is determined by a combination of the bid, the quality of the ad, and the click-through rate of the ad. Ads that display on the first SERP page and in the top positions or upper right generally perform better. Many people do not understand that their position on the page depends on ad quality and click-through rate *as well as their bid*. Improving their ad and click-through rate by refining their ad copy and landing page can actually reduce the amount they need to bid while still resulting in a good position, saving them money and improving performance.[43]

Purchasing ads is simple, and advertisers can decide how much "owning" a keyword is worth to them. Budgeting is critical. Advertisers decide not only how much to pay for a keyword but how frequently it appears. So, for example, an advertiser could use the same budget to appear in the top position with a lower frequency or in a lower position with increased frequency. Purchasing PPC ads from Google, Bing, Yahoo!, and other search engines requires little more than opening an account with a credit card. Because ad prices change every day, marketing teams need to pay close attention to PPC ads to monitor their spend.

Reaching potential buyers through an online ad network—also known as a *display network*—can be easier and frequently less expensive than dealing with all of the relevant websites individually. Ad networks vary, from the web properties (really just a fancy term for websites) owned by a single magazine publisher, to independent companies that have agreements to buy a certain amount of ad inventory across multiple publishers, to confederations of smaller sites that possess similar audiences or themes. Google itself has two networks—the "search network" that displays ads on SERPS, and the "content network" that displays Google ads on other websites that sign up with Google to make money from advertising. Finally, well-known publications and web properties typically have a dedicated advertising sales staff or, if not, a dedicated agency to handle ad buys.

Working with a Media Buyer

Many companies opt to use media buyers for advice on media mix and to strike better deals with media outlets. *Media buyers* are individuals who are responsible for purchasing time and advertising space for advertising purposes. They may work for an ad agency or for a specialized media-buying agency. Media buyers can suggest the appropriate media outlets based on the goals of your advertising campaign, taking into account demographics, reach, inventory, and other factors. Media buyers can often strike a better deal because these professionals know how much discounting is typical and who might have unsold ad inventory that you can get on the cheap.

Selecting an Advertising Agency

Whether you need an advertising agency depends on your business. Large consumer product companies almost always work with an ad agency. B2B marketers mounting a print, radio, or television advertising campaign should have an agency. Print, OOH, and banner ads created in-house are usually easy to spot: they look amateurish, and they probably lack the big idea. Some companies use a design or "digital" agency for their online banner ads.

Many aspects of selecting an ad agency boil down to common sense and chemistry. That said, your organization may require specific capabilities such as global reach or market research. Make certain you select an agency that can provide everything you need.

When selecting an agency, start with the ones that focus on your industry. We also recommend that you select agencies of similar size to your organization. If the agency is much larger than your organization, they might dismiss you as too small to be of importance. Conversely, a substantially smaller agency might lack adequate resources to manage your account effectively.

Sending out a short request for proposal (RFP) to winnow down your list is common. Here are a few questions you should ask:

- Who will be handling your account? Make certain the individual who will manage your account is not the summer intern. If working with one of the senior people is important to you, then get their commitment before you make a selection.

- How do they charge? Find out what you can expect for creative, and what's included. For example, does the agency impose additional charges for developing accompanying assets such as direct mail pieces? How do they handle change fees? Will they charge a commission for placing your ads?

- How do they hire creative talent? Inquire as to how the agency thinks about creative people, where they find these individuals, and how they retain them.

- What is the future of advertising? An open-ended question like this accomplishes two things. First, it indicates whether the agency thinks strategically. Second, it tells you how tapped in they are to the changing landscape.

- How do they measure success? When you hire an agency, *your* success will be based on *their* success. Therefore, knowing how they define success, and whether they systematically measure it, is important.

Your boss will not care that the agency you picked won a Clio award if your sales don't pick up.

♦ What have they done recently? Review the agency's recent performance, with a special focus on any out-of-the-box ideas they have implemented. Good agencies try new things, and their customers benefit.

After you have narrowed down the list of prospects based on these questions, invite the finalists to your company's office to make a presentation—the "pitch." A key point: Unless you are an immense client like Coke or McDonald's, don't expect a fully executed advertisement. Ads can be very expensive, and it's not reasonable to expect an agency to invest that much money merely to make their pitch. The agency might present sketches or a foam core *mood board*, which is a collage of images designed to express the concept. Some agencies may just pitch to you verbally.

After that, the decision is up to you. Advertising is a highly subjective game. Good luck!

Case Study

There have been so many great ads over the decades. How would we pick just one as the greatest of all time? Looking at the *AdAge* Top 100[44] makes things even harder: Volkswagen's "Think Small," which introduced the VW Beetle to the United States in the '60s (number one); the Marlboro Man (number three); Nike's "Just do it" (number four); "A diamond is forever" from De Beers (number six); the Absolut Vodka bottle campaign (number seven); "Tastes great, less filling"—quick, name the beer (number eight). These are just a few. Yet the ad in the number twelve spot is intriguing.

Apple's "1984" ad appeared only one time, on January 22, 1984, during the National Football League's Super Bowl XVIII between the Washington Redskins and the Los Angeles Raiders. Super Bowl viewership is huge (over seventy-five million then and over a hundred million today), and advertisers pay huge sums of money to use the Super Bowl broadcast as a springboard for new campaigns. But, if advertising is all about awareness through repetition, could an ad shown only once truly be effective? Would it pass Ogilvy's test of being so interesting it made you want to buy Apple's product?

The Super Bowl ad introduced the Apple Macintosh. The big idea was to pit the Mac against the incumbent IBM personal computer. The ad was a deliberate takeoff of George Orwell's novel *1984*. It was created by Chiat/Day's copywriter, Steve Hayden, and art director, Brent Thomas, and directed by Ridley Scott of *Blade Runner* fame.

The commercial opens with a dystopic industrial setting in blue and gray tones, showing a line of people marching in unison through a long tunnel lined with a string of computer monitors. A female track-and-field athlete, shown in color, is running toward a giant screen that displays pronouncements from an Orwellian Big Brother character. Chased by the thought police, she is carrying a brass track-and-field hammer, which she then throws, and it crashes through the giant screen. The ad ends with text and a voice-over: "On January twenty-fourth, Apple Computer will introduce Macintosh. And you'll see why 1984 won't be like *1984*."

The ad garnered all kinds of television commercial awards, including *TV Guide*'s Number One Greatest Commercial of All Time and *Advertising Age*'s Greatest Commercial.

Though the ad was broadcast only once, it attracted worldwide news coverage. The buzz created by "1984" was tremendous. The positioning was perfect. It was true to the brand. It was Apple—upstart innovator against IBM's machine. It holds up well after almost thirty years.

That commercial was a big idea that made a segment of the market want to join the revolution and buy a Mac. David Ogilvy would be pleased.

Learning More

+ Wells, Moriarty, and Burnett, *Advertising Principles and Practice* (Upper Saddle River:Prentice Hall, 2006).

+ David Ogilvy, *Ogilvy on Advertising* (New York:Vintage Books, 1985).

+ Andreas Ramos and Stephanie Cota, *Search Engine Marketing* (New York:McGraw-Hill Osborne Media, 2009).

Chapter 14

The Website

It's funny to think that the web, which hundreds of millions of people use every day for shopping, dating, gaming, news, and socializing, began as a technology to help improve, of all things, physics research—a topic of interest to only a fraction of the world's population. Yet today, the web is huge. According to *What Technology Wants* by Kevin Kelly, himself a chronicler of the early days of the web, it holds more than a trillion pages.

Twenty-plus years since the first website was created by physics researcher Tim Berners-Lee* at the European Organization for Nuclear Research (CERN) in 1991, we are already several generations away from its original Spartan black text with blue hyperlinks on a white page. We've moved from professional design to rich media and animation, to social media inclusion, to the requirement of usability and availability on mobile devices. All of these innovations been driven by the insatiable consumer demand for web content and the critical role the web has assumed in modern business.

With the amount of time consumers spend online and the use of the web by businesses searching for partners and suppliers, the web has become a vital marketing tool. A well-constructed website has been transformed from merely expected to an indispensable mechanism for product differentiation and competitive advantage. Despite the centrality of the web in both our

---

* In 2004, Berners-Lee was knighted by Queen Elizabeth II, joining fellow physicists Isaac Newton (1643) and James Chadwick (1945), and technologist Bill Gates (2005), as knights of the British Empire.

business and our personal lives, however, many marketing teams are not truly optimizing their websites.

This chapter will lay out the process for developing a new website from scratch, starting with the establishment of website goals; moving through the primary considerations of usability, design, and content; and then on to development. This is followed by sections that can be applied to a new or existing website: getting found, maintaining content, optimizing for conversion, and measurement. The chapter concludes with special considerations for microsites, e-commerce sites, and mobile websites.

Establishing Website Goals

The initial step in utilizing the web as a marketing tool is, of course, to create a viable website. Before you undertake any development work on the site, however, you need to identify the site's primary goals. Is the site intended to educate, inform, entertain, sell a product, or some combination of these? The goals, along with the target audience, will determine the site's functionality, design, and content. Sharing these goals with the web team, management, and rank-and-file employees will help avoid any number of artistic and functional arguments, as well as increase the likelihood that the project will be a success. You should also involve customers and partners in the process if possible—the site is intended for them, after all.

To clearly define your needs, goals, and objectives, you should ask yourself a few detailed questions:

- What are your primary business objectives, and how can the website help you achieve them?
- Who will use your website, and what are their tasks and goals?
- What information and functions do your users need, and in what form do they need them?
- How do users think your website should work?

+ What hardware and software will the majority of people use to access your site? Will they be using a laptop, a tablet, a smartphone, or some combination of these tools?

Site Fundamentals – Usability, Design, and Content

After you have agreement on your goals, you are ready to begin work on the three fundamental aspects of your site: usability, design, and content.

Usability

Usability measures the quality of a user's experience when interacting with a product or system—whether a website, a software application, mobile technology, or any user-operated device. In general, usability refers to how well individuals can use a product to achieve their goals and how satisfied they are with that process. As it relates specifically to the web, usability is the measure of the quality of customers' experiences when they interact with your website.

Usability is a combination of several factors:

+ Ease of learning – How fast can a user who has no previous experience with the website learn it sufficiently well to accomplish basic tasks?

+ Efficiency of use – Once experienced users have learned to use the website, how fast can they accomplish tasks? A site that is efficient to use will likely bring users back. This tendency, along with the quality of the content, will help achieve what web developers call "stickiness," meaning the amount of time users spend on a site and the likelihood they will return.

+ Memorability – If users have visited the website before, can they remember its setup and functions well enough to use it effectively the next time? Or, do they have to start all over again and relearn everything? When users must remember information on one web page for use on another, they can remember only about three or four items for a few seconds.

◆ Performance – No matter how intuitive or efficient the site is to navigate, poor performance is a killer. A site's performance can be affected by the servers and network that host it, the network of the user, and the content on the site. Users become frustrated if a web page does not load immediately. A study by KISSmetrics showed that 25 percent of users abandoned a website after waiting just four seconds, and the majority of mobile users would abandon a site after ten seconds.[45] In the same study, KISSmetrics found that every additional second of load time reduces conversions by 7 percent. When designing a new site, or augmenting an existingone, always test the performance to make sure the combination of content and a typical user's network speed does not cause slowdowns.

Design

The design of a website must support usability. In addition, the site is an expression of your brand, so its design should reflect your identity. Keep in mind that users will make an immediate judgment when they view your site, unconsciously assessing whether it is trustworthy, welcoming, relevant, and professional. Your design should support the image you want to portray.

Below are specific design considerations for the different parts of a website.

Home Page

A home page should concisely communicate the site's purpose, and it should clearly indicate all of the major options available on the site. Generally, on latop and desktop screens, the bulk of the home page should be visible in a single screen or "above the fold"—a term borrowed from newspaper publishers meaning the top half of a folded newspaper—and it should contain a limited amount of text. Content you want all visitors to see must be placed above the fold.

Designers should provide easy access to the home page from every page in the site so users can get back to where they started. The first action of most users is to scan the home page for link titles and major headings. Requiring users to read large amounts of text can slow them considerably. Some readers will avoid reading it altogether.

Navigation

Navigation refers to the methods people use to get to information within a website. A site's navigation scheme and features should enable users to find and access information effectively and efficiently. Create a common site-wide navigational scheme to help users learn and understand the structure of the site. Use the same scheme on all pages by consistently locating tabs, headings, and lists. Many users expect to find a site map—a kind of table of contents—in the footer of the page. Locate critical navigation elements in places that will suggest "clickability." For example, lists of words placed in the left or right panels are generally assumed to be links. Also, don't get too cute with the words in the navigation. Your goal should be comprehension, not originality.

Lastly, users expect to be able to search within a site to find what they need. Make sure to provide this capability. A search box should be located in the top right corner of the home page and subpages.

Subpage Layout

Subpages are pages that are one level down from the home page. They are sometimes called *second-level* pages, with the home page being the *top-level* page.

Well-designed headings make it easier for users to scan and read written material. Designers should strive to create unique and descriptive headings and to incorporate as many headings as is necessary to enable users to find what they are looking for. Headings should provide strong cues that orient users and inform them about page organization and structure. Headings also help classify information on a page. Each heading should be helpful in finding the desired target.

On long pages, include a list of contents with links that take users to the corresponding content farther down the page. Also, provide feedback to let users know where they are in the site. A common method to accomplish this goal is to insert *breadcrumbs* —horizontally arranged text at the top of the page, above the headline, that tells users where they are in the site's navigation and helps them find their way back "home."

A well-designed website will enable users to access important content from more than one link. Establishing multiple paths to access the same information can help users locate what they need. When you're designing the site, always remember that different users will try different approaches to finding information and may also search for information using different terms.

One fundamental rule for a user-friendly design is to display a series of related items in a vertical list rather than as continuous text. A well-organized vertical list format (e.g., bullets or grids) is much easier to scan than horizontal text, whether prose or a list.

Finally, your site's graphics should add value to and increase the clarity of the information contained on the site. Relevant pictures are often more powerful than labels in compelling a user to take a desired action.

Alt Text

Another basic design rule is to use text equivalents for all non-text elements, including images, graphical representations of text and symbols, image map regions, animations (e.g., animated GIFs), sounds, audio files, and video. Text equivalents are referred to as *alt text*, or *alt tags*, and are useful for search engine optimization as well as usability. Users will often hover their pointer over an image to read the alt text.

Content

Content is simply the information provided on a website. For a website to achieve its goals, the content needs to be engaging, relevant, and appropriate to the audience. Below are a few fundamental rules for selecting and creating useful content:

- Clear language – When you are preparing prose content for a website, use familiar words, and avoid the use of jargon, just as you would for good marketing collateral. If you must use acronyms and abbreviations, make certain they are defined on the page in language that typical users will understand. Shorten for readability—minimize the number of words in a sentence and the number of sentences in a paragraph. Make the first sentence of each paragraph descriptive of the remainder of the paragraph. Write in an affirmative, active voice. Limit the amount of prose on each page.

- Prioritize – Putting critical information near the top of the site and ensure that all necessary information is available without slowing down the user with unneeded information.

- Build for scanning – People scan before they read, so structure each page to facilitate scanning. Use clear, well-located headings; short phrases and sentences; and small, readable paragraphs. Again, use bulleted lists or grids where appropriate.

- Group – Make certain to group together all of the information that is related to a topic. This system minimizes the need for users to search or scan the site for related information. Users will assume that items that are placed in close spatial proximity, or that share the same background color, belong together conceptually.

- Visual aids –Tables, graphics, and other visuals are great for aiding understanding. Make sure to pick the best one. Presenting quantitative information in a table (rather than as a graph), for example, makes it easier to read the numbers themselves. Presenting it as a graph illustrates trends or relative size. Usability testing can help you determine when users will benefit from using graphs, tables, or other visualizations.

- Less is more – Do not overload pages or interactions with extraneous information. Displaying too much information can overwhelm users and hinder their ability to assimilate the information they need. Help users focus on their desired tasks by excluding information that task analysis and usability testing indicate is not relevant.

Building the Site

Once you have considered the usability, design, and content for a site, it's time to start building it. Here are the steps to assure success.

Content Inventory

A *content inventory* is a list of everything that is contained on your site. When you are developing a new site, you should create an inventory of the content as it is being developed. As the site matures, the inventory will keep you updated as to what is on the site, how old each page is, and when each page was revised or needs to be reviewed.

Many websites grow by accretion. Organizations keep adding pages to their sites, but few of them ever remove dated or superfluous pages. This is a serious error. After a while, if you don't keep a content inventory, the web or marketing team have a harder and harder time keeping all of the website's content up-to-date.

When you are revising an existing website, start with a content inventory of what is on the site. Then, create a planned content inventory for the new version of the site based on your site's goals and objectives.

To perform a content inventory, create a spreadsheet or use a database application to categorize and describe the information on every page of your site. Your inventory should include the following elements:

- Where the page resides in the navigation
- The page title and URL

- A short description of the information on the page

- When the page was created, when it was last revised, and when the next page review is scheduled

- Who wrote the page (if you know), who is currently responsible for the page, and the contact information for that individual

- The expiration date of the page (if there is one)

- Other pages that this page links to, and pages that link to it

- Page status—keep, delete, revise, in revision process, planned, being written, being edited, in review, ready for posting, or posted

If you use a spreadsheet or database, you can sort the inventory by any of the categories of information you have. The primary category might be the overall topic or area so that you can view all of the pages that relate to the same information. For maintenance purposes, you may also want to sort by date of last update so that you can view all of the old content on the site and review these pages to determine if they need to be updated. There are also applications that can scan your site to check for broken links. A content management system that can keep track of page versions and help web teams search for content is a good idea for larger sites.

Creating a Site Map

To help you get the content organized, you may want to create a site map. A *site map* is a visual representation of the information contained on your site. You can create a site map that looks like a company organization chart, with textual descriptions inside boxes, connected by lines, that descend in a hierarchy from the home page. Or you can create one in outline form, indenting for each sublevel. This approach has the added advantage that you can easily create a navigational site map from it. Figure 1 below shows a snippet from the site map for culinary sauce producer Kagome's revised website.

Figure 1: Snippet from a site map

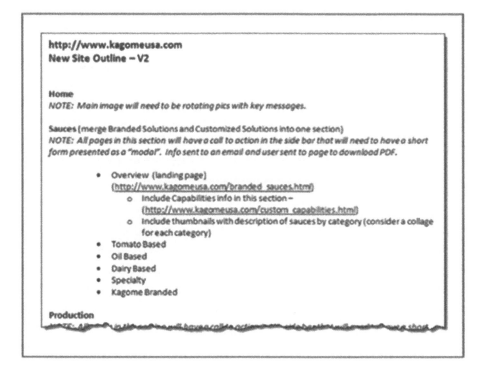

Creating the Wireframe

A *wireframe* is a basic visual illustration of a web page. The term comes from the line drawings engineers create to illustrate three-dimensional objects before they are produced. The purpose of a wireframe is to illustrate the features, content, and links that need to appear on a page so that your design team can mock up a visual interface and your developers will understand the page features and how they are supposed to work.

A wireframe indicates where each item should be placed on a page. In addition, it performs the following functions:

- Identifies all of the features on a page

◆ Prioritizes the features so that the most important ones are prominently positioned

◆ Visually communicates this information to the rest of your design team via a diagram of the page

Wireframes can range from a simple mock-up of an information-based page to an extremely complex diagram illustrating an intricate process with several steps, such as a product purchase. They do not dictate how a site should look. Wireframes can be created using various tools, from a simple word processing program to a complex diagramming program. Figure 2 below shows the wireframe created for the Kagome site.

Figure 2: Sample wireframe

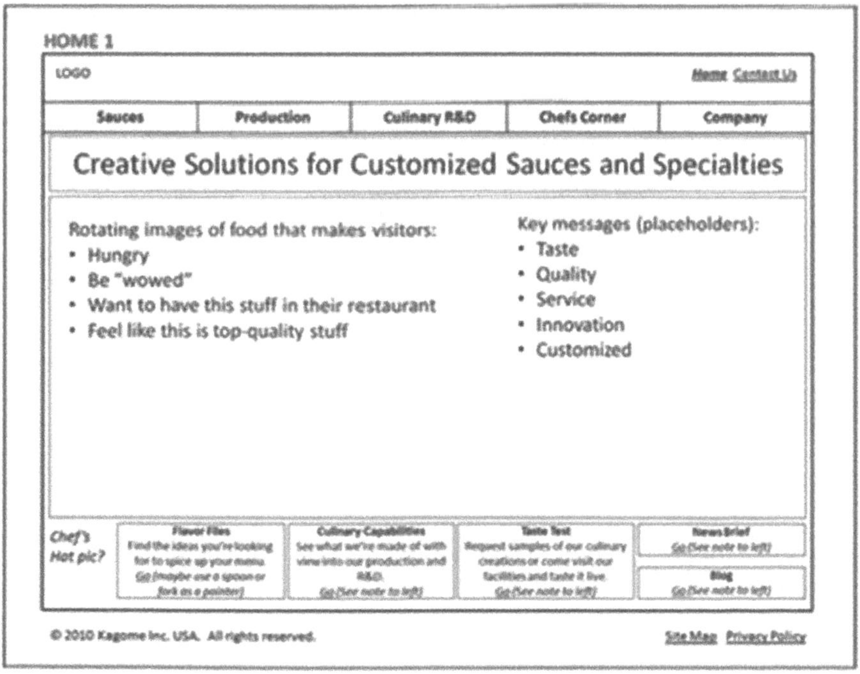

Developing and Publishing

An outside contractor or IT resource is usually responsible for taking what marketing has designed and developing it into a working website. Covering all the details involved in web development is beyond the responsibilities of a marketer and therefore outside the scope of this book. There are, however, some important things a marketer needs to remember to make the process go smoothly and without surprises:

- Developers on the team – Involving developers in the project from the beginning can save a lot of misunderstanding and finger-pointing when it comes time for development. Developers can point out potential issues early on.

- Content management – Using a content management system allows teams to preview content and save older versions of pages in case you need to roll back changes.

- Staging server – Having a staging server allows the marketing team to preview new pages before they are published to the world.

- Style Sheets – Cascading style sheets (CSS) are templates that specify the look and feel of a web page. CSS makes it easier to develop, and later to modify, web pages and can simplify the creation of sites tailored to display on specific mobile devices.

- Never assume – Make sure to spell out explicitly all integrations, compatibility requirements, and any details that are beyond the site map and wireframe. Common oversights are integration with the sales and marketing systems, instrumentation for measurement, and little things like *favicons*—the small icons that appear in the browser navigation bar, tabs, and bookmarks.

Getting Found

Building a great website doesn't guarantee that people will flock to it. Even if you are a known brand or purveyor, poorly developed sites can reduce your online visibility. Even the best websites are of limited value if searchers can't find and access them with minimal effort. This section examines strategies to enhance your site's online visibility. It focuses on three key elements: search engine optimization, maintaining links, and social media.

Search Engine Optimization

Search engine optimization (SEO) is the process of increasing the visibility of a website in search engines. Greater visibility means that the site will appear both more often and closer to the top of the list of search results. These features will increase the likelihood that a prospective customer will click on the link that points to your site. Remember that SEO refers to unpaid, or natural, search results. This process is different than search engine marketing, SEM, which we discussed in the previous chapter.

SEO is an important marketing consideration. According to the Pew Internet American Life survey,[46] 73 percent of Americans use a search engine, and 59 percent of them use one every day. Although the details of the search algorithms are complex trade secrets that are always changing, SEO can be thought of as aligning your site with the mutual goals of search engines and online users. Your content should be useful, popular (read "credible"), and, of course, easy to locate. The list below summarizes the basic elements of SEO:

- Page content – As amazing at it may sound, people forget to include keywords in their content that are important for search. Sometimes when page content is reworked, previous SEO work is overwritten. A common mistake is putting keywords in graphics and therefore hiding them from search engines. First and foremost, pages should be written so that customers find them appealing and easy to navigate. However, designers must also take into account the functionality of search engines. As one example, all images should have alt text for search engines to scan.

- Page titles – A very common mistake is the failure to include the important keywords in the page title. Many sites use the same title for all pages—for example, the company name. This is a mistake. Instead, each page that you want customers to find must have the keywords in the title—for example, the names of your products.

- Page URLs – URLs should always be written in user-readable words and not web developer shorthand. As with page titles, the URL should include the keywords. A simple way to do this for product pages is to incorporate the product name into the URL.

- Meta tags – These are descriptive tags included in the HTML code that describe the content of that page, including page title, overall description, keywords, and language. Meta tags are not as important as they used to be, because many people tried to cheat on SEO by loading meta tags with keywords that were popular in searches but not actually included on that page. Nevertheless, meta tags enable search engines to review the page content more efficiently and thoroughly. Likewise, images should have an alt tag that provides a description. For example, use the descriptive tag "red_tricycle.jpg" rather than "pic00276.jpg."

- Inbound links – The popularity of a site or a page is judged by the number of other relevant sites that link back to it. Therefore, the popularity of the sites that link to yours is important. Ensuring that other sites link back to yours is critical to SEO. Convincing the media, partners, customers, and others to link to your site—or at least to particular parts of it—is a critical component of link building. We do not recommend working with shady link-building services or "link-spamming" companies you do not have a legitimate relationship with.

- XML site maps – An XML site map is an xml file that lists all of your pages and indicates when they were updated. It displays the structure of your website and where your pages reside, and it makes the search engine spiders that crawl your site more effective.

Maintaining Links

Broken links cause two problems: they irritate users, and they prevent search engines from following a link to that page. Many websites suffer from broken links at some point, often after they have been redesigned and the navigation changed. Although your site may look fine after the redesign, all of the links into the pages may not work. This problem will reduce the number of inbound links—what some people call "link juice"—and potentially reduce your ranking in search results. To prevent this from happening, monitor your site for broken links, consider SEO impact when you modify your site architecture (and therefore your URLs), and always redirect old URLs to new ones to preserve your inbound links.

Social Media

Finally, you should incorporate social media share features into your website. Including these features will enhance your visibility in two ways. First, interested users can share your site with their friends and peer groups. As we discussed in the chapter on social media and word of mouth, these people may be influencers or connecters.

Secondly, social media sharing creates more inbound links, which helps your SEO. Actively linking back to your website from your blogs and press releases is also a good practice that can improve your ranking. See chapter 7 for more discussion on social media.

Optimizing Websites for Conversion

The previous section discussed strategies for bringing people to your website. This section addresses the next step in the process—conversion. When people locate and access your site, what do you want them to do? Going further, do you want them to be able to explore the entire site or to focus their attention on just a part of it that you designed for them with your offer? If you are in business to sell products and services, your website should have conversion mechanisms, such as lead capture forms or e-commerce functions, built in to achieve these goals. Far too many sites are informational, but they fail to move the business forward for lack of, or poor execution of, conversion features.

Calls to Action

As with other forms of direct marketing, you should include calls to action on your site. They should certainly appear on your landing pages to reiterate the offer and CTA from the direct marketing piece that drove people there. Below are some guidelines for properly incorporating CTAs into your site (for a more detailed discussion of CTAs, refer back to chapter 9 on direct marketing):

- Wording – CTAs contain words that urge the reader, listener, or viewer to take an immediate action. Common CTAs on the web are "Click Here," "Download Now," and "Register Now."

- Size and color –The CTA text should be larger than the surrounding text. Ideally the CTA is a color graphic to attract attention.

- Position – The CTA should be placed above the fold so consumers can view it on any device. Typically, the CTA is the most important element on the page, so it should get a prime spot. Web page viewers typically scan a page from left to right, top to bottom. Therefore, positioning the CTA top right to bottom right, above the fold, is ideal.

- Test, test, test – There is an ideal combination of offer and CTA wording, design, and positioning that you should strive to achieve. You should test all of these continuously until you feel a page is optimized. Even after you have completed the testing, you should continue to monitor CTAs over time and watch for declines in conversions, at which point you need to start tweaking and testing again.

Landing Pages

In online marketing, a *landing page* is a lead-capture page—a single web page that appears in response to clicking on a pay-per-click or banner advertisement, or a link in an eDM. The landing page should display copy that is a logical extension of the advertisement, for example, using the same language and graphics. Any company that links from a paid search ad to their home page, rather than a dedicated landing page, is throwing money out the window. That's because users can navigate from the home page to anywhere on the website they choose to visit—and not convert. Here are a few suggestions for optimizing landing pages:

- ◆ Make sure the copy and offer match the ad – This sounds obvious, but many organizations don't do it. When the ad copy does not match the landing page content, potential customers have a "Something's funny here" moment, or, even worse, they believe they have been misled. Either way, conversions suffer.

- ◆ Remove site navigation – Why direct potential customers to a dedicated landing page only to offer them the freedom to roam around your site? Many people leave in navigation capabilities out of ignorance or because they are too lazy to do the extra work above and beyond cloning a page that contains their navigation. Don't be one of them.

- ◆ Include a picture – If you are selling a product or offering a free white paper, include a picture of it on the landing page. Consumers generally respond well to pictures of the offer.

- ◆ Make the lead-capture form short – To minimize form abandonment, make the form short. Request only the information you need.

Measurement

Your website should be instrumented for measurement. There are many things you can measure that are useful to tuning your marketing efforts as well as to understanding your business. Some of these are total visitors, referring sites, time spent on your site, and so on. As was the case with advertising, marketers have access to a number of tools and services for measuring a website. The two most popular are Google Analytics and Adobe Marketing Cloud (formerly Omniture). You should take measurement needs into account when you design and develop a website.

An area of special focus for website measurement should be measuring conversions. As discussed in chapter 9 on direct marketing, a conversion is the completion of a desired action to achieve a business outcome. These actions include signing up for a newsletter, registering for an asset, asking to be contacted, and purchasing a product, just to name a few. Of all the things you want to be able to measure and report on, response to your marketing offers should be at the top of the list. Website measurement is covered in more detail in chapter 20.

Specialized Websites

Microsites, online stores, and mobile websites are three specialized types of websites. The core ideas above—usability, good design, interesting content, ease of search—all apply, but there are both nuances and unique attributes for each that marketers should keep in mind.

Microsites

A microsite is a small cluster of web pages that are organized around an event or a topic. When microsites are tied to an event, for example, all of the information is made available in an easily accessible location. If the event is sponsored by a company, then the microsite might reflect the show theme, even if it differs from the corporate identity. Sometimes a microsite is designed to educate on a topic. In this case, a single page would not be adequate, and you may want to give the visitor more to explore. Microsites for new product launches, education on trends or laws, and explorations of diseases are just a few examples.

There are also times when microsites have their own URLs. This practice somewhat blurs the distinction between a website and microsite. However, if a microsite is limited in size and is dedicated to a specific topic, then it qualifies as one. Pharmaceutical companies sometimes create microsites for specific drugs, like www.claritin.com or www.viagra.com.

E-Commerce Sites and Online Stores

There is an entire science behind selling online. Companies that derive a significant amount of revenue online more than likely are using an application to run their online store. Nonetheless, a number of the same web design principles apply. The store should reflect the organization's brand so users know they are in the right place. In commerce, where money is being exchanged, trustworthiness and professionalism are especially important, and the online store should evoke those traits. The site should be easy to navigate and search. SEO is vital (competitors often battle over natural search rankings) so that new customers can find your products. SEM is used to drive additional traffic.

Online stores pay particular attention to calls to action and offers. Most e-commerce teams spend a great deal of time testing CTAs and offers. Lastly, if users must make comparisons between two products, it is best to place the items being compared side by side.

Mobile Sites

Users are accessing the web in record numbers on the go from their mobile phones, and from their tablets at home and in the office. Research firm IDC predicts that by 2015, the number of people accessing the web via mobile devices will surpass the number of people doing so via PCs. Marketers need to (a) pay special attention to how people use their websites on mobile devices and (b) consider designing mobile versions of their sites.

All of the same design, usability, and content principles that we have discussed apply to mobile sites. However, there are some additional considerations that apply specifically to mobile sites. As of the writing of this book, only a minority of companies with websites had mobile-friendly sites—a missed opportunity. Below are some best practices for creating mobile sites:

- Use case – The first thing you need to learn is whether mobile users are using your site in the same way on mobile devices as they do when viewing it on their laptops or desktop computers. For example, users of sports sites and news sites may be interested only in the latest scores and headlines on their mobile phones, and not in long-form articles or archives. So, the content may be more limited and the navigation simpler. Calls to action may be changed to appeal to things people might do when they are on the go, such as use a coupon in a store.

- Screen size – Even if the use case is the same, given the much smaller screens on phones, the site will need to reduce the amount of content and the way it is displayed. Forcing users to continuously zoom in to read microscopic text is a usability no-no. *Responsive design*, also called *responsive web design*, is a method of using CSS to change the layout and amount of content to adjust to the screen size.

- Finger size – People are increasingly using touch navigation on smartphones, so navigation needs to be easy to manipulate with thumbs or index fingers.

- Dedicated mobile site – Mobile sites are increasingly using the m.company.com domain, rather than the www.company.com domain syntax. Even if users do not type the mobile URL into their phones, your website should detect that they are on a mobile device and direct them to the mobile site.

- Apps – Many organizations are taking advantage of custom applications, or apps, on smartphones and tablets. Apps improve the viewing experience, and they add useful functionality, increasing the stickiness of your organization or content. A best practice is to sense a mobile platform when a visitor hits your mobile or WWW site and offer a link to your app.

As of the writing of this book, an interesting trend was emerging. Consumers were beginning to use multiple devices to accomplish a single task. According to research by Google, not only are consumers increasingly reading e-mail, shopping, and reading news on a variety of devices, but they are doing so sequentially, moving from their computer to their phone and back again to achieve a task.[47] In fact, two-thirds of respondents stated that they used multiple devices to make a single purchase. Many consumers now "showroom," scanning prices via their phones at a retail store and then comparison shopping later that day from their tablets or PCs. What should marketers conclude from this research? Basically, that marketers need to make the user experience familiar to the user while simultaneously taking into account the differences in devices. In some instances, marketers will need to contemplate multiple devices when they determine their website goals.

Case Study – The CrowdFlower Website

I joined CrowdFlower in March of 2013. Sometimes as a CMO, you join a company because it has a great website, with a clear value proposition and a sexy brand. CrowdFlower had a sexy brand and an easy-to-grasp value proposition, but the website was poor, and I knew I could improve it.

CrowdFlower's business was growing when I joined the company, about to break the $10 million mark in annual revenue. The product was strong, the company was the market leader, and it had an amazing roster of customers, including Apple, AT&T, Autodesk, eBay, Ford, LinkedIn, Toyota, Unilever, and others.

The website, though, had some big problems. First, it was hard to grasp the value proposition from the home page. If you understood CrowdFlower's business and wanted to understand more about its product, you needed to read the documentation, which was written for developers. The design was also garish, consisting of large blocks of gray and orange (see figure 3 below). SEO and CTAs were almost entirely absent. This damning quote from our VP of sales summed it up: "Our site's so bad I try not to tell customers our URL."

Figure 3: The original CrowdFlower website

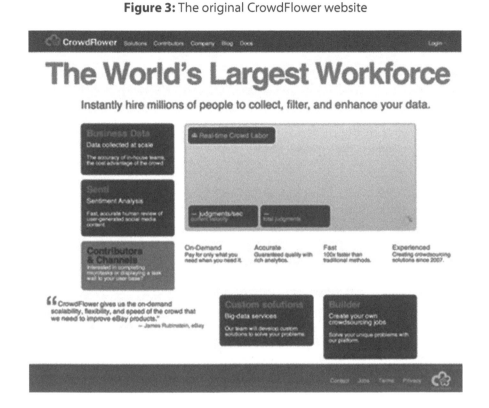

To fix the website, I first interviewed the executive team and key stakeholders in the company. I got all kinds of suggestions, but we identified four key problems that needed to be fixed: our message was not clear; we were not using any of our customers to reinforce our value proposition; we had no lead capture; and the site was, well, ugly.

During the process, I was surprised to see how deeply employees cared about the aesthetics of the site. I had worked with obsessive executives in previous jobs, but here the whole company was obsessive about the site. Between the consumerization-of-IT trend, where employees expect their own company's site and applications to match those of consumer electronics companies like Apple and Samsung, and the heavy percentage of Millennials among the employees for whom style trumped substance, I got an earful from every corner of the company. So, I made the employees part of the process and held open forums to hear everything they had to say. Not all were great ideas, but I did get some good ones. In addition, the employees were engaged and had a stake in the success of the site.

One idea from the employees was to build the new site as a trendy so-called "long site." The old school of design said that everything had to be above the fold (within one screen). People would rather click to a new page than scroll. But now, it was all about scrolling. Some sites had four, five, six screens of content, laid out in "panels" down the page. Scrolling caught on both because people were used to the continuous nature of blog sites, but more so because of mobile devices, especialy smartphones. Scrolling down a page with your thumb was faster (and easier) than clicking and waiting for multiple pages to load.

Speaking of which, mobile was a must. Even though we were not a consumer product, entertainment, or social media company, our buyers expected a good experience on their phones. Many would get annoyed if a page was not optimized for their smartphones. Plus, with an increasing percent of buyers reading e-mail on their phones, any direct marketing that led to a landing page needed to be mobile ready. So, the site was programmed for "responsive design," where the content would be displayed differently on a PC, tablet, and smartphone. On certain pages, we would simply remove content when viewed on a phone to make it easier to get to the most useful information.

I sent out an RFP to ten firms up and down the West Coast, both to get a range of design and because the tech boom in San Francisco was causing "zip code inflation" for companies like us who were based in the city. The high bid was *four times* that of the low bid for the same project! I found a great agency out of Vancouver. I went back to the executives and a few key employees and ran workshops to get to the essence of the brand. I met several times a week for several weeks with the head of product and the CEO to refine company and product messaging.

The next step was to create the wireframe and socialize it within the company. Figure 4 below shows the wireframe. The hero space was designed to simply convey our value proposition. The panel (3) below was customer pull quotes and videos of customers reinforcing our value proposition. We also designed a solutions section (4) that would focus on how we could help our five key buyers. The fourth panel (5) was a tuned-up version of the map from the original website—the engineers liked it, and it showed that work was happening live. We also expanded the footer (6) for faster navigation and SEO.

Figure 4: The CrowdFlower website wireframe

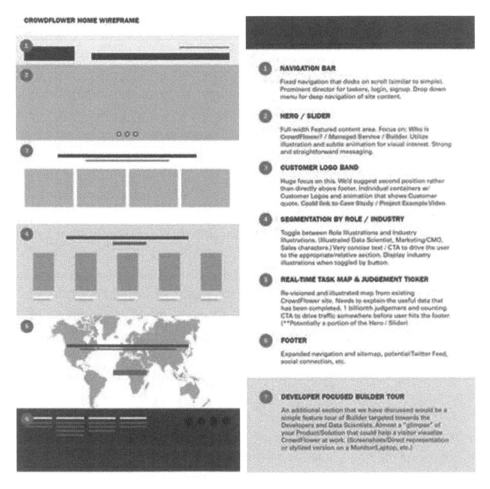

The new site was not only much more attractive, but it clearly explained what we did. Case studies and videos from key customers were added. We used "persona icons" in the solutions section for the CMO, head of sales operations, data scientist, head of e-commerce and head of product right on the home page and the navigation, as seen in figure 5 below.

Figure 5: The new website

The results were great. First, the site looked much better. I got unsolicited comments on it from customers about its awesomeness. The message was clear, too.

Performance improved significantly. In the first month, we saw organic site traffic increase over 40 percent by dint of the SEO site optimization done by the development team. Mobile traffic increased 125 percent. And, our new CTAs resulted in hundreds of inquiries in the first six months.

The cherry on top? Not only was our VP of sales happy with the site—no longer suppressing the URL—he began using it as a tool to explain our products on sales calls.

Chapter 15

Collateral and Marketing Assets

Marketing devotes a great deal of its time and money to creating *collateral*. Also known as *sales collateral* and *marketing collateral*, the term refers to the collection of documents that a company produces in support of a sale. The name derives from the "in support of" or "accompanying" definition of the word "collateral." When applied specifically to marketing, collateral most commonly consists of product data sheets, brochures, case studies, white papers, and similar documents. Marketers also use the broader, more generic term *marketing assets*, which encompass marketing collateral as well as its component parts: content, images, and templates.

The key to the effective use of collateral is to produce just the right amount to support the business. Although this sounds obvious, many marketers fall into the "collateral trap," where they accumulate an ever-increasing panoply of collateral over the years that is difficult to keep current. Obtaining maximum value from collateral requires a thorough understanding of the organization's buyers and selling process, combined with discipline in managing the right volume of collateral.

This chapter begins with a discussion about alignment of the customer journey and the assets a marketing team creates. Writing and style best practices are followed by a description of the most common types of collateral and online assets. Last is a discussion of when collateral should be freely available and when marketers should consider requiring registration.

Aligning Collateral with the Customer Journey

The most productive approach to creating the right collateral is to anticipate the buyer's needs before he or she makes the purchase. These needs, of course, vary greatly depending on the product, the industry, and the type of buyer.

Regardless of the specifics, however, the underlying principle is the same. Recall from chapter 11 that the process the buyer goes through to arrive at a buying decision is called the customer journey. This journey, which culminates in the buyer's becoming a customer, consists of four stages: awareness, research, consideration, and purchase.

A skilled marketing team achieves an understanding of the buyer by utilizing its market and persona research. It can then employ this knowledge to create the collateral that will help transition the buyer from stage to stage. To accomplish this task, marketers must determine which types of collateral are most appropriate in each stage. At the awareness stage, for example, buyers might need a presentation or video simply to demonstrate what the product is and what needs it can meet. Prospective buyers might require a spec sheet or a detailed white paper to assist them during the research stage. Later in the process, in the consideration stage, the buyer might need expert opinion pieces or detailed financial presentations to convince his or her boss that purchasing the product will benefit the company.

Asset Maps

A big job for any marketing team is maintaining all of the assets it creates. Even a relatively small organization can generate hundreds of data sheets, brochures, white papers, and other assets. Large organizations must maintain thousands. A visual representation of all of an organization's assets is known as an *asset map*.

There are two types of asset maps. The first is a detailed inventory of all the collateral that marketing has produced and maintains. Marketing uses these maps to keep track of all of its relevant documents.

This first type of asset map is necessary and can be an impressive visual display of the volume of work that marketing has generated. However, there is a second, more useful type of asset map that displays the collateral recommended for use at each stage of the customer journey. This type of asset map is useful in communicating to the broader marketing team which assets they should consider using in various marketing programs. For example, a new analyst report that portrays your product in a more favorable light might be employed in a new direct-marketing effort. Asset maps can also be used to educate the sales team, explaining when to use specific types of collateral and for what purpose.

Figure 1: Buyer journey asset map

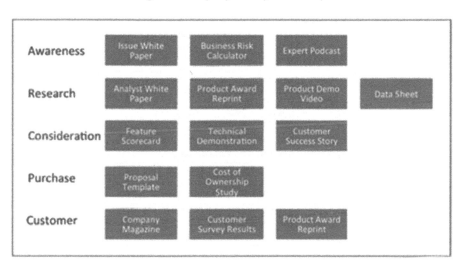

Figure 1 illustrates an asset map that indicates which types of collateral to use at each stage of the buyer journey. Notice that the assets become more specific as the prospective buyer moves closer to the purchase stage.

In the awareness stage, the assets—the white paper that explores the issue or problem, the expert speaking on the topic, and the calculator that quantifies risk—are all designed to make the buyer aware of the issue and to tie your company to the solution.

Everything in the research stage illustrates your products' capabilities at a summary level, and a white paper by a third-party analyst adds credibility.

The feature scorecard and detailed technical presentation highlight your key advantages against your competition for buyers in the consideration stage, and the customer success video—which, ideally, is from the buyers' industry or walk of life—assures buyers that other customers have benefitted from choosing your company and using your product or service.

The assets used in the purchase phase are all geared toward helping to ease the buying process and providing any financial justification that buyers might need to convince others in the buying center.

Finally, after buyers have purchased your product and become customers, you want to keep them engaged with updates in your company magazine, which may also include new products to sell them. In addition, informing them of annual survey results and any awards the product received will help keep them engaged and loyal.

Asset maps are not just for B2B sales. Anyone who has bought a car has probably been given a beautifully produced brochure with enticing photographs, detailed specifications, and color options. These brochures are meant to answer lingering questions and move buyers from the research to consideration phase by enticing them to begin choosing a car color and interior finishes. Whatever the market, adopting the asset map approach will help a company produce better, more useful collateral that will drive sales.

Content Marketing

Content marketing is the technique of creating and distributing valuable and relevant content to attract and acquire customers. Basically, content marketing is communicating with your customers and prospects without selling.

More and more marketers are turning into content marketers as their target customers are increasingly relying on the web to find, research, and buy products. Good content helps educate and persuade customers during this process. It cannot be emphasized enough that this content needs to be high quality, valuable, and *definitely not salesy*. If your content seems like advertising, it will turn off prospective customers.

Content marketing is related to a number of concepts we have covered so far. Good content needs to be found, so including the right keywords and monitoring the popularity of your content should be part of your SEO process. Blogs are a popular vehicle for content marketing, so don't overlook sharing valuable information this way. Blogs and social media are great ways for customers to share your content with others.

Ideally, you become a trusted source of good information (content), and prospects follow or subscribe to your content, even if they are not yet ready to buy. This is permission marketing, as discussed in chapter 10. Companies can build marketing lists by collecting e-mail addresses this way.

When creating a content marketing strategy, marketers should think about the buyer they are trying to reach. A good buyer persona might include a preferred form of content—maybe a funny video aimed at a teen, or a research report from a trusted researcher for a doctor. A marketing team can map out their content using the buyer journey, covered in the previous section.

General Style and Writing Tips

Assets inform. Good assets persuade. Great assets excite, moving the prospective customer quickly to the next stage in his or her journey. Bad assets, on the other hand, can confuse, frustrate, and even drive your prospective customer to buy from your competition. A few general guidelines will help you produce good, and maybe even great, assets.

Writing – The writing should be clear and free from both jargon and hyperbole, which tend to turn off readers. Use the active voice, which is easier to read. The tone will vary—informal, professional, snarky—depending on the company's brand image. Your company should codify all of these rules in a style and usage guide—a document that outlines writing and design standards for the organization.

Design – Your company should create standard templates for all of your collateral types, including audio and video assets. These templates should conform to the standards that are outlined in your style guide. Details include fonts, logo placement, standards for artwork and photos, and any standards for audio and video.

Length – In general, shorter is better. People are busy, and the longer the piece, the fewer the number of people who will read, listen to, or view it. Of course, a document needs to be substantial enough to suit the purpose, particularly if the buyers had to register before they could download it.

"Scannability" – Many people will scan rather than read, either to get the gist or to decide if they should read in full. For this reason, I recommend making all documents easy to scan. Use bullets wherever you can. Include tables and figures—at least one on every other page—to summarize the content and make it less dense and intimidating. Make sure all figures have captions that stand alone and explain the content of the figures. Examine your subheads to make certain they summarize the section and "tell the story." If you review mainstream business magazines, you will see they are written this way.

Imitate what they read –Try to discover what your prospects read, and then imitate it. Ask them in surveys what newspapers, magazines, websites, and blogs they read. If possible, visit their offices or homes and observe the books, magazines, and journals sitting on a coffee table or desk. Of course, all of your collateral items need to be authentic to your organization and follow your style guide. Reading what your prospects read, however, will generate ideas regarding content, headlines, tables and figures, the appropriate vocabulary, and much more. For example, a business magazine that a CEO reads will differ in several fundamental ways from a scientific journal that a doctor reads. Some consumers may not read much at all, in which case you need to discover which television shows or videos they watch.

I am a big fan of the Bullfighter (www.fightthebull.com). This site scores documents based on the level of jargon used and overall readability (based on the same Flesch Reading Ease Index that is commonly used to determine the grade level of writing for periodicals). These scores provide valuable feedback concerning how clear and easy to understand your collateral is.

Collateral Types and Best Practices

In this section I examine the most common types of collateral, specifically data sheets, brochures, white papers, case studies, and solution briefs. There will always be other types, and even hybrids of two asset types, such as the "video white paper." In addition to format details, I've included additional writing tips, over and above the guidelines presented above, where appropriate.

Data sheets are short documents that companies use to describe a product's technical characteristics. The optimal format is two pages, with an overview, benefits, and key features on the front; and detailed features, specifications, and integrations on the back. The front should also include a picture or diagram that depicts the product.

Brochures are longer and typically less technical than data sheets. In addition to products and services, they ideally include information about the company and its customers. Brochures are usually designed to be printed; therefore, they should have high production value.

White papers are authoritative reports or guides that address an issue or a problem. A major function of white papers is to educate readers to help them make decisions. White papers are commonly used in politics, policymaking, business, and technical fields. In commercial use, the term commonly refers to documents businesses use as sales tools.[*] The length of a white paper should be adjusted according to the specific audience, though five to ten pages is typical; longer papers likely will go unread. A useful rule of thumb is to include one diagram, table, or sidebar on every other page to make the document easier to scan. Although white papers can make the case for a particular product, they should not contain overt product pitches.

As mentioned in the chapter on WOM marketing, customers prefer to learn from other customers. A *case study* or *success story* is a write-up of how a customer is using a vendor's product or services, in the context of the customer's business, to achieve business value. For a case study to achieve maximum impact, the story must be "told by the customer." Therefore, it should incorporate customer quotes throughout.

Sometimes someone else has done the writing for you. If there is a great article, product review, or analyst report, your company can usually obtain the rights and then reprint it. Increasingly, reprints are not actually "printed." Instead, they are digital copies or links that buyers can download for free for a specified time period.

Finally, *solution briefs* are short documents—typically three to five pages—that describe a vendor's products and how customers use them to solve a particular technical or business problem, sometimes called a *use*

---

[*] A lot of people wonder why they are called white papers at all. Since most documents are printed on white paper, the modifier "white" would seem redundant, and too generic to differentiate from other documents. The term was coined by the British government to distinguish shorter informational documents with white covers from the formal legislative documents sent to Parliament with blue covers—called "blue papers." The term was adopted by industry in the 1990s to mean any short informational paper.

case. Solution briefs generalize the types of problems described in case studies, and they summarize the details usually found in white papers. For example, a software company might create a solution brief called "Automated Electronic Discovery Options for Law Firms" and a case study describing how a particular law firm benefitted from using their electronic discovery application.

Other Types of Assets

The last section covered the most common type of collateral. In many businesses, they are "must-haves." Several other online multimedia asset types are gaining in popularity. Organizations should consider using these in their customer journey.

Calculators are useful for helping prospective customers understand cost savings, return on investment, total cost of ownership, financial risk or return, and anything else that can be quantified. Their greatest value is to demonstrate the financial prudence of purchasing a vendor's product. Customers can also use them, however, to choose or configure products, thereby accelerating the sale and reducing the workload of sales and customer service. The most commonly used calculators are web tools and Excel spreadsheets. Online calculators should be simple to use, with easy-to-follow instructions, and they should provide immediate output. Customers should be given the option to have a nicely formatted version sent to them. (This policy also benefits marketing by providing an opportunity to collect additional contact information.) More detailed calculators may be better suited for Excel, with a salesperson or another company representative assisting customers in completing the computations. Calculators based on assumed costs, such as hourly wages or electrical costs, should allow customers to modify these values to increase their confidence in the results.

E-books are becoming increasingly popular, if somewhat faddish. Like a white paper, e-books can educate prospective customers and inculcate them in the organization's viewpoint. Unlike white papers, e-books are generally more graphical and have less text, and are therefore more scannable. A best practice for e-books is to serialize them so that customers can download chapters one by one—perfect for a nurturing campaign.

Prospective buyers frequently want to see your product and how it works. Videos that demonstrate your product are especially popular with people who are visually oriented and may not find a white paper or podcast a satisfying experience. For software products, these demos can be created inexpensively utilizing screen capture software and a microphone. More sophisticated demos can be created with Adobe Flash animation or even by a video production agency. Professionally produced videos cost more, but your market might require them. In some cases, however, simple screen captures or less sophisticated videos produced by your in-house team come across as more "authentic" and consequently achieve better results.

A *podcast* is one "episode" in a series of audio broadcasts. The word is a combination of "broadcast" and "iPod," even though you don't need an iPod to listen to a podcast. Rather, you can download audio files from a website and play them on your computer, your telephone, or your less cool MP3 player. Podcasts should be short, somewhere between five and fifteen minutes. The easiest way to create a podcast is to produce an interview-style episode, where you simply need to write the questions, along with some guidance on which points to stress, and provide them to the interviewee in advance. Interviews with product or industry experts are popular, as are how-to and customer case study podcasts.

Videos are an increasingly popular asset and are becoming ever easier to produce. Customers often seek product information in video form. Importantly for marketers, YouTube is the second-largest search engine after Google search.[48]

The simplest way to produce video content is to record a webcast. You can promote these recordings on your website as well as in newsletters and other communications. As mentioned in chapter 12, if your company uses a webcast syndication service, these recordings will quietly attract new viewers and prospects over time. The disadvantages of webcast recordings is that they are long and hard to edit. Short product demos are easy to create with screen capture software or simply by filming a customer or employee using the product. Many companies seek to produce viral video content and may turn to an agency for help. These approach the quality of television commercials and can be very expensive.

To Gate or Not to Gate

The majority—if not all—of your collateral will be online. Most companies limit the amount of printed collateral they produce because it is expensive and many customers prefer digital versions. Customers expect to find data sheets, brochures, and white papers on a company's website. Videos and podcasts should also be available on your website. In addition, they should be syndicated over appropriate services like iTunes and YouTube, to name just two.

Many marketers wrestle with *gating*—determining what content they should require registration to obtain. Gating presents marketers with a basic dilemma. On the one hand, registration is a very effective method of capturing leads. On the other hand, requiring registration for too many of your assets can prevent search engines from finding content, and it can turn off prospective customers who need the content to conduct their research. In general, we recommend that any content that will assist in SEO or initial awareness *not* be gated. Data sheets, for example, should be available as free downloads.

Marketers employ two strategies to help decide what content to gate and what content not to gate. The first is called *tiering*. In this strategy, the organization provides a summary document that customers can download without registering and a more detailed document that includes a registration form. Ideally, the customer will find the information contained in the summary document so valuable that he or she will register for the detailed document. One benefit of this strategy is that marketers can analyze the registration data to assess consumer interest and to score leads.

The second strategy involves cross selling. The organization inserts a quick blurb on product B in the collateral for product A, with a link to additional information. To hook the prospect, the link to information on product B should not include a registration form, or else customers will likely ignore it.

To sum up, companies should gate any content that customers highly value. Examples of content that companies should gate are calculators, how-to article reprints, and analyst reports that customers would otherwise have to purchase directly. Marketers can always measure the effects of gating on downloads and adjust what they gate by studying the results. Gating will almost invariably decrease the number of times an asset is accessed or downloaded, but it will obviously increase the number of leads. If the leads captured convert to qualified leads, then gating may make sense. If not, removing the gate to increase awareness might be a better strategy.

Case Study – The Data Breach Calculator

In chapter 8, I described how my former employer, PGP Corporation, created a sales asset by hiring an expert. PGP hired the Ponemon Institute to study and report on the costs associated with a company that has suffered a data breach and the subsequent loss of sensitive customer or employee data.

The Ponemon *Cost of a Data Breach* report was a very effective awareness asset for PGP, which got a tremendous amount of press every year when the report came out, resulting in many articles and a big bump in SOV. The report was downloaded thousands of times by existing and prospective customers who wanted to understand their potential risk and costs.

My team and I started to think about how the annual report could be used to continue the conversation with the buyer. We wanted to create an asset that we could promote year-round. We also wanted to make the risk numbers more specific to a prospective customer so that our sales reps could have a discussion that was targeted to address top-of-mind issues.

The team came up with the idea of creating an online calculator application based on the report findings. The calculator would output a detailed risk and cost estimate by combining the underlying data in the report and inputs from the person using the calculator. The calculator was an ungated web application. The customers answered a short series of questions—company size, industry, country, presence of security team, number of laptops—and the calculator combined this data with report data, then displayed their estimated risk of a breach occurring and estimated costs.

My team went a bit further to turn the calculator into a lead-generation tool. If prospects wanted a customized risk report, with details about the calculation, they could fill out a short form with their name, company name, and e-mail address. Then a six-page personalized report would be sent directly to them. This appealed to individuals who wanted to share the information with others inside their organization.

The form asking for name, company name, and e-mail address was short by design, to minimize abandonment, but it gave us the three key pieces of information we needed. Together with what we knew from the report itself—company size, industry, presence of a security team, number of laptops, whether they had protective software on their endpoints, and a few other details—we could give our sales rep a detailed profile of the prospect.

Figure 2: Symantec Data Breach Calculator

Even more important than the profile data, we generated a highly qualified lead for our inside sales team. Requesting the report showed intent and interest. This is the power of tiering assets, as discussed above.

The calculator was a huge success. In the first year, it generated thousands of visits and more than twelve hundred custom reports sent.

After our initial investment to develop the tool, there was minimal annual maintenance. The Ponemon Institute gave us updated baseline numbers for our calculation each year after their report was published. The cost per acquisition was less than forty dollars and continued to decline. We eventually added additional data and languages for our European prospects, which increased our reach.

Learning More

◆ Ann Handley and C. C. Chapman, *Content Rules* (Hoboken:Wiley, 2012).

Chapter 16

Presentations

Presentations are used in every marketing program. Your CEO may burnish your brand at an industry conference as part of your reputation programs. Webcasts may be a critical part of your demand generation, and your field sales force may need to learn the company pitch as part of sales enablement. Presentations are used all the time by analyst relations teams as part of market intelligence programs. But for as important as they are, why are there so many bad ones? Think about it—how often have you been utterly bored to tears watching someone drone on, or annoyed when a presenter tries to jam a hundred-slide presentation into thirty minutes?

But then again, there are speakers you remember. Presentations you remember. Maybe they were profound. Inspiring. Or maybe they just gave you exactly the information you were looking for—succinctly. This is not an accident. Good presentations do not occur by luck. Great presenters think long and hard about what they plan to say, prepare diligently, and *practice, practice, practice.*

The marketing team is responsible for creating presentations, presenting them, and training presenters from other departments. This chapter will cover the key areas of creating and delivering good presentations. A few alternate presentation mechanisms will also be discussed.

Creating the Presentation

Before creating a single slide, there is important work to be done. A presentation needs a purpose, a story and structure, and a clear sense of how it will open and end. These are covered here first, before we move on to design in the next section.

Purpose

Before effective presenters create any slides or write a script, they consider the *purpose* of the presentation. Are they looking to educate the audience concerning a new technology or technique? Are they attempting to demonstrate thought leadership by proposing bold new ideas? Is a salesperson trying to persuade a customer to select his or her product over the competition? Or, is the presentation an internal document intended to convince the CFO to increase the marketing budget?

An easy way to identify the purpose of a presentation is to ask yourself what you want your audience to be thinking as they leave the room. Your answer should frame your delivery and content. In this section, I will cover some of the more common elements you should consider when you define the purpose:

- Educating
- Selling
- Convincing
- Inspiring

Let's take a closer look at each one.

When the purpose of your speech is to *educate*, make sure your pace is not too fast, use plenty of examples, and leave time for questions. Presenters who are trying to educate often hand out copies of their slides prior to the presentation. These handouts contain blanks next to the slides to encourage the listeners to participate by filling them in.

If your purpose is *selling*, then keep in mind that people do not like to be sold to, so your audience may put up a defensive mental barrier. To overcome this resistance, you should avoid over-the-top salesmanship, jargon, and smarmy behavior. Provide plenty of examples of how happy customers are using the product. Let these stories do the selling.

Convincing is a close cousin to selling. It applies to scenarios such as requesting a greater budget, more headcount for your department, the green light for a new project, or a donation to your cause. In such cases, make certain your business case or cause is rock solid, check and double-check all of your facts and numbers (errors are killers in these situations), and present a clear plan of how you will use the time, people, or money you are seeking.

Finally, presentations intended to *inspire* can be the most difficult type to execute effectively. To a greater extent than the other types, they frequently rely on the presenter's charisma more than anything else. If you are giving an inspiring presentation, make certain you have great stories that take your audience where you want them to go.

Story and Structure

Good presentations have a story. They have an arc. The purpose of a story arc—which is a standard motif in television dramas and movies—is to move a character or a situation from one state to another. The story arc need not be high drama. However, it must have a beginning, middle, and end. Ask any movie screenwriter, and he or she will tell you there's a reason plays and movies have three acts—the format works. The key to creating the presentation, then, is to visualize that arc and how you are going to get the audience through your beginning, middle, and end in whatever time you have been allotted.

Brainstorming the Story

Two common methods to brainstorm stories are to use whiteboards and Post-it notes. Once you have a general idea of what you are going to talk about, sketch it out on the whiteboard. How you do this depends on your personality. Linear thinkers might use a timeline arc, highlighting the beginning, middle, and end, with all the points in between. Visual thinkers might prefer to draw a series of boxes to represent the slides, filling them in with key points and rough diagrams. Post-it notes can work the same way, but they are easier to reorder. Also, they enable you to discard ideas that don't work.

Opening the Presentation

The worst opening to a presentation (next to silence and mortified stage fright) is something like this: "Hello, my name is John Smith, and I'm going to present to you on the history of axle grease." Telling the audience the same thing that appears on your title slide does not add much value. In addition, you have likely been introduced already. Moreover, if you are at a conference, then your name will be in the program. Below is a much better method to begin a presentation:

- ◆ Opening statement: Begin with a statement—perhaps your ultimate goal, a challenge to the audience, or a value proposition.

- ◆ Summary: Briefly explain what you are going to cover—the bullets of your agenda.

- ◆ Provocation: Make a controversial or challenging statement to get your audience's attention.

- ◆ Experience: Talk a bit about yourself, focusing on why your audience should listen to you.

- ◆ Conclusion: Tell the audience where you will end up. This will automatically get your audience thinking about where you are leading them, predisposing them to listen carefully, even if they may disagree with your conclusion.

This structure is often shorthanded as "Tell them what you are going to tell them, tell them, and then tell them what you told them." Reworking our bad axle grease example above, an effective opening might sound something like this:

Axle grease is one of the most important petroleum deriva-
tives ever invented. It helps our cars run, our farms harvest,
and our factories produce. Yet, we are at risk of underinvest-
ing in the production of this vital resource, which could have
a massive, if unknown, effect on our economy. To help you
understand this issue, I'm going to give you a bit of a crash
course on axle grease. I'll highlight the main areas of the
economy that rely on it and explain why we face a potential
shortfall. I've been working in this industry for twenty years,
most recently as the CEO of the largest producer, and this is
the biggest crisis I have ever seen. At the end of our sixty minutes, I hope you understand why I say this and why it's vital
we fix this problem.

Admit it, even a mundane topic like grease comes alive when it is presented this way. The presenter has summarized his case, told you a bit about
himself, and let you know how he's going to be communicating with you over
the course of the next hour.

The Meat of the Presentation

Make sure the presentation itself—the meat—matches the introduction
and supports the key points you are trying to make. Resist the urge to load
everything you could possibly think of into it (a common sin when presenters
are creating new presentations by mixing and matching slides from existing
presentations). A concise presentation that gives exactly what is promised is
always better. And, you will avoid the presentation sin of rushing through
your slides to try to finish within the allotted meeting or speaking slot time.

Closing the Presentation

A good closing ties back to the opening. Repeat the parts you want them
to remember. Restate your provocation: "Now all of you understand why a

shortage of axle grease would be catastrophic to our economy." Some presenters use a journalistic technique known as the "kicker," where they echo
a theme from their opening in their closing. Our axle grease CEO might get
cute with a kicker like: "I'm not just being a squeaky wheel. An axle grease
shortage would be bad for all of us." Use one of these two techniques and then
thank the audience. You can display your contact information, but there's no
need to read it.

Presentation Design

There are an infinite variety of ways to design slides. Below I present some
guiding principles that will maximize your presentation's impact.

> Create a template – Your organization should have a standard tem-
> plate that all presenters use. It should be created by the marketing
> department or an outside agency, and it should properly reflect your
> identity, including the logo, color palette, font, design elements, imag-
> ery, and whatever else is important to your brand image. In addition,
> it should include commonly used slide formats—bulleted lists, charts
> and graphs, transition slides, photographs, and so on. Templates will
> help prevent what many designers call "ransom note" presentations, a
> reference to the jumble of unmatched fonts in a kidnapper's ransom
> note.

> Avoid clutter – This is one of the most abused principles in design. To
> avoid a cluttered appearance, limit the use of bullets to a maximum
> of three or four per slide, with no more than six to eight words for
> each bullet. And please, no sub-bullets. They add clutter. Remember,
> the purpose of the slides is to *summarize*. After all, as the presenter,
> your role is to contribute additional information, so you don't need to
> read every word. Also, large, complex diagrams should be simplified
> or broken up.

> Pictures – Humans respond to and remember pictures better than
> text. According to brain researcher John Medina, people retain 65

percent of what they see in images versus just 10 percent of what they hear. So, use as many images as you can. These images can be photographs, diagrams, or any other visuals that will capture the audience's attention. Using clip art is not recommended, because it will make the presentation look shoddy or amateurish.

Charts and graphs – Nothing beats a chart or graph for conveying financial or other numeric data. However, cramming an entire spreadsheet into a slide is never a good idea. The basic rule for charts and graphs is, keep it simple! Going further, highlighting key numbers, cells, and graph segments helps the viewer follow along (and not focus on the wrong part). Finally, make sure to check your math—one mistake will kill your credibility for the rest of the presentation.

Design for the back row – Make certain your slides can be read by someone sitting in the back row who isn't blessed with 20/10 vision. I recommend large pictures, large charts, and large type.

Avoid superfluous transitions and sound effects – Although these elements seemed innovative when they were introduced over a decade ago, today they come off as gimmicky. Always follow this adage: you should be more interesting than your sound effects.

Scripting – If you are creating a presentation that other individuals—for example, your sales force—will deliver, then scripting is a good idea. Type out the narrative in full in the notes section to provide the presenter with context and material to draw from.

"Sliduments" – One of the most common uses today for PowerPoint is for internal planning. People find it easier to express their ideas in presentation form. Perhaps it's easier than writing a business plan in prose. We bring this use up because many presenters use the same "sliduments" designed for reading when presenting in large settings. This lazy approach leads to cluttered slides, lack of a story, and little practice.

Engaging a Designer

Organizations should consider hiring a designer to create their presentation template. Not only will designers provide you with several creative options, but they can create all of the standard slides—bulleted lists, charts, graphs, tables, transitions—that you will likely need. They will also be familiar with the nuances (often maddening) of Microsoft PowerPoint, Apple Keynote, Prezi, or whatever tool you select.

You may also want to hire a designer to create your "standard" presentations, such as your corporate overview or sales pitch. Presentations used by your executives for keynote addresses or financial analyst presentations also often need the polish a designer can bring. However, sending all of your updates and edits to a designer can get expensive. Therefore, we recommend you format your slides so the presenters can make edits themselves, or someone on the marketing team can make the edits for periodic updates.

Giving the Presentation

With the presentation story and structure in place, beautifully designed slides ready, it is time to consider the act of *presenting*. Anyone presenting should think about the presentation setting, the audience and their expectations, and how he or she as the presenter can most effectively convey the information.

Setting

Before you start to build your presentation, you should consider where and how you will deliver it. The setting will have a lot to do with how you present, the content you present, and the medium you use. The most common scenarios are:

- medium group setting;
- large group setting;
- webcast; and
- meeting.

The setting most people envision when they plan a presentation is the *medium group setting*. Imagine a room bigger than a small meeting room, for example, presenting to a department or conducting a breakout session at a conference. One advantage of this setting is that listeners will feel comfortable asking questions. Therefore, you need to pay close attention to your audience and interact with them.

The dream of every CEO, and every marketer who supports him or her, is to be the keynote speaker at the biggest event in his or her industry, with a packed house of prospects and industry followers who are hanging on to his or her every word. This scenario describes the *large group setting*. There is no hard-and-fast rule as to when a group becomes "large," but certainly any group of one hundred or more would qualify. Some keynotes have thousands of people in the audience.

If you find yourself in this situation, make sure the presentation lives up to the billing. These presentations usually try to impart just a few key ideas. Therefore, don't clutter the screens with bullets and tedious slide builds. Make the visuals bold and thought provoking. Use a few highlighted words to get the idea across. Very important: make certain the people in the last row can see everything clearly.

As discussed about events in chapter 12, in today's digital world, companies increasingly are selling their products via *webcasting*, or presentations on the web, using tools like WebEx or GoToMeeting. Since viewers are looking at their computer screens, this format has the advantage of readability, so there is more latitude for text on the screen and detailed diagrams. Many webcasting applications, however, lack the capabilities for builds, where elements on the slide appear one by one, or animations, so don't put them in. Also, if the presentation is going to be recorded, that is all the more reason to practice.

The *meeting* setting presents a special set of challenges. It is often difficult to deliver a thirty-slide presentation from start to finish across a conference table with only a few people watching. In this setting, the participants may prefer a conversation to a presentation. To accommodate these participants, focus on just a few anchor slides that can drive a conversation. For meeting with prospective customers in a sales situation, it's also a good idea to have a slide up front that summarizes the customer's needs—it helps to ensure the meeting will be relevant.

Keeping the Audience with You

Humans are prone to distraction. In today's world, smartphones are addictive little distractions that sit (and sometimes chime, flash, or vibrate) right in our pockets. So, even if you are a good presenter and your topic is interesting, there may be times when it makes sense to check in with the audience to keep them with you.

In their book *Conversations That Win the Complex Sale*, messaging gurus Erik Peterson and Tim Riesterer call the pattern of people's attention "the hammock." Why? Because, as illustrated in figure 1, it peaks at the beginning, when you have 70 percent of a listener's attention, sags in the middle when you have only 20 percent, and, depressingly for the presenter, is highest at the end when you have 100 percent. This assertion is not based solely on the authors' experiences and observations. Research in neuroscience confirms that people pay attention to the beginning and the end, because they are using a part of their brain called the "reptile brain" that controls the fight-or-flight instinct. They pay attention at the beginning because they are deciding if the information can contribute to their survival. They pay attention at the end because they know they are about to be freed. Even if you lose them in the middle, the words "in conclusion" wake up the reptile brain. All the more reason to recap your key points at the end—you have the listener's full attention.

To fight the hammock effect, you need to bring people back every ten minutes. That is the time increment during which people pay attention, according to brain researcher John Medina in *Brain Rules*. (Some observers would argue that people's attention spans are shrinking, so even ten minutes is too long these days.) How do you bring your audience back? The standard method is to insert a "spike" at least every ten minutes. Figure 1 shows what the hammock looks like when you add in spikes, or "grabbers," as Peterson and Riesterer call them.

Figure 1: Human attention: the hammock and spikes

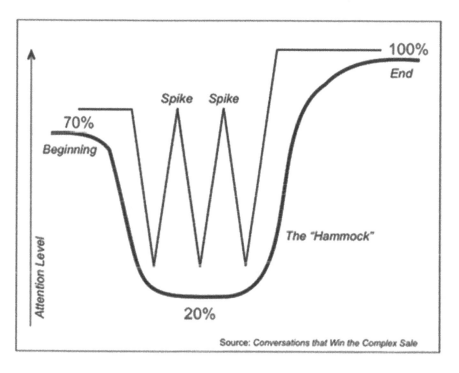

Here are a few spikes you can use:

- Facts and figures – Adults love facts and figures. They will often pause to take a note if a compelling fact is displayed on-screen.

- Questions – Asking the audience a question can keep them with you. Whether you are looking for an exact answer or examples you can use in your talk, asking questions encourages your audience to participate and thus helps to keep them engaged.

- Show-and-tell – People like to see new things. Presenting or displaying a new product to see and experience can excite the audience. Steve Jobs was a master at this approach.

- Video – Video can be tricky. Though it will likely perk up your audience, a well-produced video can make the switch back to your presentation look bland by comparison. Ideally, the presentation should critique or comment on the content of the video. Simply using the videos to display company advertisements or as a water break for the presenter will accomplish very little.

Preparation

Why is it that we expect actors, musicians, politicians, and other public performers to practice, but most people who give presentations feel no such need? Practice—rehearsal—is a vital aspect of being an effective presenter. Most great presenters practice. Winston Churchill practiced his speeches all the time—even in the bathtub! Steve Jobs prepared for weeks before his famous product announcements. Martin Luther King Jr. worked hard to become a great speaker. All presenters realize that their role is to entertain, to captivate, to inspire. Although rehearsal is time-consuming and tiresome, it makes them better presenters and allows them to inspire, convince, or entertain.

Before you give a public presentation, you should, at the minimum, practice it once out loud. Pay attention: This does *not* mean flipping through the slides and thinking about what you are going to say. It means actually *giving* the presentation. The upside to this approach is tremendous. You will become more comfortable with the material. You will discover the tongue-twisting phrases, which you then have the option of practicing or replacing. Finally, you will also learn how long the presentation will take, which enables you to work on the timing. When you consider all of these benefits, there are no valid reasons *not* to rehearse.

If you want to become really good, you should practice in front of a few coworkers and ask for constructive feedback. (An interesting side benefit is that it's often more intimidating to present in front of coworkers; speaking in front of strangers is much easier.) Another option is to record yourself, preferably using video, although audio can work, too. Listening to the playback can be humiliating and humbling, but it always pays dividends by helping you make adjustments that will improve your presentation. Finally, perform one final rehearsal either the night before or morning of your presentation so that it's fresh.

If you are speaking in a large group setting, request access to the actual room to practice. Executives giving keynotes should absolutely practice in the venue where they will be speaking. This strategy enables you to identify and adjust to potential distractions before your actual presentation. For example, you want to be aware of any spotlights, which can be unsettling and even blinding. In addition, you will need to get used to the down monitor, which is a monitor at or below stage level that shows a presenter their slides, or teleprompter. If the session is being videotaped or simultaneously projected on large screens for people seated in the back, there may be limits to where you can move onstage. In that case, request that tape be placed on the floor to demarcate the boundaries. All of these aspects are unfamiliar to even experienced small- and medium-group presenters at first, and they take some getting used to.

Exactly how many hours of practice you need depends to a large extent on who you are and how much experience you have as a presenter. In his book *Outliers*, Malcolm Gladwell cites the "10,000 Hour Rule," which posits that an individual requires ten thousand hours of practice to achieve success in a given field. Excellent presenters master the art of presentation over years of practice.

Of course, as material changes, a presenter needs to learn it and master presenting it. This is why actors and singers rehearse for weeks. US presidents spend weeks with a coach prepping for the annual State of the Union address. Steve Jobs, one of the most captivating product presenters of his time, was said to have spent hours and hours over several weeks rehearsing—and this was *after* the presentation content was written. In contrast, most amateur—and mediocre—presenters spend all of their time creating slides rather than practicing delivery.

Physical Presence

After you have mastered your delivery, you need to consider how you behave. Even a well-crafted presentation can be undermined by actions you perform on the stage or at the podium. Some of these actions are simple; in fact, many are things our mothers have been telling us since we were kids.

To start, regardless of the physical setting, pacing back and forth is never a good idea. Neither is swaying back and forth. Many of our mothers no doubt told us to "stand still" or "stop fidgeting." Unfortunately, presenters frequently don't realize they are doing these things until they see a video of themselves. Also, always keep your hands at your side, not in your pockets. Gestures are okay, as long as they are not frantic.

Next, have a delivery strategy. Will you be standing behind a podium, with access to notes and a piece of furniture to anchor you? Or, will you be alone onstage, with nothing physically separating you from the audience? If you don't have a podium, you will either have to memorize the material or carry note cards for reference.

When you are presenting without a podium, establishing a presence and rhythm is important. A common technique is to move to a spot, deliver a slide or section, and then move to a new spot and repeat. Moving can also create a spike to regain the attention of your audience. Establish eye contact with the audience, and move your gaze around when you move to another position. Don't focus just on the front row. Focus on people in the back as well. They will know you are looking at them, and they will pay attention. It will also make you more connected with the audience.* To deal with people who are talking or not paying attention, simply move to a position close to them. Don't say anything. They will get the message. More importantly, everyone in the room will be looking at you and at them—peer pressure can help.

Additional Dos and Don'ts

Dos

- Practice before you present. Good presenters rehearse their presentation several times over many days beforehand. (Am I making my point?)

---

* Several research studies have also proven that eye contact increases trust—something we inherently know from encounters with people who won't look us in the eye. If your goal is persuasion or selling, eye contact is especially important.

- Get to the room early, and make certain everything is set up. Use the restroom, get some water, adjust the temperature—do whatever you need to do early so you are not stressed out.

Don'ts

- Do *not* read your slides. The audience can do that. In addition, reading your slides conveys the impression that you don't know your material.

- Do not turn your back to the audience to look at or read your slides. You should be talking to them.

- Never start the presentation by apologizing—for the A/V, heat, cold coffee, whatever it is. Start with something interesting and exciting. Bring them in.

- Please don't use laser pointers. Not only are you looking away, but it's very distracting. If the presentation truly requires a close-up, then build it into the presentation.

Training

As we discussed in the introduction, the marketing team is responsible for training presenters. Creating nice-looking slides and then relying on the sales team or executives to deliver them well is irresponsible. Here are a few suggestions on how to train presenters:

Examples – If a presentation is to be given repeatedly by a large group of presenters, such as your standard sales pitch, then the marketing team should provide a recording of a skilled presenter giving it.

Tips on giving the presentation – Many of the presentation skills listed above, common sense as they may be, are not known by those who do not present frequently. Hold a session with presenters—on a periodic basis as part of ongoing skills training, at the annual sales kickoff, or in a recording—and cover the basics.

Certification – Giving the presentation to a group of peers can be intimidating, but it is a very effective way to learn. Require that presenters give the presentation to an internal group, whether members of the marketing team, or in the case of sales, to a sales manager or director who has already been trained. Some companies formalize this concept and "certify" presenters once they have done this to their peers' satisfaction.

Recording and coaching – Anyone who will be presenting frequently, such as an executive or product evangelist, should go through presentation training where they are recorded with a video camera and coached. Sometimes it is easier to bring in an outside consultant to perform this training, as they both have the skill and are not afraid to give feedback to an executive that might be career limiting to someone on the internal marketing team.

Alternate Presentation Media

Sometimes a situation calls for something other than the usual "slide deck." Here are a few other presentation media you may want to try.

Whiteboarding

One way to stand out is to be different. The term "death by PowerPoint" has become as clichéd as the medium it set out to pillory. So, what is the alternative? Increasingly, marketers are turning to the whiteboard.

One common strategy is to create a "gold standard" whiteboard presentation and then standardize it. Teaching the entire sales, marketing, and executive teams—and even partners—to deliver the same whiteboard can be a very effective strategy. Whiteboards function best in small situations, but there are opportunities to use them in webcasts and large-format meetings using an interactive tablet and a projector rather than an actual whiteboard. A salesperson can even draw them on a napkin, place mat, or butcher paper tablecloth when he or she takes a customer to lunch.

The key to success is to design a frame-by-frame training guide, including the script, and then train the company to use it.

SlideShare, Prezi, and Other Tools

Since WebEx and webcasting shook up the world of presentations, there have been two notable additions. The first is online slide sharing. Sites like SlideShare allow organizations to upload presentations so they can be viewed in a web browser. Sharing slides increases the reach of your presentations. In effect, it represents a new type of marketing collateral.

The second innovation is Prezi, a "zooming" presentation tool that gives a fresh look. Prezi is cloud based, and it makes it easy to download and use presentations anywhere. This tool is especially popular on tablet computers, but the visual effects of panning and zooming differentiate it from most PowerPoint presentations. As one of our colleagues quipped, like all powerful new weapons, Prezi can be easily misused, but it can work in the right setting.

Case Study

Can the story and presenter alone carry the day, even without beautiful slides? The answer is yes. The higher your status within the organization, the more the presentation should be about you and your words, not the details on the slides. To illustrate, studying a great speech with no visual aids can teach us a lot.

Martin Luther King's "I Have a Dream" speech, which he delivered on the steps of the Lincoln Memorial during the historic March on Washington on August 28, 1963, is one of the greatest speeches in US history. You may even be able to remember the closing—talk about recall!

King's speech stands at the acme of public speaking not only for its significance but for its construction and delivery. Although you may never be called upon to speak on anything as significant as achieving racial equality in the United States, understanding how King delivered such a powerful, persuasive, and moving oratory can help any speaker. Here is a breakdown of some of his techniques.

Context – First, the speech was delivered on the steps of the Lincoln Memorial, a setting of historical significance for ancestors of former slaves fighting for civil rights. King echoed Lincoln by beginning, "Five score years ago," an allusion to the opening of Lincoln's Gettysburg Address, and he referenced the Emancipation Proclamation, which gave slaves in the Confederate states their freedom. Opening with a tie to history, place, or person is a powerful technique that sets the context for what is to come. It signals to the listener: "Something important is coming, so pay attention."

Cadence – King started slowly and calmly. His opening did not have the volume, power, or gestures of his famous closing. Following along with his mountaintop metaphor, King was taking you there with him, slowly but surely, until everyone reached the pinnacle together. Picking up the pace, varying the pace, and even varying the volume can be very effective strategies.

Repetition – King repeated "I have a dream" several times as he moved into the heart of his speech. He repeated "Let freedom ring" more than ten times to create a strong closing. Known as *anaphora*, repeating words found in neighboring clauses is a powerful rhetorical device. Speakers don't have to repeat ten times, though. A CEO repeating a word like "focus" or "customers" to introduce each of three sections of his talk would make it more memorable and impactful.

Language – King employed beautiful language in "I Have a Dream." Importantly, it was not complex language, which would have been beyond many of the people he was trying to reach. Here are a few of my favorites:

> "...the Negro lives on a lonely island of poverty in the midst of a vast ocean of material prosperity." A great contrasting image.

> "In a sense, we've come to our nation's capital to cash a check. When the architects of our republic wrote the

magnificent words of the Constitution and the Declaration of Independence, they were signing a promissory note to which every American was to fall heir...It is obvious today that America has defaulted on this promissory note... America has given the Negro people a bad check, a check which has come back marked 'insufficient funds.'" King casts rights in terms of money—something everyone can understand.

"Let us not seek to satisfy our thirst for freedom by drinking from the cup of bitterness and hatred." A great sentiment and clear directive, with a biblical reference to Jeremiah 2:13 that was true to King the minister and that resonated with his followers.

Closing – For those who cannot recall it, here is King's closing: "Free at last! Free at last! Thank God almighty, we are free at last." The closing of the speech was great not only because it was rousing but also because it was presumptive: it was a call to action, tying back to King's "And when this happens, when we allow freedom to ring." Many talks, by contrast, close with a whimper.

Authenticity – For all of King's devices, he was speaking from the heart, for a cause he truly believed in. Audiences can sense passion, expertise—and imposters.

Practice – King delivered most of "I Have a Dream" without notes. He drew from material he had used in other addresses and sermons in the months and years before the March on Washington, much as a great musician improvises after years of experimentation and practice. King may have been born a great orator, but he became perhaps the greatest by practicing.

No matter who you are or what you are presenting, no matter who the audience is or how well they know you, no matter if you are educating neophytes or converting nonbelievers, you can reach the promised land of oration by learning the techniques of Dr. King.

Learning More

- Nancy Duarte, *Slide:ology* (San Francisco:O'Reilly, 2008).

- Carmine Gallo, *The Presentation Secrets of Steve Jobs: How to Be Insanely Great in Front of Any Audience* (New York:McGraw-Hill, 2009).

- Garr Reynolds, *Presentation Zen: Simple Ideas on Presentation Design and Delivery* (Berkeley: New Riders, 2008).

- Corey Sommers and David Jenkins, *Whiteboard Selling:Empowering Sales through Visuals* (Hoboken: Wiley, 2013).

Chapter 17

Sales Enablement

Recall from chapter 1 that Peter Drucker defined a successful marketing strategy as one that sells the product without the involvement of the sales force. Drucker's thoughts notwithstanding, in reality, very few products are so wonderful that they sell themselves. As a general rule, selling products and services requires a sales force that is well prepared to answer questions and lead a prospective buyer to a sale. In most organizations, the marketing department's role is to arm the sales team with whatever resources they need to close a sale. We refer to this function as *sales enablement*. In short, sales enablement is providing the tools and training a sales force needs to win business.

Moreover, especially in B2B selling, the sales team is the most visible carrier of a company's marketing message and value proposition. Your salespeople and channel partners spend more time in front of a prospective buyer than any banner ad or industry analyst. Therefore, it's essential to provide your salespeople with the best possible training. For some reason, this seemingly obvious reality is lost on many marketing professionals who find training a required drudgery and would rather be working on a cool advertisement. Smart marketers understand that sales enablement is a competitive advantage. This chapter will provide an overview of good sales training content, using a sales playbook to teach salespeople, and developing sales tools to help them move prospects to customers.

How to Train a Salesperson

There are two types of sales training. The first type involves training in basic sales skills such as discovery, qualification, and negotiation. The sales organization manages this process. Sales management usually brings in an outside sales instructor to train the sales force in these fundamentals, either on an annual basis or as part of new-hire orientation. This training typically involves one of the well-known sales systems, whether SPIN, Sandler, target account selling, or the newer Challenger Sale.

The second type of sales training involves helping the sales force identify and relate to the target buyers for your products. This is the training that marketing is responsible for. Essentially, marketing needs to convey all of the work it has performed to identify an attractive market, help spec the product, and package it up with an attractive value proposition. A best practice is to put all of this information into the context of the sales system your company uses. SPIN selling, for example, is a questioning methodology, so the training that marketing conducts should include questions aligned with SPIN. (SPIN is detailed later in the chapter.)

Finally, salespeople need to be motivated. Of course, they are motivated by their compensation plans, but a team that feels fired up and is well prepared is a dangerous weapon. Good sales training is equal amounts education and motivation.

Below are the essential components of sales training:

Identifying a buyer – Knowing the ideal buyer profile is a very powerful tool for sales reps. It helps them to avoid wasting time with the wrong person and to navigate inside an organization to find the right person. This information should be a distillation of the profiling conducted in the marketing plan, vetted with sales leadership to make sure it aligns with real-world successes. Ideally, it should include important points from the buyer persona and the buying center.

How to qualify – Related to the buyer profile is the question of what the sales reps should look for. This is where qualification is important. Do prospective customers have the problem you solve? How do you avoid wasting time with tire kickers? Many companies use the BANT qualification mnemonic: budget, authority, need, and timeframe. A qualified prospect should have the money to spend, the authority to spend it, and a need that fits your product or service. Salespeople understand how to qualify in general from their own experience and sales skills training. Marketing needs to train sales on qualification related to the product and buyer profile.

Anatomy of a win – The best way to teach sales reps is by example. And, like your buyers, sales reps prefer to hear from and learn from their peers. Using examples of sales wins, presented by the reps who closed the deals, is an excellent method for training your sales force. Marketing usually collaborates with sales management to recruit these reps and to prepare their materials.

Product knowledge – Understanding the products to be sold is, of course, critical to the sales process. Studies have demonstrated that sales reps who understand their products and how they relate to customer problems are more effective than the proverbial back-slapping "relationship" account managers.[49] Training should focus on how product capabilities map to customer problems and how they differ from the competition.

Pricing and licensing – Once your salespeople understand how to find prospects and have gotten them interested in your product, they need to price the solution. Alternatively, the issue of pricing may come up in general terms during the sales process. Yet, many companies neglect to train salespeople and partners in this step in the sales cycle. Pricing is critical, so don't make this mistake. Some companies train their sales reps on the value of their product to help mitigate the knee-jerk reaction to offer discounts when pressed by a customer.

Handling objections – Your salespeople will learn how to handle objections generically in their sales skills training. Prospects spurn their pitches every day. Marketing should arm them with answers to common objections specific to your product or service. Ideally, these responses should help educate, establishing the sales rep as knowledgeable in the eye of the prospect.

The ordering of these components is intentional. Many organizations make the mistake of spending too much time on the product and product details. Yes, good sales teams tend to have deeper product knowledge than their peers, but they do *not* need to be product experts. Teaching a team how to find opportunities and motivating them to find as many as they can is much more valuable to an organization's top line.

Sales Playbooks

If you ask heads of sales what they desire most in their job, the answer will likely be a repeatable, predictable sales process. The more one deal can look like another, the better a sales manager, director, or vice president can predict the likelihood of a win, and the better his or her forecasting will be.

This objective is difficult to achieve when different salespeople are selling in different ways. Though every customer situation is unique and every sales rep has a distinctive personality and style, more often than not there are common points in a sale as well as common mistakes or pitfalls to be avoided. Making your sales team aware of the critical points in a sale and how to avoid common mistakes will smooth out the process and improve sales efficiency.

This is where sales playbooks come in. A *sales playbook* is a collection of one or more sales *plays*—a series of steps to move an opportunity to a closed deal. The concept is analogous to a football team's playbook that contains a number of plays for different situations (In contrast to a football playbook, however, sales playbooks should be simple and contain only a limited number of plays.) Whether a company should employ multiple plays depends on the number of products they sell and the range of buyers they sell to.*

All playbooks should include three critical pieces. The first is the description of the play. This is essentially a quick overview of the play and how it works, including the market, the buyer profile, and key trends. The second piece is comprised of step-by-step play activities. This information typically is presented as a workflow diagram that displays all of the stages involved in the play as well as the activities associated with each step. The final piece describes the tools and assets by step. This is essentially a list of sales tools and customer assets, mapped to a particular step in the sales play, with guidance on how to use them.

A play starts at the point a sales qualified lead has been handed off to sales, or when a salesperson has created a sales generated lead. The steps of a sales play should be aligned with the sales stages that sales management uses to track progress within their pipeline. These stages are not the general stages of awareness, research, consideration, and purchase that are part of the customer journey, as discussed in chapter 11. Rather, these are specific stages that sales management has defined for a specific organization, its products, and its customers.

Many of the steps in a sales play are sales fundamentals that focus on qualifying opportunities, discovering specific customer problems, obtaining agreement or quid pro quo from prospects, and preparing to close the deal, also known as "the close." Each step should be completed in sequence and include a corresponding set of tools that will aid a sales rep in getting to the next step.

---

* A caution on the use of the term "playbook" with international sales teams. American football, despite the NFL's aspirations, is not yet an international sport. Not all sports have playbooks, so the term may not translate. Be sensitive to this, and use another term if need be. And whatever you do, don't use the gridiron's iconic "Xs and Os" play illustration as a graphic on the cover of the "playbook."

Figure 1: An actual B2B sales play

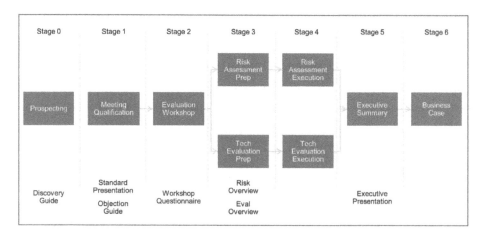

Figure 1 shows a play that was employed very effectively by a team I worked with while at Symantec, generating over $500 million in software sales (I genericized the play to mask some of the team's secrets). Without giving too much away, the play worked because sales had gathered specific information to qualify the customer, reps obtained certain quid pro quos from the customer in advance, and the security risks discovered by the product were presented back to customers in a compelling format. Sales leaders swore by the play, and they would lower the likelihood of closing a deal if they discovered a rep had skipped a stage.

Sales plays and playbooks are a great tool to align sales and marketing. After each play is defined and agreed to by sales and marketing management, a set of key assets needed to accomplish the sale will emerge. This will quickly net out the needed customer assets and internal sales tools. The assets listed in the sales play stages may be a little different from the asset map we presented chapter 15, which included the awareness and research stages of the customer journey. For example, a sales play would include internal assets, such as checklists for salespeople and pat answers to customer objections, that would never be used as part of a demand generation program. In figure 1, note how the sales tools used in each stage are listed across the bottom.

A caveat on sales plays and playbooks: Without support from sales management, playbooks can involve a lot of work for very little gain. The best sales teams enforce the process, just as a coach would insist on running a play the way it was drawn up on the board. A well-designed sales play will have milestones that, once achieved, increase the probability of a sale and help sales management improve their forecasts.

Aligning Sales Training with Sales Methodology

As mentioned, many direct sales organizations use a specific sales methodology. SPIN selling, Scientific Selling, Target Account Selling, the Challenger Sale, and Sandler are just a few of the more popular ones. Although each methodology is quite general, they all include prescribed methods for discovering sales opportunities, qualifying opportunities, handling objections, and negotiating.

People who sell for a living often consider training on sales skills to be more valuable than product training. It's a part of their professional development, and it may help them close more deals than learning the latest product features. In addition, it adds to their overall sales skills, and it will serve them well even after they have left your company.

To better engage with salespeople and to align with their sales skills development, truly effective sales enablement should be conducted in the context of their sales methodology. Mapping information about your product or service into their sales methodology bridges the gap. Marketing will be speaking sales' language and giving them tools that they can use in the field right away. Plus, why would you leave it up to your field sales organization to do the mapping? Mapping is most effective when it is performed centrally and only once. This approach ensures consistency. More often than not, if you leave mapping to individual field reps, they will not do it at all, or they will attempt to do it on the fly, with mixed results.

To understand the specifics of alignment, consider the following example. The product marketing group in a company that employs SPIN selling creates a set of questions that connect customer problems discovered using SPIN with the company's product capabilities. SPIN is a mnemonic that reminds salespeople to ask the following questions:

- Situation – Questions concerning the overall business or organization
- Problem – Questions aimed at uncovering problems or issues
- Implication – Questions intended to identify the potential negative impacts of the unsolved problem
- Needs-Payoff – Questions designed to highlight the positive impact of solving the problem

When the product marketing team conducts sales training that is built around SPIN, they teach the sales rep not only the specifics of their product but also how to communicate with customers concerning the product.

Certain sales methodologies also use charts, tables, or scorecards to qualify opportunities or to plan account strategies. Companies can create sales tools for their products that align to these elements. These sales tools can be included in the appropriate stage of their playbook. For example, the "Top Objections Guide" from stage 1 in figure 1 above was written in the style of Sandler, the sales methodology used by the sales team.

Aligning with a methodology may not work for companies that sell through the channel. The partners will have their own sales strategies; in fact, some of them might not subscribe to a methodology at all. If you have a large partner that does a significant amount of business, it might be worth dedicating the time to align a channel sales tool to their methodology. Otherwise, you can generalize qualifying questions and methodology-specific tools. (We discuss channel enablement further in chapter 19.)

Other Training Methods

In addition to formal training at sales kickoffs or academies, there are a number of other methods to train a sales force. In this section, we will review four widely accepted approaches:

- ◆ Webcast series

- ◆ Online training

- ◆ Podcasts

- ◆ Whiteboard training

Webcasts are not only for customers. A regular series of webcasts on an expected cadence, or schedule, is a great way to reinforce training. In many organizations with large sales teams, however, webcasts and live training by themselves cannot provide the necessary training. For these companies, recorded training, delivered online with built-in testing, is an effective strategy to scale out training and build in certification. Some companies also employ this strategy with channel partners to get them up to speed and set a gate—meaning they have to take the time and pass the built-in test—to become certified to sell the product.

Podcasts—sometimes called "drive-time training"—are an excellent medium for reaching a large sales force and allowing them to train on their own time, like when they are driving to the office or to an account. Podcasts are most effective when they are kept short. Producing a series of podcasts enables you to cover more material. With the proliferation of iPods and smartphones, pushing out training information in MP3 format allows reps to learn even while they are on the treadmill.

Finally, training via whiteboards provides two benefits. First, teaching sales reps to reproduce a standard whiteboard presentation—created by marketing—gives them a useful sales tool for customer meetings. As we covered in the last chapter, whiteboard presentations are great for small, interactive meetings. Second, because reproducing a standard whiteboard presentation requires practice, sales reps will absorb the material, in contrast to a PowerPoint presentation that they may never read until they are in front of a customer. Figure 2, below, is a step-by-step whiteboard presentation guide created to train sales and channel partners at PGP Corporation. The guide covered what to draw, in what order, and what points to emphasize.

Figure 2: Step-by-step whiteboard training guide created by PGP Corporation for training direct sales and channel partners

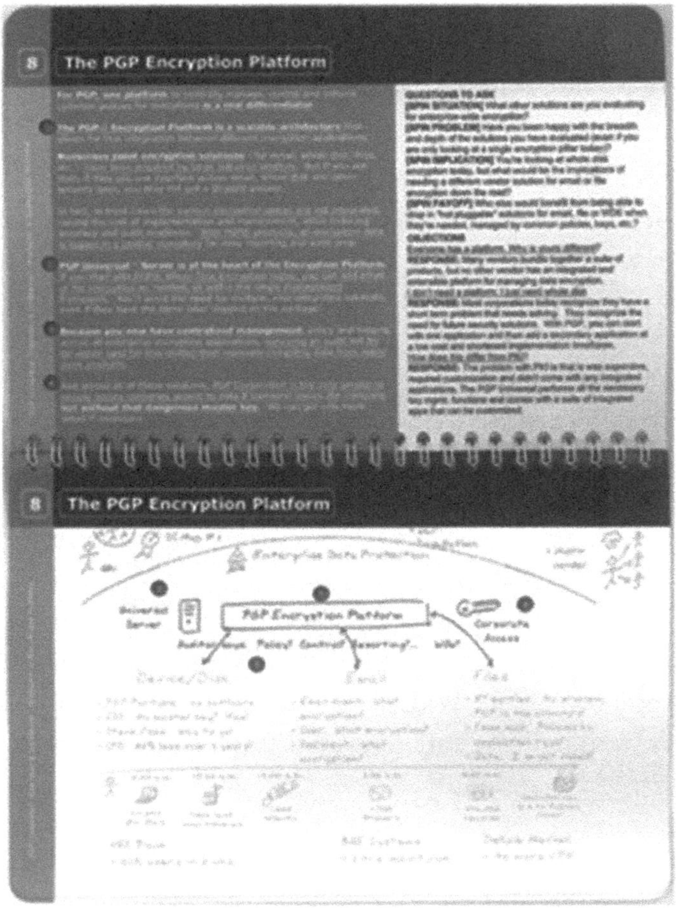

Sales Tools

In addition to customer-facing collateral like data sheets, brochures, and presentations, marketing—specifically product marketing—is often called upon to create tools to assist the sales team in winning. The tools can take many forms. One widely used tool is the call script, an example conversation a sales rep would have with a customer. Another popular tool is the calculator, which usually calculates potential cost savings a customer would gain, used by a sales rep to prepare for a customer call or to complete while sitting down with a prospective customer. This section examines some commonly used sales tools in more detail.

Call scripts are prepared scripts used by telemarketing or inside sales for prospecting on the phone. These scripts should contain a value proposition, an offer to interest the prospect, and a next step to commit the customer. They should also include answers to common objections. In addition, they frequently contain "branches," or discussion paths, that a telemarketer or an inside sales rep can follow based on the answers customers give.

Discovery guides consist of a series of questions that a sales rep can utilize to discover customer problems or issues. A good discovery guide should offer a range of questions that reps can ask during meetings and phone conversations, along with a short description of how the organization's products address the issues or problems.

Regardless of whether a prospect has sent out a request for proposal (RFP), he or she may be evaluating multiple products. The best tool for comparing products is a *scorecard*, which is a spreadsheet of criteria, weighted for importance, that outputs a score for each vendor. Creating and providing prospective customers with a scorecard weighted to your organization's strengths can also be a very effective sales tool.

Creating RFPs can be a lot of work for customers, and slanting the requirements toward your company's strengths can increase your odds of winning. For these reasons, high-performing organizations provide *sample RFP templates* to prospects early on in the sales cycle. Sales teams prefer to avoid RFPs because they extend the sales cycle and increase the salesperson's workload. However, many customers insist on using this process. When they do, your company generally will fare better if the RFP template resembles yours.

Providing satisfactory answers to common objections is critical in moving the sales process forward, and no organization wants its reps to be caught flat-footed. Therefore, marketing should prepare *objection handling guides* that provide a standard set of answers to common objections. Top-performing organizations will actually practice using these guides to answer objections in live training sessions.

Prospects are often seeking to quantify the size of the problem or the value of the solution. *Calculators*, whether spreadsheets or small applications, are the ideal tools to provide these answers. Calculators can be provided by the selling organization, based on estimates or data from other customers or by a third party with an objective stance or a comprehensive knowledge of the market. Calculators should enable customers to customize the inputs, weight the key variables, and generate a report that they can share inside their organizations.

Battlecards—one-page summaries of how your organization lines up, or goes into battle, against the competition—are a common request from a direct sales organization. Battlecards typically list key selling points, discovery questions, competitive differentiators, and traps to set for the competition.

Case Study – The Vontu Playbook

Vontu was a security software company founded in 2001. Based in San Francisco, the company hoped to grow based on what was, at the time, a radical idea. Rather than designing software to keep out the bad guys, Vontu wanted to prevent employees from inadvertently or foolishly exposing confidential information from the inside.

At that time, this inside-out, rather than outside-in, approach to security was unheard of, and no one was looking to buy it. This constituted a major obstacle for a fledgling company whose objective was not simply to sell their software, but to sell it at a premium in six- and seven-figure deals.

Vontu was dealing with a significant business issue—how to sell a brand-new security product, for a lot of money, that no one knew they needed. The company's founders were confident that they could sell their product if they could communicate directly with customers and show them all of the confidential data their employees were exposing. The challenge was to convince prospective customers to meet with someone who was selling a product that solved a problem they didn't know they had.

To overcome this hurdle, the company developed a play: offer the customer a risk assessment free of charge, and then have the sales rep follow up with a report that revealed all of the data that were leaking out of the customer's organization. The sales reps now had an offer (the free risk assessment) and a natural follow-up (the report) that demonstrated a pressing need for the product and thus justified the high price. Significantly, Vontu had designed its software so that it was easy to drop off an appliance with the software already loaded, connect it to the prospective customer's network, let it scan the e-mails employees were sending out over a period of two weeks, and then print a report of all of the confidential data that were being exposed.

The play was developed by one of Vontu's founders, Kevin Rowney, and its head of product marketing, Maureen Kelly. These two executives rolled out "the playbook" at an optional session during the company's quarterly sales training. After a few reps reported success with this strategy, sales management made "running the play" mandatory. Management would question reps on weekly calls not just about their forecasts but specifically where they were with the play *on every deal.* The risk assessment, or RA, was so effective in closing deals that it became a leading indicator—sales management could predict the odds of quarterly revenue attainment based on the number of RAs.

Along the way, Rowney and Kelly made adjustments to the play. One problem arose when some reps rushed to offer the RA without properly qualifying the opportunity, thereby wasting both their time and valuable sales engineering resources. To address this problem, Rowney and Kelly incorporated qualifying questions to step one of the play. Now, a prospective customer had to be qualified before the rep would agree to have the first meeting. Qualifying also made this meeting more effective, because the rep had collected a lot of valuable information up front.

Another issue confronting Vontu was that the report was not being seen by the right people in the account, such as the chief information officer, the general counsel, and the head of human resources. These were the people who really understood the business risk posed by exposing sensitive intellectual property, customer information, and employee details. Vontu alleviated this problem by adding another crucial gate to the play. Before Vontu would perform the risk assessment, the customer had to agree to invite these key executives to the meeting where Vontu revealed the results. This quid pro quo, although uncomfortable for many reps, aligned perfectly with Vontu's use of the Sandler sales methodology, which emphasizes the use of these "up-front contracts." Requiring the businesspeople, and not just the security team, to attend the meeting assured that the report received proper exposure. As a result, deploying Vontu's technology frequently became a company priority.

In the end, Vontu helped define the market for what is now known as data loss prevention (DLP). The market mushroomed to almost $500 million by 2011,[50] and deploying DLP has become the highest priority for security teams in large companies—quite a contrast to the early days. In 2007, Vontu was acquired by Symantec for $350 million. The play is still in use today.

Learning More

◆ Corey Sommers and David Jenkins, *Whiteboard Selling: Empowering Sales through Visuals* (Hoboken:Wiley, 2013).

Chapter 18

Marketing and Selling through a Channel

ost Americans know Kellogg's Corn Flakes, Viagra, and the Apple iPod. They probably also know the manufacturers of these products—Kellogg's, Pfizer, and Apple—and the name of their local supermarket, drugstore chain, and big-box store where they can buy them. Most of them, however, probably have never heard of the McLane Company, McKesson, or Tech Data. These three firms are multibillion-dollar companies that distribute Corn Flakes, Viagra, and the iPod, respectively.

Distributors are a key part of the channel, which is the set of companies that delivers a product or service to market. In many cases, the only way your product will get in front of a customer is via the channel. Understanding how the channel works is essential for marketers because they need to design go-to-market strategies and marketing programs that work with the channel. Recall that the channel is a key component of McCarthy's fourth P—place (if this reference doesn't sound familiar, then you might want to review the discussion of the Four Ps in chapter 1).

This chapter is meant to help marketers understand the overall purpose of the channel and how to choose the right channel partners. It describes the various players in the channel that a marketer can utilize in his or her route to market, contrasts selling through the channel and working with a company's direct sales force, and covers how to profile channel partners to help select the right ones.

Purpose of a Channel

Quite simply, the *channel* is the set of parties that combine to move products from the manufacturer, producer, or developer to the business or consumer that purchases them. These parties are known as your *channel partners*.

An organization's channel and channel partners, along with its own salespeople and online store, are its *routes to market*. Field salespeople, inside telesales reps, and a company's online store are known as *direct* routes to market. Channel partners are *indirect* routes to market, sometimes called *indirect channels*.

Understanding the channel is critical for marketers, because it will affect all of an organization's marketing programs. An organization that has both direct and indirect routes to market will need to adjust its programs to compensate for both. Even an organization with only indirect routes to market, but different types of channel partners, will need to make adjustments. Generally speaking, adding indirect routes to market adds work for the marketing team.

So why bother with a channel? In some industries, the channel is the only way to reach the end customers, which is discussed later in the chapter. There are also cost advantages in many cases. Sometimes a channel partner performs functions your company or your customers need, known as *value add*. Below is a list of common value-add functions performed by channel partners:

- Ordering – A helpful channel partner makes it more convenient for your end customer to purchase your product or service, sometimes by offering attractive payment terms.

- Shipping and handling – Partners frequently possess expertise in handling and shipping certain types of products, from perishable produce to multiton excavation equipment.

- Storage – Some partners provide warehouse space to store your products, ideally in a location that is close to your customers.

- Display – In the case of retail sales, how and where your products are displayed is critical. Having stores where your customers shop, and attractive shelf space for your products, are vital.

- Promotion – Partners may be adept at promoting products like yours through diverse media ranging from newspaper circulars to direct mailings to financial incentives.

- Selling – Naturally, you will rely on channel partners to sell for you.

- Services – Some partners have skilled consultants that can provide services, such as installation and maintenance, for your products.

- Information feedback – Partners are the ones who interact directly with your customers, and they often serve as surrogates for customer feedback.

Although a channel offers many benefits to marketers, it also poses several challenges. The most fundamental challenge is that you are relying on people who don't work for your company to sell your products and services. To compound this issue, they may also carry your competitor's products, in which case you need to convince them to sell yours. Further, as with your sales force, your partners need to be trained and motivated to do the job. This challenge frequently involves moving your product or service to the "top of the sell" rather than being treated as a "throwaway" product that is bundled with others. This is one of the most challenging tasks that a channel marketing manager must perform.

Figure 1: Cost and value add of routes to market

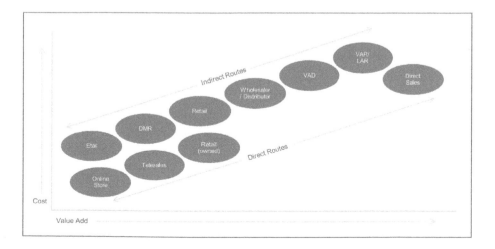

Channel Players

There are many pieces to the channel. A channel will look different for different businesses and different geographies, and it can change over time. Understanding the different players in the channel is critical to building a route to market that fits your business. In this section, we will focus on the following key players:

- Direct marketing reseller
- Distributor
- Large account reseller
- Original equipment manufacturer
- System integrator
- Value-added reseller
- Wholesaler

A *direct marketing reseller (DMR)* is a company that sells directly to businesses or consumers over the phone or online without operating storefront operations of any kind. DMRs fill the gap between big-box retailers, who may also sell online, and distributors, who sell to resellers and retailers. DMRs offer their customers convenience in that they carry thousands of products, can take orders quickly, and can streamline purchasing. CDW is a DMR that sells technology products to businesses and government organizations. Amazon is an example of an *e-tailer*, a company that sells goods or commodities to consumers electronically over the Internet.

Sometimes called a "disty" for short, a *distributor* is a company that moves products from the manufacturer to resellers—both wholesalers and retailers. Distributors play a key part in the supply chain between manufacturers or suppliers and their retail channels. *Value-added distributors (VADs)* add a number of services in addition to distribution, such as recruitment, training, centralized quoting, and financing for their "downstream" reseller partners. Tech Data, mentioned in the introduction of this chapter, is an example of a

VAD. In the international market, companies rely on VADs not only to resell their products but also to support, train, and develop solutions for the products in a particular region.

A *large account reseller (LAR)* is a company that sells hardware and software to large organizations, typically those with more than 250 employees. Because LARs deal in bulk quantities, they can offer volume discounts and special leasing and purchasing programs that resellers geared to small companies cannot. Some LARs also operate as DMRs. CDW, for example, is an LAR of technology products.

The *original equipment manufacturer (OEM)* is a company that builds products or components that are purchased by a company and retailed under the purchasing company's brand name. ACDelco and Bosch are well-known automotive OEMs. Intel and Samsung are two of the largest personal computer and tablet computer OEM chip providers. The term OEM is also used by software companies who integrate rather than manufacture software components. A *system integrator (SI)* builds computing systems for clients by combining hardware and software products from multiple vendors. SIs typically recommend products rather than resell them. In this sense, SIs are important influences and can be part of an organization's influencer marketing efforts.

A *value-added reseller (VAR)* adds features or services to an existing product and then resells it—usually to end customers—as an integrated product or a complete solution. VARs are common in the electronics, computer hardware, and software industries. While there are many large VARs, it is not uncommon for them to be smaller, regional businesses. VARs offer specific product expertise and valued services, such as installation and ongoing maintenance.

Finally, a *wholesaler* purchases goods in bulk to obtain a favorable discount and then distributes them to other wholesalers or to retailers. Wholesalers typically operate in B2C markets. They may buy from a manufacturer, a supplier, a distributor, or another wholesaler. Wholesalers exist in almost every market segment—food, beverage, timber, fuel, chemical, fabric, and on and on. Many specialize. For example, Segrest Farms is a Gibsonton, Florida, wholesaler that supplies tropical fish to over a thousand pet stores across the United States.

Profiling Partners

What kinds of channel partners do you need, and how many of them do you need? These questions have been around channel selling forever. To answer these questions, companies rely on several basic criteria, which we discuss below.

Customer fit – Do these partners have relationships with your target customer, and does your target customer purchase from these partners? Geographic coverage, customer relationships, and government buying contracts are all examples of customer fit.

Industry fit – Oftentimes, a particular partner is the deemed "expert" in the industry and is the first choice of end customers within that industry. Understanding who these partners are and how you can best utilize their services is essential to winning sales in specific industries. Health care, for example, is a common industry specialization for VARs. Their added value to customers stems from knowledge of how hospitals operate, health and privacy regulations, and new advances in medical technologies.

Product fit – Do these partners have experience selling products like yours? Or, if your partners provide value-added services, are these services a good fit with your products, and are your products a good skill match with the partners' consulting teams?

Economic fit – Are the price point and revenue potential attractive to the partner, and can the partner realize a profit by selling your products? Some partners, like DMRs, can make money selling large volumes of low-dollar orders, whereas others have more expensive cost structures and need larger deals.

Capacity – Can the partner effectively manage the amount of business that you will direct toward it?

Determining Routes to Market

As mentioned above, although the principles that underlie all channels are similar, channels can appear quite different for different businesses. Obviously, for example, there is no need for a system integrator to distribute food products to grocery stores. Likewise, a commodity electronics wholesaler makes no sense in the software business, though it may benefit companies that manufacture the hardware the applications run on. How an organization builds a channel depends on the nature of its business, its maturity, and what the competition is doing. For a mature company, for example, mimicking the competition's strategy might be sufficient. If the organization is operating in a new market, however, or if it is not mature enough to emulate the strategy of a larger competitor, then it may have to start from the bottom and build over time.

In the software business, a common pattern is for companies with a direct sales force to first recruit SIs to install and configure—but not resell—their software. Only after they have captured sufficient market demand would a software company consider recruiting VARs to install, configure, *and* resell. Finally, when the software company starts taking orders from large business or government customers, they can add LARs.

DMRs are usually signed on when a company has a commoditized product—easy to understand and sell—with significant enough demand from customer organizations of all sizes to be profitable. The company would add a VAD when it has a sufficiently large number of VARs and/or LARs to manage. There may also be a regional need for a VAD if the supplier does not have a significant footprint in a particular region.

By contrast, selling through retail stores usually requires distribution, either wholesalers or distributors, depending on the product. This route to market is well established, and marketers may find themselves working to gain the attention of wholesalers and distributors who control distribution to their desired retail outlets.

Tiers of Distribution

A channel not only is comprised of various players, but it can consist of multiple levels, or *tiers*. The number of tiers typically increases with the size of the business. When handling more and more resellers or retailers becomes a strain on a supplier, the supplier can add distribution tiers. These tiers provide additional reach and logistics capacity. In addition, they offer practical benefits that the supplier itself cannot; for example, a distributor's business model or capitalization may allow them to offer attractive financing programs. Channels can consist of one, two, or three tiers. Each is described below.

In *single-tier distribution*, resellers—VARs, LARs, and DMRs—purchase directly from the supplier. The supplier is responsible for recruiting, training, and collecting revenue from the resellers directly.

In contrast, in *two-tier distribution*, resellers—VARs, LARs and DMRs—purchase from a distributor who purchases directly from the supplier. Depending on who the distributors are and whether they add value, they may also recruit resellers, train them, provide quoting and ordering assistance, and offer attractive financing programs, for example, sixty days for payment. Selling through wholesalers is also considered two-tier distribution.

Some businesses add a third tier of distribution, such as when wholesalers buy via distributors and then resell to retailers. Alternatively, a company can set up a *master distributor*, who in turn sells to other distributors. Table 1 summarizes single-, two-, and three-tier distribution.

Table 1: Tiers of distribution

Type	Description
Single Tier	LARs, VARs, DMRs, and e-tailers buy directly from the manufacturer or supplier.
Two Tier	LARs, VARs, DMRs, e-tailers, and retailers buy from a distributor, who purchases directly from the manufacturer or supplier.
Three Tier	Distributors buy from wholesalers, or a master distributor sells to other distributors. Resellers, e-tailers, and retailers still buy from distribution.

Mixing Direct Sales and Channel Partners

A fundamental challenge confronting companies considering indirect routes to market is to determine the optimal mix of channel partners and direct salespeople. Most companies base this decision on their go-to-market strategy, which was covered in chapter 4. As mentioned previously, a company can rely on its channel partners to augment a direct sales force in specific geographic regions or market segments that are not sufficiently covered by its direct sales force. Channel partners can also help scale the business faster, with their established sales teams, distribution networks, and order processing systems. In many cases, companies cannot hire and train salespeople fast enough, or they do not want to invest in the creation of a large direct sales force. Particularly in smaller markets, the costs of setting up a direct sales force can far outweigh the margin the company must pay to the channel (margin will be discussed further in the next chapter).

Ideally, channel partners and the direct sales force should augment each other. This is also known as a *leveraged sales model*. Channel partners give the direct sales force more reach and allow it to focus on key accounts or markets.

Unfortunately, in the real world, tensions between channel partners and the direct sales force frequently materialize. These tensions are generally referred to as *channel conflicts* and typically have two causes. The first occurs when the direct sales force becomes convinced that the partners are not working hard enough for their business, but instead are merely waiting at the trough for sales to "flip" deals to them for fulfillment. Sales and executive management may have similar feelings, wondering what they are paying the partners for. To avoid this common bias, it is important (1) to appreciate the contributions of partners in handling contracts, product fulfillment, installation services, and financing, and (2) to incentivize partners to identify their own opportunities.

The second cause of tension is the channel partners' concern that the supplier's direct sales force will "cherry-pick" the best opportunities for themselves and leave the less desirable deals for the partners. *Opportunity registration*, also known as *deal registration*, helps resolve this problem by allowing partners to claim any sales opportunities they identify. These opportunities are "hands-off" for the direct sales force for an agreed-upon period of time. Deal registration is covered in greater detail in the next chapter.

Some companies resolve their channel conflicts by segmenting their customer base. A common strategy is to assign their direct team to oversee large strategic accounts, where sales are complex or maintaining loyalty through contact is paramount. Smaller accounts—say, midsize companies—are managed by value-added resellers who specialize in providing services needed by these size businesses. Finally, small transactional deals can be handled by a company web store or a DMR. Figure 2 below shows this type of coverage model.

Figure 2: Coverage model

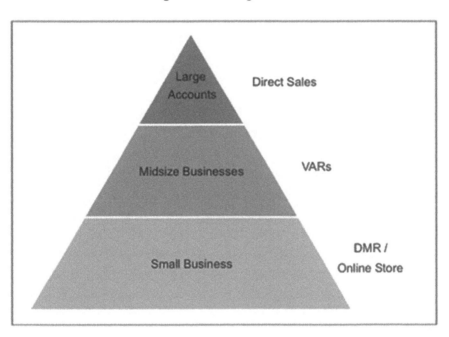

The decision to integrate channel sales can also be motivated by cost. Partners are typically 15 to 40 percent less expensive to maintain than a direct sales force.[51] Calculating this differential can take a bit of work, and it is not an exact science. The easiest method is to compare the company's *sales, general, and administrative (SG&A)* cost, usually expressed as a percentage of revenue, against the combined margin and other benefits a channel partner would receive.

Case Study

Most Americans probably don't recognize the name Avnet. In fact, the $26 billion dollar company with more than seventeen thousand employees distributes thousands of computer and electronic products that touch our lives just about every day. Interestingly, over its history, Avnet's distribution network was critical to building up three media that marketers rely on today: radio, television, and the Internet.

In 1921, Charles Avnet, a Russian immigrant, began selling surplus radio parts in New York's "Radio Row." This portside area located in Manhattan's Lower West Side was a mecca for ham radio enthusiasts. Significantly, Avnet entered the radio business just as it was about to take off. In 1922, roughly one hundred thousand radios were sold in the United States. By 1924, that number had increased tenfold.

In 1929, Galvin Manufacturing introduced the first car radio, the Motorola, short for "motor Victrola." Avnet started assembling and selling antenna kits, his first attempt at value-added distribution.

Then the Great Depression hit. Like so many people, Avnet found himself in debt. Despite the severe economic crisis, however, the demand for radios remained robust. In addition, the newest novelty—television—was beginning to make inroads. Responding to these trends, Avnet closed his retail operation to cut costs and moved into electronics wholesale. Then, as the United States geared up for WWII, Avnet shifted his attention to military and government requests, supplying military antennas and electronics connecters.*

Following the war, Avnet expanded to supply critical components to aviation and missile manufacturers on the West Coast. He later distributed critical transistors and microchips to the new breed of computer manufacturers in Silicon Valley in the 1960s.

Throughout the 1970s, 1980s, and 1990s, Avnet continued to represent the "who's who" of the computer industry—IBM, Texas Instruments, Cisco, HP, Sun, and Microsoft, to name a few. By 2000, Avnet was making $1 billion in

---

* Avnet's supplier/partner Galvin Manufacturing did well in WWII as well, manufacturing walkie-talkies for Allied troops. In 1947, it changed its name to Motorola.

revenue every month. Quite a journey from Russia to Manhattan to Arizona, and from the brink of bankruptcy to an international high-tech distribution powerhouse. Avnet reinvented itself from a so-called "box pusher" by adding value to the sale through training, service, quoting, and other services. The result? Avnet became one of the first VADs in the computer industry.

Learning More

• Lawrence Friedman and Tim Furey, *The Channel Advantage* (Oxford: Butterworth-Heinemann, 1999).

Chapter 19

Channel Partner Programs

The last chapter explained what channels are and why so many companies choose to utilize them. In this chapter, we will focus more specifically on *channel partner programs*, which are formalized groupings of sales and marketing activities designed to attract and retain channel partners. Many of the foundational elements of channel partner programs are table stakes for playing the game of channel distribution. Smart companies understand that well-executed channel partner programs can create a competitive advantage. The financial incentives, materials and tools, and other perks included in a channel program can motivate a partner to sell more of your product than a competitor's product.

Components of a Channel Partner Program

Although every company has a unique channel program, all partner programs contain several common components. Not every company is in a position to offer all components, and not all channel partners will meet the company's established criteria for receiving all of the benefits. A standard strategy for evaluating your program's components is to examine your competitors' programs to ensure your program is attractive by comparison. Below we discuss the most common program components.

> Discounts and margin – Partners buy products at a discount from the supplier and then sell them for as close to the list price as the market will bear. The difference between their buy price and the sell price is

their *margin*. Generally speaking, the deeper the discount, the greater the partner's profit. Margins vary by industry. They can range from 5 to 30 percent.

Education and training – Suppliers want competent partners, and partners want suppliers who can teach them the skills they need to open up new markets. Training courses conducted by the supplier for the partner's sales and technical staff are therefore a win-win endeavor, and they are critical for any partner program. Many companies offer formal certifications for their partners' employees who have successfully completed a training program. The partners can use these certificates to market their expertise.

Technical and sales support – In addition to training, suppliers should offer support for their partners' technical and sales staffs. Technical support is designed to assist the partner's technical staff in installing and configuring the supplier's products. Sales support is often oriented toward quoting and ordering.

Sample products and demo equipment – Sample products to show prospective customers, or demo equipment for more complex products like software applications, can help channel partners move the sales cycle along. Partners appreciate when suppliers provide these assets for free or at deep discounts.

Partner marketing funds – In addition to discounts on their products, many companies offer funds to help partners generate demand. Companies distribute these funds in one of three ways:

- As discretionary grants, known as market development funds (MDF)

- As a percentage of product sold, known as contra-revenue funds

- As cost sharing, called co-op funds

Partner marketing funds are covered in more detail later in the chapter.

Marketing and promotion activities – Many partners are small businesses that have little or no marketing staff. Therefore, providing marketing programs that promote partners is beneficial to their business. Some companies provide *turnkey marketing collateral* to which a partner can append its logo and contact information, thus supplying the partner with professional-looking assets it otherwise might not have been able to produce. The partner benefits from the "halo effect" of being co-branded with the supplier. Suppliers also benefit because their marketing teams maintain control over their brands in the market by avoiding the slapdash partner materials that come in for approval, and gain a better idea of how their partner marketing funds are being spent.

Deal registration – As explained in chapter 18, *deal registration*, or *opportunity registration*, is an online process that allows partners to register deals that they discovered and are working directly. This policy benefits partners by giving them exclusive rights to work opportunities for a period of time, without the supplier's direct sales team cherry-picking deals or other channel partners swooping in. It also gives the supplier greater insight into the partner's pipeline.

Rebates – Finally, rebates are additional incentives that further increase a partner's margin. Companies frequently offer rebates in exchange for a partner's meeting or exceeding a certain sales goal. The money is returned (or equivalent payments owed are forgiven) when the target is met. In other cases, they provide rebates for a limited time to promote a designated product. We examine rebates in detail later in this chapter.

Tiering Partner Programs

Many old channel hands invoke the Pareto principle, better known as the 80-20 rule, when they discuss the top-line contributions partners make: 80 percent of your revenue will be generated by 20 percent of your partners. For this reason, most channel programs are tiered. The most productive partners occupy the highest level, which has the greatest margin, marketing funds, and other benefits. The purpose of tiering is to reward the top 20 percent of your partners for the business they bring in. Other partners receive less, depending on their contribution.

Most channel programs have one or two levels; some have as many as three or four. These are relative levels of importance and benefits within the channel program itself. (Make certain not to confuse *program tiers* with the multi-tiered *distribution* we discussed in the previous chapter.) As we descend from the upper to the lower levels, both the margin and the partner program benefits decline with each tier. For example, partner marketing fund accrual will decrease, and deal registration may not be available to the lowest-tier partners.

A common naming scheme for partner tiers is "precious metals": gold is the top tier, followed by silver and bronze. Some companies have a fourth, lowest level for "registered partners," who may sign up just to sell a single deal. The most significant factor in determining a partner's level is its revenue contribution. This contribution can be based on either historical performance or contractual agreement, where partners sign up for a specified level of revenue. In addition to a revenue commitment, suppliers usually require a certain number of the partner's sales and technical staff to have completed formalized training and become certified. This demonstrates a partner's investment in the supplier's business. Table 1 illustrates typical benefits for a four-level program, with gold partners receiving the highest margin and the most benefits.

Table 1: Example partner program overview with four levels

Benefit	Gold	Silver	Bronze	Registered
Margin	30%	25%	20%	No
Partner Marketing Funds	Yes	Yes	No	No
Partner Portal	Yes	Yes	Yes	Yes
Online Training	Yes	Yes	Yes	Yes
Certification	Yes	Yes	No	No
Partner Logo	Yes	Yes	Yes	Yes

Channel programs should be designed to allow channel partners to "graduate" to the next tier if their revenue can justify it and if they are willing to commit the requisite sales and technical resources. The opposite is also true—channel sales management may need to downgrade a partner that is not hitting its targets. In some cases, partners are "sunsetted"—removed entirely from the program.

Creating and Building a Channel Partner Program

Creating and building a channel involves a great deal of work. Companies need to locate the best partners in the market (based on the profiling discussed in the last chapter), train them so they are effective, and keep them happy so they stick around and don't defect to the competition. A well thought-out channel partner program can help accomplish these objectives. A simple framework that encapsulates these is *recruit, ramp,* and *retain.* Channel partner programs must address all three of these steps, and they must have assets and activities designed for the partners when partners reach each step. A function within marketing called *channel marketing* is often responsible for creating and managing the channel partner program.

Partner *recruitment* can be conducted directly by the company or by a VAD who performs this task on behalf of the company. In the latter arrangement, the VAD selects the VAR from its existing stable of resellers. Once the partner managers have agreed on a profile of a desired partner, they meet with prospective partners to recruit them into the program. To expedite this process, suppliers should create a brochure aimed at prospective partners, along with a presentation that they can use during recruitment meetings. These materials should contain details on market opportunity, business opportunities for the partner—including the margin and any value-added services the partner can expect to sell—and a description of the program's benefits.

Once the partners are on board, they need to be *ramped*, meaning brought up to speed or made effective, as quickly as possible. Because partners have businesses to run and are likely selling products from several vendors, training them to be effective will probably take several months or fiscal year quarters more than training a company salesperson. Training is the most important aspect of ramping. Partners should receive both sales and technical training. In-person training is ideal in the beginning phases of a partnership. After partners have mastered the fundamentals, they can receive follow-up training via online courseware. Ideally, sales or marketing will route a few opportunities to the partners to get them started and to excite them about the business.

After the partners are up to speed and have transacted some business, the final step is to *retain* them. Retention is often referred to as "channel loyalty," and companies often incorporate specific channel-loyalty activities into their overall channel marketing programs. Many companies make the mistake of leaving partners to fend for themselves after they have been ramped. They maintain they have done more than enough and they are paying the partners good money, but they see the relationship sour. Again, just like salespeople, partners need to be praised and motivated. Marketing and the partner managers should collaborate to help the partner create demand generation campaigns utilizing the company's channel-ready assets. In addition, many supplier companies create partner loyalty programs that award the partners' sales reps cash or prizes for successfully selling the companies' products. They also offer rebates and other financial incentives to top partners with impressive track records to encourage them to do even more.

Funding Channel Partner Marketing

Though channel partners can buy products at discounted rates, vendors still need to invest to help them generate demand. Recall that we identified three basic models for funding channel marketing activities: market development funds, contra-revenue funds, and co-op funds. These are distinctive models, but businesspeople commonly confuse them. Therefore, you must be careful to specify to the partner exactly what kind of funding your company offers.

Market development funds (MDF) are distributed to partners in advance of sales. Their purpose is to help develop the market or markets a channel partner serves. To receive MDF, partners are expected to submit a plan that explains how they will utilize these monies, and they must seek approval from the vendor's channel marketing or sales team. Vendors typically employ MDF to spur growth efforts in new markets, such as new territories.

In the simplest case, companies allocate MDF funds before a channel partner achieves a steady run rate selling the company's products. The key word is *develop*. To help partners establish a pipeline, a company makes MDF available for activities such as renting marketing lists, creating direct marketing materials, and running ads. The funding amount is negotiated between the vendor and partner, with the partner usually providing a simple marketing plan for the vendor to approve.

In contrast to MDF, *contra-revenue (contra) funds* are distributed to vendors who are already selling the company's products at a steady clip. Partners accrue these funds as a percentage of the total revenue they generate by selling these products. The percentage is usually low single digits—typically 1 to 3 percent—and is tied to the partner program tier. In tiered partner programs, the highest-level partners receive the largest percentage of funds. This arrangement both rewards the most productive partners and incentivizes them to maintain their status. It also ensures that the vendor invests its contra funds in partners that have a proven track record and that the vendor feels confident will effectively move its products.

Even though contra funds are automatically accrued, partners need to be held accountable for how they spend these monies. When a partner wants to redeem/get paid, it submits a request for approval. To avoid frustration, the partner program should have guidelines in place for acceptable marketing activities and programs. These guidelines are entirely up to the supplier. A company might decide, for example, that purchasing tee shirts or branded tsotchkes is not something they will authorize. Contra funds also expire after a certain period, typically six months, to limit the supplier's financial liability. CFOs don't like unclaimed and growing liabilities on the books.

Finally, companies use *co-op (cooperative) funds* for shared-cost initiatives, such as advertising and direct mail. In most cases, the supplier and the channel partner split the total costs fifty-fifty. Perhaps the best known co-op program is the Intel Inside advertising co-op program, where Intel assumes some of the advertising costs for PC manufacturers. In return, the manufacturers agree to include the Intel Inside logo in their print ads and to incorporate a three-second, five-note Intel Inside tone into their television commercials.* Though the distinctions can be a bit blurry, vendors usually allocate co-op funds for activities it prescribes, like including a logo in an ad. In contrast, it makes MDF funds available for activities proposed by channel partners.

This distinction notwithstanding, partners can utilize MDF, contra, and co-op funds for a variety of activities, including events, direct marketing, and promotions. They can also use these funds to purchase demo equipment, not-for-resale (NFR) software licenses, and, in some cases, necessary training that the vendor does not provide as part of the partner program.

A word of caution on all of the partner marketing fund types. Many people use the term MDF generically to mean any type of partner funding. Some confuse contra-revenue and co-op funds. Make sure you clarify in your materials and discussions to avoid potential frustration down the line.

Other Incentives – Rebates and Funded Heads

In addition to co-op funds, MDF, and deal registration margin incentives, companies offer rebates to motivate their partners and create channel loyalty. A *rebate* is an amount paid by way of reduction, return, or refund on monies that have already been spent or contributed. In the specific context of the channel, rebates are monies a supplier returns or refunds to a channel partner after the sale if the partner has reached certain milestones or targets. Rebates are in addition to the agreed-upon margin a partner receives.

Vendors typically employ rebates to drive certain sales behaviors—typically hitting clearly defined revenue targets. For example, a gold partner for table 1 above would always get a 30 percent margin on products sold. The supplier might, for example, decide to pay an *additional* 5 percent rebate to gold partners to drive sales of a certain product during the final quarter of its fiscal year to boost revenues. Rebates are usually expressed as percentages,

---

* The advertising results were stunning. Intel's research indicated that only 24 percent of European PC buyers were familiar with the Intel Inside logos as of late 1991. One year later that figure had grown to nearly 80 percent, and by 1995 it had soared to 94 percent and continues at these high levels today.

and they are redeemed "on the back end"—in other words, after deals have been sold. In the above example, the partner would receive its 30 percent margin (the difference between the partner's buy price and the list price) as soon as it is paid by the customer, and receive the 5 percent after the sale from the supplier.

Companies should structure rebates so that partners need to claim them, as opposed to paying them out automatically. This system ensures that partners remain engaged and avoids situations where checks just show up and confuse partners who inadvertently hit goals (which does happen). Rebates can be stacked, so that a partner that hits 105 percent of target keeps going to hit a rebate incentive for 110 percent of target. Rebates can also be structured to drive other types of behavior, including close rate, product mix, accreditation course score increases—even MDF utilization.

Suppliers will sometimes go so far as to pay the salaries of employees of a VAD, LAR, or VAR. This arrangement is known as a *funded head*, and larger resellers and distributors will often seek this benefit from a new supplier. The benefit for the reseller or distributor, who both are very sensitive to their margins, is the obvious cost offset. The benefit for the supplier is to have someone dedicated to its business inside the partner. Despite this benefit, however, some suppliers perceive funded heads as an extortionist tactic by their partners, who are already making a good margin. Whether the competitive and mindshare benefits warrant the cost of a funded head is a business decision that each company needs to make.

Partner Scorecards

Every company measures the total bookings brought in by each channel partner. However, most companies do not do a good job of measuring the value add of each partner. This deficiency can create problems down the line, when management is reviewing the costs of supporting the channel—both margin costs and channel partner program costs. As discussed, many companies exhibit a bias—inherited from the sales team—that the partner is not earning its keep. Rather, the partner is essentially taking deals that sales already worked and getting paid simply for creating the quote and sending an invoice.

In reality, there are channel partners who do just this, and they are probably not the ones you want to work with. Rather, you should pursue channel partners that are actively engaged in your business, investing in it, and finding new opportunities.

So, how do you differentiate the proactive partners from the passive ones? The answer is to utilize a practice known as *partner scoring*. This process scores channel partners on an ongoing basis based on both their skills and their involvement in deals. Partners can be scored on a number of measurable attributes:

- Total revenue generated

- Number of deals or opportunities originated

- Number of installations completed

- Number of certified technical staff

- Number of certified sales staff

- Utilization of partner marketing funds

Scoring is usually a combination of automated scoring from the sales automation system and scores entered by the *channel account manager (CAM)* for that partner. The particular scale a company uses to score partners is not important. What is most important is the *relative* score compared to other channel partners. For example, a partner that books a lot of business, but has a relatively low score, may not be adding much value in terms of business originated or services provided to customers. In contrast, another partner might generate a bit less revenue, but achieve a higher overall score, by training more salespeople and registering more opportunities. In this case, you may want to direct more business or marketing investment to the high-scoring partner and instruct your CAM to find out why your low-scoring but high-bookings customer is not doing more. Utilizing a good CRM and partner portal will help you achieve a better understanding of exactly what a particular partner is contributing to the sale and how. Table 2 presents an example of a *partner scorecard* that a company would use to assess (score) the performance of a value-added reseller of a technical product.

Table 2: A basic channel scorecard for a value-added reseller

Criteria	Performance	Average Performance	Score (1–5)
Revenue	$17,540,000	$12,500,000	4
Registered Opportunities	35	50	2
Installations	120	110	3
Certified Sales Staff	20	15	4
Certified Technical Staff	15	12	4
Marketing Fund Utilization	80%	91%	2

The scorecard lists seven metrics that this supplier uses to track the performance of value-added resellers. Some suppliers employ more detailed metrics, such as average discount and the amount of value-added services sold. The best approach is to keep things simple to start and then add metrics as the need arises. In many cases, it is not feasible to get detailed information from channel partners. For example, if there is a distributor between you and a reseller, or if a reseller chooses not to share detailed information about their business.

This scorecard displays the performance of the partner ("Performance"), along with the average performances of all of the supplier's other resellers ("Average Performance"). The last column lists assessments by the CAM, using an ascending value scale of 1–5. In this example, although the partner is outperforming the average in revenue, it is underperforming in terms of opportunities it originated, shown as "Registered Opportunities." This partner also is utilizing only 80 percent of the available partner marketing funds. The partner seems to have sufficient certified sales and technical staff, and it is capable when it comes to installations. Based on this information, the CAM may conclude that this partner needs to generate more of its own demand by spending more partner marketing dollars. The CAM would then discuss this issue with the partner. Alternatively, seeing its performance compared with its VAR peers could spur this partner into action.

Partner Marketing Plans

Putting in place a joint marketing plan is an effective strategy for aligning channel partners with the supplier. This effort can comprise a part of a joint business plan, which many channel sales leaders ask their partner managers for anyway. The plan should not be onerous to the partner, but detailed enough so that it can be executed and measured..

A good plan should focus on the specific activities needed to drive the business, which typically involve demand generation. The goal is to determine how many leads and opportunities a partner needs and then recommend appropriate marketing activities. Demand generation expertise is a value add from the supplier. A supplier's channel marketing team may even create turnkey programs partners can execute using contra funds, complete with email, direct mail, landing pages or whatever other templates would be needed. The effort required will be paid back just in the reduction of crazy ideas and "bad creative" coming back from partners.

Sharing Information – Partner Portals and Communications

Partner portals are web applications that provide centralized access to information that partners need. Each supplier has its own partner portal. A portal should have all of the product information, pricing detail, training, and opportunity management that a partner needs to transact business. Partner portals are sometimes referred to as *partner relationship management (PRM)* systems, and they may be built on top of the customer relationship management systems that internal salespeople use. Partner portals should contain the following elements:

Detailed product information – Partners should have unfettered access to detailed product information, including configuration options, technical details, and competitive information.

Pricing information – Prices change over time, so the partner portal should contain an up-to-date price list. Because partners may sell products from several companies, they need to access each company's pricing quickly and easily. Companies may also provide pricing and licensing guidelines and calculators to assist partners with pricing issues.

Special promotions and discounts – The details of special discounts and pricing promotions should be prominently displayed to ensure that the partner's reps are aware of them.

Links to training – Online training required for certification, or training on new product offerings, should be easy to access and register for. Companies may also include a schedule for upcoming partner webcasts and regional training events.

Opportunity registration – Partners should be able to enter new opportunities and check on the approval status of their entries directly from the portal.

Links to marketing materials – Any marketing materials that a partner's sales reps need should be accessible, as well as turnkey marketing collateral and other assets. Turnkey marketing programs that allow partners to redeem marketing funds in exchange for a program executed by the supplier on the partner's behalf are becoming increasingly popular.

Links to partner marketing fund information – Partners should be able to access information about their accrued co-op marketing fund balance. They should also be able to submit requests for reimbursement of approved marketing activities from their funds.

In addition to creating and maintaining portals, companies should engage in regular communications with their channel partners. These communications typically take the form of a monthly or quarterly newsletter that includes information on new products, promotions and discounts, selling tips, and other useful information. Going further, most companies are contractually obligated to communicate new product pricing information within a set period before a new product release—usually one to two months.

Channel-Ready Collateral and Programs

Companies should provide marketing collateral that partners can co-brand and pass on to their customers. These materials are commonly called "co-brandable" or "through channel" assets. *Through channel* describes an asset, like a data sheet, that a vendor creates and a channel partner passes *through* to the end prospect. Assets designed for the channel, like recruiting brochures, are called "to channel" assets. The most common through-channel assets are data sheets, product brochures, and direct mail pieces, but in reality, any asset can be made co-brandable. The simplest method is to provide partners with editable files, including design guidelines, into which they can insert their logo and contact information. Some companies produce slightly different-looking brochures or mailers for their partners, to denote a channel offering or a certified partner, or to give partners a sense of exclusivity.

For smaller partners that do not have a marketing department, or even any marketing staff, providing through-channel assets may not be enough. Some partners may not have staff who are skilled at using the professional design tools needed to add their logo and contact information to a data sheet. More commonly, partners can handle these basic tasks, but they lack experience in managing demand generation activities.

To address this problem, companies should develop turnkey demand generation assets for their partners. For example, the company can create a through-channel direct mail piece, complete with an offer. The partner's only responsibility is to decide who to send the direct mail to. In the case where the partner also needs a list of contacts, companies may provide the services of a list broker as well. The most advanced companies allow a partner to select a piece, upload or purchase a list, and have it managed by a bonded mail house—all from the partner portal. Although these services involve a lot of work, companies that provide them to their partners understand they will be getting a much better return on their partner marketing dollars while providing their partners with better service. In addition to direct mail pieces, complete kits for webinars or "seminars in a box" are effective.

Case Study

The luxury watch industry is larger than you might think. According to the Federation of the Swiss Watch Industry, Swiss luxury watch manufacturers—including well-known brands like Rolex, Omega, Cartier, Longines, and Patek Philippe—generated over $23 billion in sales in 2011.

Luxury watch brands sell via the retail channel. Some have showcase stores that help burnish their brands, but by and large, watchmakers sell through department stores and local jewelers. These retailers are known as "authorized dealers" or "authorized agents." Many luxury watch brands choose not to sell via the online channel—a choice made to limit distribution and price competition while sustaining the exclusivity attached to their brands.

Authorized dealers buy watches at a discounted wholesale price and sell them at their manufacturers' suggested retail price (MSRP). Depending on the watch manufacturer, there may be a distributor that represents the brand for a state, country, or region. Luxury watch brands and their distributors have sales representatives, or "reps," that help train authorized dealers, answer their questions, aid with inventory replenishment, keep an eye on their sales, and help make sure the retailer is properly displaying their products. Many watch brands also employ anonymous "secret shoppers"—people who pose as customers and report back to the manufacturer on the experience.

Luxury watch brands are very particular about their authorized dealers. First, the number of retailers—or "doors"—is limited, to create exclusivity as well as to limit price competition. Second, retailers typically must agree to carry a certain minimum number of a brand's models to allow for a good shopping experience. The retailer's sales staff needs to be trained on the watches so they can knowledgeably answer questions.

Luxury goods manufacturers manage their brands very carefully. Items as expensive as a Rolex Submariner or Patek Philippe Reference cost in the neighborhood of $225,000 and require a brand that can support the cost. Authorized dealers must provide an in-store experience that meets a luxury brand's standards. Luxury brands, for example, have a say in store design—giving input to sections of the store that showcase their watches. Luxury watch brands require authorized dealers to commit to store design and watch display requirements in their contracts. Some brands require a certain case size—measured in linear feet—dedicated to their watches. Rolex pushes for the display of the Rolex logo on the wall closest to the watch display case, and that certain materials and finishes are used on the wall. Luxury watch manufacturers usually send window and in-case displays to retailers several times a year, reflecting new lines or seasonal themes.

Luxury watch brands also provide marketing support. This is especially important in a channel made up of small businesses that typically have no marketing staff. Also, luxury watch channel programs usually offer co-op advertising money. In the case of local retailers, this is usually spent on newspaper and out-of-home advertising. I recently noticed a Patek Philippe billboard on my commute home from work. The billboard also highlighted the name and address of a local jeweler—an authorized Patek Philippe door. Knowing how expensive billboards can be, I asked my local jewelry store owner about it. The watch brand and the jeweler split the cost fifty-fifty. Watchmakers can also tailor newspaper advertisements to include a local retailer's address, and even help with ad insertion.

Channels are important to just about any business, from low-price commodities to luxury goods. Though the products and markets are very different, the basic functions—distribution, training and support, demand creation, and quality control—are remarkably similar.

Chapter 20

Test and Measure – Lather, Rinse, Repeat

"You can't manage what you can't measure" is a favorite management maxim. It is commonly attributed to the legendary manufacturing quality guru William Deming, although nobody is certain who really coined it. Regardless of whether Deming actually said it, however, he would no doubt agree that in marketing, as in any process-oriented task, measurement is a natural precondition to improvement. Professional marketers should take heed. Marketing efficacy can be improved only through continual testing and measurement.

Marketers should utilize empirical tests for two fundamental purposes: to make informed decisions and to track progress over an extended period of time. There is no shortage of marketing elements to test. Among the most basic are the following:

- E-mail subject lines
- Ad headlines and copy
- Calls to action
- Offers
- Lead capture form length
- Landing page design
- Web page design

Put simply, the amount of marketing data that can be analyzed represents an embarrassment of riches. Practically every buyer behavior—whether call, click, search, or scan—is at our disposal.

This chapter opens with a discussion of the culture of testing and measurement and how to shift an organization toward it. It then describes specific test methods, followed by methods for measuring different marketing programs. It concludes with an overview of marketing benchmarks for comparing your marketing effectiveness with your competition's and how to use these assessments to adjust your overall marketing mix.

Shifting to a Test-and-Measurement Culture

A major challenge for most marketing teams is to make testing and measurement a standard component of their culture. Marketing is not manufacturing, after all. Testing and measurement cannot be performed on an ad hoc basis. Rather, they have to be continuous, with the end goal of refining the marketing program over time.

In Benjamin Cheever's novel *The Plagiarist*, a marketing executive becomes an industry legend by adding one word to shampoo bottles: repeat. This single action doubles shampoo sales overnight. You will find this advice on shampoo bottles today. It has stuck in our lexicon as a humorous way of saying that a certain set of instructions should be repeated until an explicit goal is reached. The same instructions apply to a test-and-measurement culture: test, measure, repeat.

There are several good reasons for marketers to test as much data as they can, as frequently as they can. Here are just a few:

- ◆ To outperform the competition – If your competitors don't conduct ongoing testing, they may be wasting money, producing ineffective marketing materials, or both. For this reason, integrating testing into your marketing culture can provide your marketing team—and your company—with a key competitive advantage.

- To spend money more wisely – Understanding which ads, creatives, web pages, or other elements appeal to customers will enable you to allocate more dollars to them.

- Avoid costly missteps – Imagine a scenario in which your CEO is in love with an ad concept, but it falls flat with your customers and prospects. Unfortunately, you have already paid the agency to create and place the ad. Testing in advance can help you to avoid these very expensive mistakes.

- Bring empirical proof to your peers – When marketing programs are not supported with test results, their quality and impact can be discussed only in a subjective way, where everyone's opinion carries equal weight. To avoid opinion-based debates, provide all involved parties with test results. Which ads did the focus group prefer? Which creatives pulled better?

How to Test

Testing in marketing is not rocket science. In fact, as simple as the two primary test methodologies are, it's surprising they are not employed more often.

A/B Testing

A/B testing—also known as *split testing* and *bucket testing*—is a very simple tool that marketers use to evaluate which of two versions of a marketing asset is more effective. The process is straightforward: Create two variants of the asset you want to test, and then measure the response for each variant. The variant with the higher relative performance is the winner and should be used. If you are testing an online asset, chances are your marketing automation tool can help you measure views, clicks, opens, conversions, or whatever responses you are looking to assess.

In the case of direct mail, rather than simply splitting your list of potential respondents in half, start with a subset. That way you are not sending 50 percent of your total list the losing variant, just 50 percent of the smaller subset. After measuring which version of the direct mail this group preferred, use that variant for the balance of your total list. For example, select one hundred contacts from a list of one thousand; then send version A of the direct mail to fifty, and version B of the direct mail to fifty. Measure the response. Send the winning version to the remaining nine hundred.

Figure 1 below shows two banner ads created for a North Carolina–based hospital. The A version of the ad showed a nurse, and the B version showed a cancer survivor and her child. All other copy stayed the same. The version with the nurse outperformed the other with 63 percent more click-throughs. The nurse showed compassion and confidence. Changing just one element of an ad can have a significant impact.

Figure 1: A/B testing banner ads

Effective marketing teams adopt an iterative approach, constantly tweaking and testing, using best practices, and incorporating knowledge gleaned in previous tests into all future marketing work. Building on the direct mail example above, a second test comparing the winner of the first A/B test versus a modified variant of that winner should always be done. Significantly, although A/B testing is simple in concept and relatively easy to execute, many marketing teams lack the discipline to conduct it. Test, measure, repeat.

Focus Group

Gauging opinion before investing significant sums in a marketing effort is always a good idea. Though marketers sell to buyers located outside their walls, they make the mistake of talking only among themselves. Remember: No one in your building is a proxy for a customer. Talk to a real one!

The best strategy for communicating directly to customers is via a focus group. A focus group is a form of qualitative research in which the individuals conducting the exercise ask a group of people about their perceptions, opinions, beliefs, and attitudes toward a product, a service, a concept, an advertisement, or an idea. The first focus group—then known as "the focused interview"—was conducted by sociologist Robert K. Merton at Columbia University's Bureau of Applied Social Research.* In 1943, Merton and his colleague Paul Lazarsfeld conducted the first focused interviews to measure the effects of "mass persuasion" radio announcements aimed at selling war bonds, on what was to become Voice of America.[52]

Focus groups can take a number of forms. Typically they are small groups comprised of six to ten people, plus a facilitator. The group setting helps spark conversation, and the facilitator keeps the conversation moving, prevents any single participant from dominating, and ensures that all of the questions or topics are covered. A marketing or research team typically observes the session through a one-way mirror.

In recent years, online focus groups have become more popular. A common format is for the facilitator to ask questions or show visuals online—using an application similar to one used for webcasting—and for the participants to reply using online chat or voting tools. Major benefits of online focus groups are lower costs for the marketers and greater convenience for the participants. The major drawback is that the marketers observing the session lose the ability to observe body language, facial expressions, and other forms of nonverbal communication, which can be as revealing as spoken language.

---

* The focus group was but one of Merton's contributions to the world. He also coined the terms "role model" and "self-fulfilling prophecy."

The results gained from focus groups can be very powerful. Companies can utilize the feedback to make decisions ranging from how to package an individual product to how to frame an entire campaign. They can also get ideas for new products or features. Importantly, focus groups bring the customer's voice back into the company. This ensures that the opinions of insiders—even powerful executives—do not overshadow those of the target customers. Even obtaining feedback from a handful of existing customers via phone or e-mail can have a powerful effect.

How to Measure

Web Measurement

Website statistics are an indicator of customer behavior, though they generally need to be interpreted. Most marketing teams use these data to reveal online awareness trends and optimize both online advertising spend and lead capture and online purchases. Marketers have access to a number of tools—some free, like Google Analytics—that can measure and report on web statistics. The frequency of reporting will vary by business, with online businesses reporting daily or weekly, and other organizations reporting on a monthly basis. Below we list some of the most common measures:

- ◆ Pageviews – The total number of pages viewed during the time period.

- ◆ Visitors – Typically the total number of visits, unique visits, and the location of the visitors.

- ◆ Time on site – The amount of time a user spends on the site. A high score can be a good sign (your site is so useful that people spend a long time on it) or a bad sign (it is difficult to navigate, so customers take a long time to find what they're looking for).

- ◆ Bounce rate – The percentage of single-page visits, or visits in which the person left—"bounced"—from your site back to the page he or she came from. Marketers use this metric to measure visit quality: a high bounce rate generally indicates that site entrance pages were not relevant to your visitors.

+ Form or shopping cart abandonment – The percentage of visitors who abandon a form while they are in the process of signing up for an offer, or who fail to complete a transaction and abandon their shopping cart. The major reasons why visitors abandon forms is that they are too long or the offers they contain don't stand out. Visitors abandon shopping carts for assorted reasons: Shipping costs are too high, visitors discover better offers through comparison shopping, the transaction requires too much personal information, or the process takes too long. Sometimes buyers simply change their minds. E-commerce sites devote a great deal of time to analyzing their checkout process to reduce shopping cart abandonment.

+ Referrals – A list of websites that refer people to your site. The most common sources of referrals are search engines, online news sites, advertisements, blogs, and partner sites. Effective marketers use this information to shift their ad spending to sites that generate referrals, work on linking with more popular referrers, or optimize content to align with likely referrers.

+ Popular pages and links – A ranked list of the most popular content on your site, whether a page or a link to an asset. This information is a good indicator of which content may no longer be useful, which content may need to be moved or highlighted, and which content or products buyers are most interested in.

+ Top site-search terms – A ranked list of the popular search terms visitors use once they are on your website. This information can reveal which items the market is looking for, which search terms buyers are using, and which information the company should highlight, or uplevel, on its site so that prospects and customers can find it more easily.

- Backlinks – Inbound links to your website or to a page on your site. Having a large number of backlinks from high-quality sites increases the likelihood that search engines will direct visitors to your pages. Tracking backlinks and working to build more of them is a common SEO strategy.

- Site rank – The ranking of the popularity of a website by a third-party service, such as Alexa or comScore. Site rank is generally more important for companies whose web presence is vital to their business, such as e-commerce, gaming, and news organizations. It can also be used to gauge how an organization's online presence compares to its competitors'.

There are many, many more measurements. Which ones you use will depend on your company, whether you sell online, and the level of detail you need.

Measuring Demand Generation

A company should measure all of its lead information in a standard fashion to identify which activities are contributing the most to the funnel. What exactly should they measure? The following list identifies the key variables:

- Source – the program or source of the lead

- Conversion rate – the percentage of inquiries that converted to marketing qualified leads, or MQLs

- Lead flow – the total number of MQLs

- Cost per lead – the amount each MQL cost to generate (Recall from chapter 9 that this is also known as cost per acquisition, or CPA.)

- Velocity/time to conversion – the number of days from inquiry to opportunity

Table 1: Reporting on effectiveness of marketing activities

Source	Inquiries	Cost	% MQL	Velocity (Days)	MQL to Opp. Index
3rd Party Email Blast	9,049	$36	20%	32	0.5
Trade Show	3,786	$36	22%	29	1.8
Trade Show – Virtual	3,125	$18	17%	48	1.0
Paid Webinar	1,971	$71	26%	33	0.7
PPC Advertising	1,494	$135	45%	15	1.8
Salesforce AppExchange	1,128	$41	72%	3	2.4
Content Syndication	881	$69	18%	29	1.2
Social Media	588	$94	33%	16	0.2
Other Paid	1,645	$45	25%	32	0.9
Website/Inbound	5,133	NA	58%	9	1.9
Referral/WOM	564	NA	21%	32	1.4
Sales Prospecting	349	NA	19%	71	3.9

Used by Permission of Marketo, Inc.

Table 1 provides a good example of how a company can identify which marketing tactics are performing well and which ones are not. In this example, the marketing team has set high, average, and low performance thresholds for each measure, shown in green, black, and red, respectively.

Total inquiries ("Inquiries") and cost per lead ("Cost") are shown in the second and third columns. Right away, you can see, based on the color-coding, that pay-per-click ad costs (in red) are significantly higher than the hundred-dollar threshold for cost per lead, whereas third-party e-mail blasts, trade shows, and virtual trade shows (in green) are significantly lower than the forty-dollar threshold (note that these threshold values are just examples;

every company will have its own). The table does not display explicit costs for "run rate" activities (website/inbound leads, referral/WOM leads, and sales generated leads) since there are ongoing costs.

The percentage of inquiries that convert to MQLs in the fourth column (% MQL) is similarly color-coded, with less than 20 percent being low, 20 to 40 percent being average, and above 40 percent being high. We can see that PPC, while costly, is effective: nearly half of the prospects became MQLs. In contrast, content syndication is not cost-effective, nor does it convert well. Although there are more elaborate graphical models for illustrating program effectiveness, I prefer this color-coded tabular representation, which I became aware of via the work of Jon Miller at Marketo.

In addition to the above, table 1 illustrates two other interesting metrics. The first—*velocity*—represents the average number of days required to convert a lead to an opportunity. Understanding velocity is important when deciding when to employ various tactics. For example, if sales management feels its pipeline is low and needs more quickly, then marketing should shift investment to tactics with a high velocity that will generate more pipeline quickly, even if they are more expensive. In the example above, an organization could easily reallocate budget to PPC advertising, which has a velocity of fifteen days.

The second metric—the *MQL-to-opportunity index*—indicates the likelihood of conversion *relative* to other programs. In table 1, virtual trade shows was selected as the baseline index, and normalized to equal 1. The MQL-to-opportunity indexes for all of the other sources were then normalized using the same weighting. The idea is to pick a source and make its index equal 1 to make comparison among sources easier. Relative to virtual trade shows, then, trade shows are 1.8 times more likely to convert, and leads from the Salesforce AppExchange are 2.4 times more likely to convert. Social media and third-party e-mail blasts have a lower than average likelihood of converting.

Marketers can use the combination of cost, velocity, and lead-to-opportunity to make informed decisions about their marketing mix. Rather than discuss tactics in the abstract, direct comparisons of cost and efficacy can be made. Social media, while trendy, is not very cheap and not very effective, as shown in the example above. PPC advertising is very expensive, but also very effective (high conversion, high velocity, high MQL-to-opportunity-index). Sharing these metrics with sales management is a great way to show how marketing is driving the business, and to avoid uninformed requests from sales for new marketing efforts.

Measuring PR and Social Media

Chapters 5 and 6 covered measurement of press and social media in detail. To recap, the marketing team should measure the following media elements on a regular basis:

- Share of voice and press sentiment
- Total press mentions
- Clicks on the press releases, blogs, and web pages linked to from press releases and blogs
- Social media stats – tweets, retweets, Facebook "likes," social sentiment, and others

Measuring Advertising

Depending on the type of advertising your company is running, you may already be measuring its effectiveness. Referrals to your website may be coming from SEM keyword or banner ads. You may also be measuring the conversion rates of direct-response advertising in direct mail offers you send out—hopefully evaluating different subjects and offers in your A/B testing.

Below are the most common metrics, which were discussed in chapter 13. Unless your specific goal is to raise awareness of a new product or brand, you should focus on conversion rates, because they are the most precise measurement of qualified leads:

- Impressions, aka ad views – The total number of times an ad is available for view.

- Share of voice – The percentage of available ad inventory your company purchased. Measuring SOV online, sometimes called *impression share*, is easier. The percentage of times an online ad unit appears compared to the number of times it could have been shown, based on the total available ad space inventory, is the SOV. Off-line, companies calculate estimates based on the total amount of money spent, for example, the amount spent on print advertising in national newspapers.

- Click-through rate – The percentage of viewers of an online ad who clicked on it.

- Conversion rate – The percentage of viewers who took the desired action to achieve the business outcome, whether subscribing, registering, or actually purchasing something.

Marketing Program Mix

Using the metrics discussed above, a head of marketing can measure each program's effectiveness and return on investment. Certain programs will stand out as winners, while others will drop to the bottom. Analyzing the mix of programs on a regular basis will help marketing to optimize its spending and enhance its contributions to the top line.

Analyzing the marketing program mix will also help battle two common marketing problems—the "sacred cow" and the "budget rut." The sacred cow, or "we always do that show," can be a problem in marketing. People get attached to certain events, reports, tools—even vendors. Program analysis can help break this counterproductive pattern by providing statistical evidence that these treasured programs are not as effective as others.

The budget rut occurs when individual marketing teams get comfortable with their annual budgets and expect to receive the same level of funding in the coming years. Becoming accustomed to an annual budget—the rut—can squeeze other, potentially more successful tactics and programs. Using statistics to demonstrate a lack of efficacy on the part of these programs can help justify budget shifts.

There will always be marketing activities that don't contribute directly to a lead and therefore to revenue. A head of marketing can assign a value to a program based on its contribution to a "marketing-assisted lead," which contributes indirectly. Alternatively, he or she can set aside a certain amount of funding for "keeping the lights on" functions, such as maintaining the website, as well as awareness and influence programs like PR and AR.

Marketing Benchmarks

Tracking performance over time will, of course, let you know if your marketing performance is improving or worsening. In addition, using A/B testing to identify the relative performance of assets, headlines, web pages, and other tools. The questions remain, though: How will your organization know where it stands against industry norms, and how much potential improvement is possible? That's where marketing benchmarks—norms collected from a number of marketing organizations—come in.

There are a number of organizations that produce annual benchmark reports, including the Corporate Executive Board, Forrester Research, MarketingSherpa, and SiriusDecisions. These companies create benchmarks for a broad range of categories, including lead conversion, time spent on websites, ad click-through rates, direct marketing efficacy by media, and many others. Some organizations—and publications—also survey buyers on how they like to be marketed to, what they pay attention to, and how they find information about products they buy.

Marketing benchmarks are also very useful in the budgeting process. Based on these data, you may decide, for example, to shift funds from an area that is performing above average to one that needs more help. Benchmarks can help defend your overall marketing budget by demonstrating that your organization is more effective, and hopefully more cost-effective, than your competition.

Learning More

◆ Eric Peterson, *Web Site Measurement Hacks* (San Francisco:O'Reilly, 2005).

Chapter 21

Showing Results – ROMI, Dashboards, KPIs, and Forecasting

Many marketing teams struggle to demonstrate their value. Marketing is often judged by executives who have no marketing experience and operate under basic misconceptions concerning the marketing function. Moreover, these biases can affect marketing's working relationships with other teams. For these reasons, it is critical for marketing to objectively demonstrate its contributions to the business. Creating cool ads and splashy events may be fun, but metrics have a longer-lasting and harder-hitting impact on corporate decision makers.

Heads of marketing need to understand that one of their fundamental responsibilities is to demonstrate to the executive team or the board of directors what these executives are getting for their money. Beware the CFO who perceives marketing essentially as a giant cost center. Truly effective marketing heads use metrics to their advantage by turning the conversation around, demonstrating how additional investments in marketing can grow the top line. These are conversations CFOs can understand, just as they understand the impact of hiring more salespeople or opening a new factory. These conversations must involve numbers, however, because numbers are the language that executives understand. This is why metrics are so important.

In the last chapter, we discussed the range of activities that marketing can measure. These measurements are all metrics, but they may not be metrics that a CEO or VP of sales cares about. For example, far too many B2B marketing teams show their CEOs monthly website traffic stats without exhibiting a discernible connection to revenue generation. Though marketing benchmarks are critical to demonstrate the science of the marketing profession, trying to dazzle executives with too much marketing jargon can backfire. Rather than attempting to overwhelm your executives with impressive aggregations of data, I recommend that you select a few key metrics, or *key performance indicators (KPIs)*, and share them via a dashboard. I also recommend that you choose KPIs that are both indicators of marketing's contribution to the business and data that marketing tracks on behalf of the business.

This chapter will discuss marketing and business metrics that a head of marketing should consider tracking. It will also explain how to use these metrics in dashboards and forecasts to demonstrate marketing's value to the overall business.

Marketing Metrics

This discussion of metrics is divided into two sections—marketing metrics and business metrics. *Marketing metrics* measure the effectiveness of marketing efforts on the business. *Business metrics* are measures of the business collected by marketing.

ROMI

Return on marketing investment, or ROMI, is a straightforward metric that directly addresses the question of what marketing is doing to drive the business. Just as return on investment (ROI) is a measure of the profit earned from any investment, ROMI is a measure of the profit earned from marketing investment. ROMI is calculated as:

$$\frac{(\text{Incremental Revenue Attributable to Marketing} \times \text{Margin} - \text{Marketing Investment})}{\text{Marketing Investment}}$$

The first variable, incremental revenue attributable to marketing, is exactly as it sounds. A CMO should take care not to include recurring or guaranteed revenue, since it would come in even if marketing did nothing. Also, any revenue from opportunities that were not marketing sourced or influenced should not be included.

Multiplying this revenue number by margin gives you your gross profit. It is important to use gross profit, and not total revenue, because there are other costs involved in generating revenue, such as salespeople, channel margins, and the cost of manufacturing the product. These other costs are known collectively as *cost of goods sold*, or COGS, and is usually expressed as a percentage. Margin is 100 percent minus your COGS. You can obtain COGS and margin from your CFO.

For example, a marketing campaign costing $100,000 that brought in $800,000 for a company with a margin of 75 percent would be calculated as follows:

$$\frac{(\$800,000 \times .75 - \$100,000)}{\$100,000} = \frac{(\$600,000 - \$100,000)}{\$100,000} - 500\%$$

The $600,000 represents $800,000 in new revenue less 25 percent COGS (75 percent margin).

ROMI needs to be utilized carefully so it does not appear as if the marketing department is taking credit for work done by an organization overall. Make sure you can tie a ROMI calculation to a discrete marketing initiative with measurable, incremental revenues, such as a holiday campaign. In general, measuring ROMI for demand generation is more concrete than for other programs.

Some companies prefer to use the *customer lifetime value (CLV)* instead of gross profit. CLV is the expected revenue a customer will generate during his or her time as a customer, or "lifetime."* This methodology is well

---

* There are many ways to calculate CLV, and the math can get a bit hairy, so I will spare you the details. Basically, CLV is an average expected revenue for the first year, minus some attrition for the second year and beyond, plus any increase in purchase behavior for the average remaining customer. You can segment customers based on their CLV as well, say by grouping big spenders and average Joes. Building a CLV model with your CFO and VP of sales is a good idea.

suited for service-oriented businesses that charge an annual subscription, or services that customers typically remain with for a long period of time, such as credit cards and bank accounts. The formula for calculating ROMI using CLV is:

$$\frac{(\text{Customer Lifetime Value - Marketing Investment})}{\text{Marketing Investment}}$$

ROMI is easier to calculate on a per-initiative basis than for the overall marketing spend. That's because many of the activities paid for in the overall marketing spend are indirect influences on buyer behavior, such as brand advertising. ROMI is obviously a good way to compare one program to another, and measuring ROMI for each program is a good marketing discipline. It may also prove useful to compare year-over-year improvements in ROMI for the marketing function as a whole to indicate its overall effectiveness.

Awareness

As covered in previous chapters, share of voice is a term used both in public relations and in advertising. It refers to the exposure of your company or product (your share) compared to that of your competitors. In PR, it is the number of stories written or aired about your company or product. These stories can appear in newspapers, trade publications, television, radio, and, increasingly, blogs and other online media. The idea is that you want your voice to stand out among all the other voices flogging products or ideas.

SOV can be measured by your PR or advertising agency for articles and ads, respectively. There are also a number of services that you can subscribe to that will track and measure SOV. The metric is typically illustrated as a pie chart that compares your SOV against your top competitors'. Some services also measure cost per thousand people reached. You can utilize this metric to evaluate the efficacy of your PR efforts. Figure 1 is an SOV report for Symantec versus its top three competitors in the data loss prevention market, gathered by our PR team during my tenure there. Based on our majority share, we kept the PR activities steady and worked on beefing up other areas of our marketing mix.

Figure 1: Share of voice (SOV)

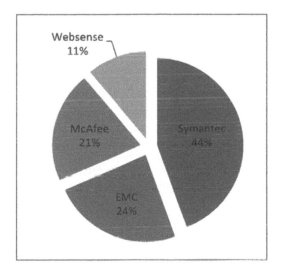

Marketing-Sourced and Marketing-Influenced Pipeline

Marketing-sourced pipeline measures the percentage of leads in the pipeline that were uniquely created by marketing. Specifically, these are MQLs that turn into SQLs. The average runs from 10 to 50 percent, and it depends greatly on company size and industry. Newer, smaller companies with no reputation or large installed base of customers will rely more heavily on marketing for demand generation. By way of contrast, established companies with sales representatives dedicated to a discrete list of accounts will shoulder more of the new business generation load. Marketing-sourced pipeline is one of the most direct measures of marketing impact, so every head of marketing should track it closely.

In contrast, *marketing-influenced pipeline* is the percentage of leads touched at least once by marketing during a set period of time; for example, a prospect sourced by a salesperson attends a seminar that furthers the sales process. The average for marketing-influenced pipeline ranges from 25 to more than 75 percent. An important word of advice: Never show marketing-influenced pipeline without also showing marketing-sourced pipeline. The reason? Marketing-influenced pipeline is a softer metric, because it can't prove the lead was actually sourced by marketing. Consequently, it can call into question marketing's overall efficacy. Its lack of precision and provability may also turn off some of the more analytical members of the executive staff. The idea is to use marketing-sourced pipeline to demonstrate marketing's direct contribution, and marketing-influenced pipeline to illustrate how marketing is moving deals along. Ideally, a marketing team can indicate some impact on marketing-influenced pipeline, such as shorter time to close.

Marketing-Sourced and Marketing-Influenced Revenue

Taking things a step further, *marketing-sourced revenue* measures the percentage of closed deals in the pipeline that were uniquely created by marketing. *Marketing-influenced revenue*, in contrast, is the percentage of closed deals that were touched at least once by marketing. Many marketers prefer to show sourced and influenced pipeline metrics over the equivalent revenue metrics, because they provide direct evidence of marketing's contribution without the x factor of sales execution. Creating a "closed loop" reporting on revenue presents a major challenge, because there are factors beyond the control of the marketing organization, like proper input and labeling in the CRM system and the inability to track a sales all the way through the channel.

Investment to Revenue

Finally, *investment to revenue* calculates how many dollars of revenue are generated by every dollar invested in demand generation. Investment to revenue can be more effective than ROMI in executive settings, because it presents the return in dollar terms rather than percentages. Like many things in marketing, presentation matters. The industry average ranges from five to twenty dollars in revenue for every dollar invested in demand creation.

Business Metrics

In addition to data on marketing effectiveness, there are other metrics that marketing ideally should track and report for the business. I will call these metrics "business metrics" as opposed to "marketing metrics," for lack of a more formal term. Let's begin with a fundamental—and rather obvious—metric, namely, market share.

Market Share

As the name suggests, *market share* is the percentage of an industry or market's total sales that a particular company earns over a specified time period. Although market share is not exclusively a measurement of the marketing organization's overall effectiveness, it does reflect how well a company is executing against the Four Ps of marketing. It is also a great tool for sparking executive-level discussions and—in some cases—for increasing your marketing budget if, say, your company is falling behind or sees an opportunity to take share from a competitor.

Large companies in established markets can usually turn to an industry analyst for market share numbers. These data usually come out annually. In smaller industries, marketing can create market share estimates by piecing together the competition's estimated revenue or customer count. Marketers can obtain a great deal of relevant information by examining SEC filings, by polling salespeople who may have recently come over from a competitor, and by talking to partners and consultants who sell or recommend products. A more detailed discussion of market share calculation can be found in chapter 3.

Look-to-Book and Other Industry-Specific Metrics

A *look-to-book* ratio is the number of people who visit a travel website compared with the number who actually make a purchase. This is really a conversion rate that is phrased specifically for the travel industry. Look-to-book is a valuable metric, because it ties so closely to the business. For similar reasons, effective marketers in any business should utilize any industry-specific metrics in their reporting.

Customer Satisfaction and Net Promoter Score

Chapter 7 covered customer satisfaction and Net Promoter Score. Because these metrics are so important to the marketing plan, the question arises: Should marketing own the tracking and reporting of these data? There are other functions in an organization, like customer service, that may be directly tied to these metrics, and perhaps compensated on them. These observations notwithstanding, these data are an overall indicator of the company's strength, and someone needs to own them across the company.

Given the chance, a head of marketing should jump at the opportunity to track and report on customer satisfaction, for a couple of reasons. First, it is a great indicator that marketing is tied directly to the business. Second, satisfied customers are the most powerful advocates a company or brand can have. It is in marketing's interest, therefore, to have as many net promoters in the market as possible. Including these metrics in a dashboard makes sense as a measurement of both the customers' pulse and the likelihood of referrals, renewals, or repeat purchases. Figure 2 shows NPS reporting for a company, overall and individually, for its four business units: BU A, BU B, BU C, and BU D. The results for the current quarter are in gold, and the previous quarter in blue. BU B has a good overall NPS and is improving. BU D does not look so good.

Figure 2: Reporting Net Promoter Score (NPS)

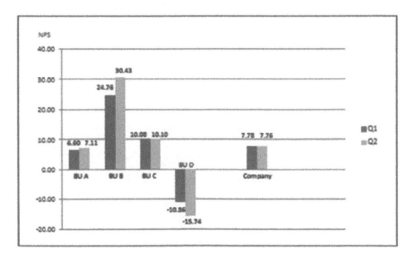

Share of Wallet

Share of wallet is the measurement of a customer's spend within a category that is captured by a given product, brand, or company. Increasing the share of a customer's wallet a company receives can be a more economical strategy for boosting revenue than increasing market share by selling to new customers. Share of wallet is also more insightful than customer satisfaction or net promoter score, because it reflects actual customer purchases. Remember, customers can be very satisfied with a company's product but ultimately select their competitors' products instead. Companies can utilize share of wallet percentage to assess their competitive position, that is, the relative importance of their product or company within their industry. Based on these assessments, they might undertake initiatives to capture a larger share.

Although share of wallet data are extremely valuable, accurate data may be hard to come by. The best method for calculating share of wallet is to survey your customers directly. Unfortunately, not all customers will share this information. In these cases, companies can utilize the services of analysts who provide annual spending information for industry segments. These numbers may not be perfect, but companies can estimate customer spending on their products against them.

A study in *Harvard Business Review* identified another, simpler method for calculating share of wallet.[53] The study discovered that the rank customers assign to a brand, product, or company relative to competitors in the category strongly correlates to that brand, product, or company's share of wallet. Known as the *wallet allocation rule*, this method enables a company to predict its share of wallet based on customer rankings.

Shown in figure 3, calculating share of wallet using the wallet allocation rule can be done in three steps. First, determine how many companies/brands are competing for share of wallet. The example below shows three brands: Acme, Summit, and Pinnacle. Highly fragmented markets will likely have more than three. Next, survey customers, or obtain satisfaction surveys from third parties, and convert the scores into a rank. Collecting this information might be difficult and may warrant hiring an outside firm to conduct the survey. However, asking customers to rank a vendor is more palatable to them than asking how much money they are spending with each. The example below shows rankings of three customers: Tom, Dick, and Harry. Once the rankings are collected, use the wallet allocation rule formula, which will result in a percentage. This is the percent share of wallet for each customer. Finally, simply average each customer's share of wallet for an overall share for each company/brand. As can be seen, Acme has 17 percent, Summit has 44 percent, and Pinnacle has 39 percent.

Figure 3: Wallet allocation rule

Step 1: Rank each company/brand for each customer, based on their relative rank in the survey being used.

	Acme	Summit	Pinnacle
Tom	3	1	2
Dick	3	2	1
Harry	3	1	2

Step 2: Calculate share of wallet for each company/brand and customer combination, using the Wallet Allocation Rule formula below. The first calculation for Tom and Acme is shown at right.

$$\text{Share of Wallet} = \left(1 - \frac{\text{Rank}}{\text{Number of Brands} + 1}\right) \times \left(\frac{2}{\text{Number of Brands}}\right)$$

$$= \left(1 - \frac{3}{3+1}\right) \times \frac{2}{3}$$
$$= \left(1 - 0.75\right) \times 0.67$$
$$= \left(0.25\right) \times 0.67$$
$$= 0.1675, \text{Rounded to } 17\%$$

Step 3: Once calculations for each combination are complete, average across all customers to calculate wallet share for the product/brand.

	Acme	Summit	Pinnacle
Tom	17%	50%	33%
Dick	17%	33%	50%
Harry	17%	50%	33%
	17%	44%	39%

Product Portfolio Owned

Most companies sell more than one product. However, rarely do customers buy all of a company's products at the same time, if ever. The average number of products that a customer or customer segment owns is valuable information.

The opportunity to sell additional products to existing customers is significant to any business. When a company already has a relationship with the customer—assuming the customer is satisfied—then opportunities, in the form of meetings or direct marketing, exist to sell more. Recall that selling additional products is a cost-effective strategy for increasing share of wallet.

Salespeople often use the term *white space* to describe the opportunity to increase sales within the installed based. Marketers refer to a product's *attach rate*, which is the number of complementary products the company sells for each primary product. Marketing teams use white space and the attach rate as inputs to what is known as *installed base marketing*. They frequently design promotions to sell additional products, either by allowing sales reps to cross sell or by allowing customers to upgrade to more advanced or feature-rich products. The latter strategy is known as an *upsell*. Some businesses even set annual goals for the average number of products they want their customers to own.

Using Marketing Benchmarks

How would your CEO answer this question: So, how is your marketing team doing? What would he or she use as the basis for answering the question? Will the answer be subjective, based on certain assumptions concerning what marketing is supposed to do? Or, even worse, will it be based on an unfair comparison to a company with a huge advertising budget that the CEO sees in the *Wall Street Journal*? Hopefully, at the very least, the CEO's opinion will be informed by the pipeline contributions that you have been showing him or her. The best way to answer that question, however, would be to evaluate marketing's contributions to the business and to the industry overall.

Fortunately for marketers, benchmarks are available for all kinds of marketing metrics. Demonstrating that your averages for pipeline contribution, revenue contribution, and investment to revenue are higher than the industry average will give the CEO confidence in the output of the marketing team. Combined with a good market share and market share growth, as well as a positive SOV, these numbers will make him or her smile. Good sources of marketing benchmarks are MarketingSherpa and SiriusDecisions.

Marketing Dashboards

Communicating the effectiveness of marketing programs, whether to your CEO or to the rest of the organization, is a critical skill that any head of marketing needs. Dashboards simplify the task by visually displaying what marketing is doing and how well they are doing it. In addition, the marketing department can use dashboards to facilitate communication across different marketing teams.

A well-designed marketing dashboard starts with an agreement on the key functions of marketing within the organization. Does marketing drive innovation? Customer retention? Brand awareness? Demand? A combination of the above? Sometimes arriving at the answer is an interesting exercise in itself—part cross-functional education on what marketing does, part discussion on what the business requires from marketing. Both activities are positive outcomes in and of themselves, even before the dashboard is created.

After the company achieves a consensus regarding marketing priorities, the next step is to identify KPIs that measure these priorities. An effective dashboard displays these KPIs in a format that is easy to understand. Figure 4 presents a sample dashboard for an organization that sells to other businesses. It combines both marketing and business metrics.

Figure 4: Sample marketing dashboard

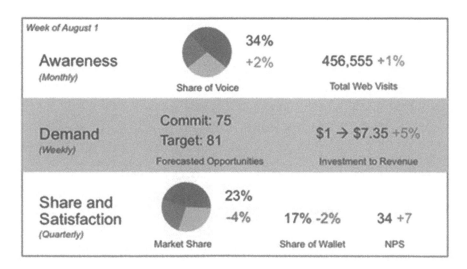

This dashboard has several important design characteristics. First, it includes only seven KPIs. These are the metrics that the company has decided are most important for assessing both marketing's performance and the overall state of the business. Second, the KPIs are clearly categorized by marketing program: awareness (reputation), demand generation (demand), and share and satisfaction (market intelligence). Finally, to reduce clutter, the dashboard employs graphs only where necessary to indicate relative share.

An executive team could use this dashboard as the basis for a productive discussion. Both PR share of voice and website visits—a metric this company values because their customers research their purchases online—seem healthy and are trending upward from the previous month. Demand generation also seems healthy, with the chief marketing officer targeting more opportunities than he or she actually needs to hit the revenue target. Going further, the positive NPS score suggests that the company's customers are satisfied. Despite these positive indicators, however, market share and share of wallet are decreasing. What can account for this discrepancy? Perhaps it is a delay in production. Or, a competitor could be undercutting their price or selling via more distributors. Another possible explanation is that the revenue plan was set too low, enabling competitors to outpace (take more market share) the company's sales teams. Overall, however, figure 4 reflects well on marketing's performance, and it provides information to help the executive team diagnose marketing- and sales-related problems.

Notice that figure 4 does not itself contain all of the underlying data, nor does it display the historical data. These numbers can be provided as needed. Also, share of voice and website visits are marketing metrics, but the table presents them in the context of the business, in a sequence that maps to a typical prospective customer journey (starting with awareness, moving through demand, to measuring the satisfaction of customers). Finally, investment to revenue is included to inform the other executives that marketing is performing efficiently and is generating business rather than simply spending money.

Forecasting

There is a reason why the sales department often has the most prominent role at executive staff and board meetings. The most important topic, regardless of the company's size, is the sales forecast. However exciting the new brand strategy, website, or advertising campaign, sales are a company's lifeline.

Forecasts matter, and accurate forecasting is what executives look for. Sales leaders live and die by the accuracy of their forecasts. Sales leaders are, however, limited in their ability to predict beyond the current quarter. This presents an opportunity for a CMO to step in and present a longer-range forecast. A *marketing forecast* is a multiquarter prediction of opportunities marketing expects to add to the pipeline. In contrast, a sales forecast is a prediction of opportunities that will close in the current quarter (And don't confuse "marketing forecast" with "market forecast," which is a long-term prediction of the growth of a market, usually done by a third-party analyst.)

Table 1: Marketing forecast

	-4	-3	-2	-1	Cur.	+1	+2	+3
Commit	76	79	82	82	85	88	92	94
Target	80	83	86	89	91	94	97	100
Forecast	81	83	86	89	88	90	97	103
Actual	80	85	95	86	91	--	--	--
Attainment	100%	102%	110%	96%	100%	--	--	--

Source: "Marketing Forecasting," Marketo

Table 1 presents an example of a marketing forecast. This format shows forecasted opportunities for the current month ("Cur.") and the next three months, shown as +1, +2, and +3. The table also shows the previous four months as -1, -2, -3, and -4 for comparison purposes. The forecast tracks the following:

Commit – Shown in the top row, the number of opportunities a CMO feels certain he or she can achieve.

Target – Shown in the second row, a higher total than the commit that he or she will drive the marketing team toward. The target is also a hedge: if the marketing team misses the target, they should still hit the commit.

Forecast – The CMO's best estimate, based on current information, about the number of opportunities in the current and next three quarters. The forecast will float either higher or lower than the target and the commit. A CMO would, for example, shift resources if the forecast in any of the next three quarters slips below the commit.

Actual – The actual results allow for evaluation of performance. For example, in the previous month (-1) this CMO's team generated 86 opportunities against a commit of 82. Actuals are not shown for the next three months, as they are not yet known.

Table 1 projects forward using the same calculations the CMO used to calculate how many leads he or she needed: the average MQL to SAL and SAL to SQL conversion rates (you might want to review the discussion of leads in chapter 12). In the current month, the CMO beat the commit of 85 and hit the target of 91. For the next month, shown as +1 across the top, the CMO has a commit of 88, a target of 94, and is forecasting 90. This format can be extended to show revenue in the pipeline by multiplying the opportunities by the average selling price or deal size.

In sum, then, better forecasting by marketing will help any business, regardless of the industry in which it operates. It will also help the marketing department to better justify its budget, particularly when marketing requests additional funding in midyear to help drive the business. Going further, other departments will have more respect for marketing if it provides long-range forecasts. By framing marketing in terms of outputs (revenue) rather than inputs (the marketing budget), marketing can position itself as a revenue center, and not a cost center to be cut.

Learning More

- Patrick LaPointe, *Marketing by the Dashboard Light* (2005).

- Paul W. Farris et al., *Marketing Metrics: 50+ Metrics Every Executive Should Master,* (Philadelphia:Wharton School Publishing, 2007).

- *MarketingNPV Journal* (www.marketingnpv.com)

Chapter 22

Marketing Budgets

V ery little happens in marketing without money. Securing enough money to support an organization's goals is a fundamental responsibility of a CMO or a VP of marketing. Most heads of marketing learn from experience how to get what they need. Unfortunately many of them have to learn the hard way, through errors and inadequate budget allocations. The reality is that many marketing executives simply lack basic skills in building, presenting, and defending budgets. Remember that when an executive team makes budgeting decisions, it needs to consider whether investing in new research, more salespeople, or a new marketing initiative is the best way to spend money. An effective marketing head must be able to convince the team that this is the way to go.

How can marketing accomplish this task? Successful CMOs understand that when they communicate with management, a key strategy is to change the focus of the budgeting conversation from "cost" to "investment." Through experience and demonstrated results, they properly portray the marketing department as a team that can drive growth. With the digitization of marketing, CMOs are better armed than ever before with credible data to demonstrate marketing's impact and to garner the investment they need.

In addition to obtaining funds, heads of marketing must possess the knowledge and expertise to effectively manage these funds. Note that these two roles are inextricably connected. Specifically, the failure to properly utilize marketing funds can have repercussions on funding decisions in subsequent fiscal years. To avoid this scenario, marketing leaders should put into place procedures to ensure the budget is used properly and tracked diligently.

Running a tight ship will burnish the marketing head's reputation and make him or her a more effective leader.

This chapter will cover the entire process of marketing budgets, from the planning cycle and the methodologies used, through funding allocation to programs and marketing teams, and ending with the all-important functions of defending and tracking budgets.

The Budgeting Cycle

Most organizations plan the next year's budget a few months before the end of their fiscal year. Every organization is different, but executives that are well prepared and can justify their requests always come out ahead. High-performing heads of marketing have mastered the budgeting cycle—the process of planning, justifying, spending, and tracking their budgets. The steps are outlined in table 1 and then discussed in greater detail in the following sections. As you study the steps, remember that budgeting is a cycle, not an event—you are never finished.

Table 1: Steps in the budgeting cycle

Step	Components	Comments
Planning	Understand the business objectives. Gather marketing effectiveness reports from previous years.	Start with the business plan, not last year's marketing plan. Though this takes a bit more work, it will ensure that marketing's goals and the overall business goals are aligned. Otherwise, you might simply be going through the motions.

Building	Pick a budgeting methodology. Decide on a high-level marketing mix to achieve your goals.	If this is a new company or a new assignment, you may need to start from the beginning. The percentage of revenue methodology is recommended (discussed below). Provide high-level guidance on the mix and goals to your team, and have them build it from the bottom up.
Justifying	Compare proposed investment to peers and industry benchmarks. Align program spend, marketing goals, and overall business objectives.	Spend a lot of time here. Get as much outside information as you can. You may find yourself educating other executives on industry norms.
Using	Allocate budget by department, by month or quarter. Ensure marketing department leaders utilize fully.	Believe it or not, some people have a hard time spending what they say they will. Make timely, within-budget spending a basic consideration in evaluating your personnel.
Tracking	Designate an individual in finance or marketing operations to track spend and produce budget-tracking reports.	An ongoing dialogue between the person tracking the spend and the department head avoids end-of-quarter surprises.

Reporting	Demonstrate the efficacy of investment against stated marketing goals and business objectives.	Use the reports discussed in chapter 21 to demonstrate the business value of the company's marketing investments.
Adjusting	Adjust budgets periodically based on changes in the marketing mix, "belt tightening" across the company, or opportunities for additional investment.	Keep an eye on what's working and what's not. Don't be afraid to change the mix. Do your duty if business conditions require you to trim a bit. But, don't be afraid to ask for more money if you can justify the investment.

Budgeting Methodologies

There are four primary methods for determining the marketing budget. We examine them in this section, beginning with the most widely used method, the percentage of revenue:

- Percentage of revenue – The marketing budget is derived as a percentage of the overall organization's expected revenue for the fiscal year.

- Competitive comps – The marketing budget is derived by estimating the competition's spend. This task is easier to perform for public companies, which must disclose how much money they spend on sales and marketing.

- Activity-based – This bottom-up approach begins with the organization's revenue number and works backward. The budget is calculated based on how many leads are needed to hit the number. In addition to lead-acquisition costs, other expenses, such as customer retention, awareness, branding, and run-rate costs (see below), need to be factored in.

◆ What you can afford – The least favorite approach, this "hand-to-mouth" method is sometimes just a reality for smaller companies. Needless to say, it is always a good idea to show the CEO, president, owner, or founder the budgets derived from competitive comps and activity-based methods to influence their ideas of what they can afford.

Even if your company uses percentage of revenue for setting the marketing budget, creating a bottom-up, activity-based budget makes your funding requests easier to defend. For example, if your team is effective at generating MQLs that convert to SQLs, then the money you request for demand generation will be difficult to challenge. Going further, an activity-based budget will include certain "keeping the lights on" costs, or *run-rate costs*. This term refers to activities and programs the marketing team cannot do without, such as PR agency retainers, collateral production, and website maintenance. Any big-ticket items like advertising and event sponsorships must be closely tied to corporate awareness and demand generation goals.

Marketing Spend Benchmarks

Most executives outside marketing do not have a solid working knowledge of how much money they should allocate to their organizations' marketing efforts. Perhaps, they have a general recollection from their experiences at a previous company. Or, they might have seen the sales-and-marketing operating expense line on an SEC filing. In some cases, of course, they simply have never dealt with marketing budget allocation before. All of the above scenarios occur in the business world, and none of them is good news for a head of marketing. Without an informed discussion, your marketing department will likely get less, and not more, than it needs.

For heads of marketing who are confronted with these scenarios, perhaps the best strategy is to expose these executives to current marketing budget benchmarks. Fortunately, there are many sources that provide this information. Included here are industry research firms like the Corporate Executive Board, analyst firms like Forrester Research and IDC, and specialized marketing research firms like SiriusDecisions and MarketingSherpa. The range of spend on marketing has remained quite wide over the years, from as little as 1.5 percent of revenue to slightly more than 10 percent of revenue. Despite these disparities, however, an overview of marketing spend benchmarks reveals some fairly consistent patterns:

> Consumer products vs. B2B products – Not surprisingly, consumer product marketers spend more than B2B marketers. This pattern is due largely to factors like the cost of advertising and spending in support of the brand.
>
> Company size – Small businesses frequently spend proportionally more than larger businesses, because they do not enjoy the economies of scale, yet they need to provide many of the same marketing programs and services. As a VP of finance colleague of mine once explained, "We're not fat, we're short." He meant that we were spending proportionally more on marketing because we had not reached the revenue heights of our competition.
>
> Industry – Some industries spend more than others on marketing. In B2B, for example, software companies spend more than mining companies. Similarly, beer and soda manufacturers spend more than most other consumer products. Marketing spend in the insurance and pharmaceutical industries notably increased starting in the late 1990s due to their increased use of advertising to reach consumers directly.*
>
> Business growth stage – Companies in growth mode spend more than those in slow-growth or maintaining mode. This should not be a surprise. After all, acquiring new customers is the most expensive marketing task.

---

* According to *AdAge*, US ad spend by pharmaceutical companies increased from $700 million in 1996 to $5.4 billion in 2006.

Regardless of where your company falls within these various patterns, it is essential that when you utilize industry benchmarks, you compare your company to the appropriate profile. Large companies with an established brand name and "cash cow" products that rely heavily on renewals rather than new sales will spend less on marketing. So, if you work at a start-up, don't let your CFO use data from a large company to talk you down to a spend level that does not fit your business.

Budget Allocation

Once the total budget is secured, a CMO's job is not over. The next step is to allocate the money to the various marketing activities, departments, and/or individuals. CMOs typically distribute funds based on three considerations:

- The marketing mix
- People versus marketing programs
- Across individual marketing teams

All three will be examined in this section.

Marketing Mix

An essential component of budget planning is to analyze the prior year's marketing mix to identify the most effective tactics and programs as well as the ones that provided few benefits for the business. Marketing should maintain or increase funding for successful tactics or programs and decrease or eliminate funding for unsuccessful ones.

In addition, if a company changes its go-to-market strategy, then marketing needs to add appropriate promotional and enablement budget. If, for example, the company reduced the price of a product to increase market share, the appropriate increase in demand generation and/or distribution would need to be added to compensate. Using the forecasting techniques described in the last chapter, CMOs should come prepared to ask for more money for demand generation if they can demonstrate that it will help to grow the top line.

Programs versus People

Don't forget about people: They make your department function. At the same time, however, they may be one of your most expensive budget categories. For all of these reasons, it is essential that you carefully review how much you are spending on people versus programs. You may be allocating too much to one or the other.

A standard rule is that a well-run marketing department should spend more on programs than on people. There are companies that spend a great deal on people, in some cases more than they do on programs. This allocation as upside down. You lose a lot of flexibility and reduce the money you have to leverage channel partners and third-party agencies. A ratio of 60:40 programs to people seems about right. If your people spend exceeds 40 percent of your total expenditures, then you should review your budget for activities you can outsource.

Calculating the programs-to-people ratio is straightforward. Simply add up all your personnel costs—typically salary and benefits, or "fully loaded cost"—and all of your marketing program costs, including outside vendors. The total of the two is your overall marketing budget. The percentage of the total budget spend on programs versus the percentage spend on people is the programs-to-people ratio. For example, a company that spends $6 million on programs and $4 million on people, for a total of $10 million, would calculate its programs-to-people ratio as follows:

$$(\$6,000,000 \div \$10,000,000) = 60\%$$
$$(\$4,000,000 \div \$10,000,000) = 40\%$$

Allocating across Marketing Teams

Marketing budgets should be allocated after each marketing team—or person, in a small company—has completed and presented a marketing plan for the upcoming year. These plans should include run-rate costs. They will also contain requests for budget to achieve the annual marketing goals, which should be tied to the company's annual business goals.

Finally, the marketing plans inevitably will contain requests to fund new initiatives.

The job of a head of marketing is to ensure the marketing plan supports the business and the marketing budget supports the plan. The final decisions concerning budget allocation across marketing teams can be arrived at via one of three methods: by consensus, through collective bargaining, or by CMO fiat. Consensus is the preferred model, although things don't always work out that way, and a strong hand may be required.

It may also fall upon the head of marketing to ask hard questions if changes to the marketing mix are required. For example, if live events have not generated a satisfactory ROMI, then shifting those dollars to another activity or program makes sense. Taking money away and changing "how we've always done things" is not easy—and is usually accompanied by keening from the marketing group and its constituency—but it frequently is necessary. Doing the same things year after year, while expecting an uptick in budget along with revenue increases, can cause marketing to become flabby. Adjusting and readjusting the marketing mix helps your team and your business avoid "marketing ruts."

A CMO may also want to take the opportunity to adjust spend ratios. For example, if the marketing budget is running high as a percentage of revenue, then it is the CMO's responsibility to adjust it downward. The CMO essentially has two options for performing this task. The first is the "haircut" approach in which he or she reduces all functions by the same amount or percentage. The second is to target the reductions specifically to underperforming or overfunded areas. In addition, when marketing areas request additional staff, the marketing head needs to review the programs-to-people ratio to ensure those requests won't create serious imbalances.

Finally, a CMO should also not be afraid to request additional funds if an opportunity presents itself in the market. If a competitor falters, for example, or there is a competitive advantage in the product line to be exploited, then increasing the spend on promotion is a logical strategy. In scenarios like these, marketing can employ predictive forecasting to present a likely positive outcome if management agrees to allocate the additional sums.

Budget Formatting

Creating an appropriate annual budget is essential, but by itself, it is not sufficient. In addition, marketing must present the budget in an accessible and reader-friendly format. The ideal approach is to produce the budget in a summary form, with additional details available as needed. The most common method is to create a series of linked spreadsheets. The top sheet displays the marketing budget by department—or by geography—by quarter. The linked spreadsheets should provide details by department or geography. The departmental spreadsheet should contain a summary by program, by quarter. Collapsing rows provide a summary view of each program or major activity. Expanding rows enable executives to drill down for any detailed information they require.

Figure 1: A summary view of the overall marketing budget

2009 Marketing Budget - Programs

			Q1	Q2	Q3	Q4
Corporate Marketing NA	$	1,250,000	$ 292,583	$ 569,583	$ 259,083	$ 126,750
EMEA Marketing	$	1,153,000	$ 228,880	$ 356,480	$ 305,130	$ 262,510
Channel Marketing - Programs	$	894,000	$ 222,275	$ 357,075	$ 255,825	$ 58,825
Channel Marketing - MDF	$	1,139,800	$ 215,000	$ 153,000	$ 250,000	$ 321,000
Corporate Communications	$	1,102,600	$ 288,150	$ 363,150	$ 293,150	$ 258,150
Japan Marketing	$	91,000	$ 10,000	$ 26,000	$ 25,000	$ 30,000
Product Marketing	$	178,000	$ 18,000	$ 60,000	$ 50,000	$ 50,000
E-commerce and Advocacy	$	100,000	$ 25,000	$ 25,000	$ 25,000	$ 25,000
	$	5,908,400	$ 1,299,888	$ 1,810,288	$ 1,463,188	$ 1,132,235

Figure 1 represents my marketing budget at a midsize software company. I created the budget in Microsoft Excel; the summary view reproduced in the figure is the top sheet. Each of the eight departmental budgets comprises its own sheet and is linked to the summary (channel marketing had separate programs and MDF budgets, since program dollars were allocated, while MDF accrued). I selected this format because it is easy both to maintain and, when necessary, to adjust.

Figure 2 represents the European marketing budget. Notice how the "Lead Generation/Awareness Programs" and "Alliances" sections have been expanded to reveal the details. The Microsoft Excel Outline feature does an excellent job of displaying programs at a summary level while allowing readers to drill down by clicking on the + sign to reveal the individual tactics.

Figure 2: The European marketing budget with detail exposed for lead generation and awareness programs, as well as for alliances

			Q1	Q2	Q3	Q4
1	EMEA Marketing					
2						
3			**Q1**	**Q2**	**Q3**	**Q4**
4			**$228,880**	**$356,480**	**$305,130**	**$262,510**
5	Press Retainers & Programs		$ 62,000	$ 63,000	$ 66,000	$ 63,000
9	Events		$25,000	$170,000	$101,000	$115,000
24	Lead Generation/Awareness Programs		$65,700	$60,800	$69,950	$49,230
25	*Telemarketing*		*$6,400*		*$6,400*	
26	*Webcasts*		*$10,000*	*$5,000*	*$10,000*	
27	*Content Syndication*		*$30,000*	*$35,000*	*$30,000*	*$30,000*
28	*Integrated Marketing Programs - Online/Offline*		*$11,300*	*$11,300*	*$11,300*	*$11,300*
29	*Advertising*					
30	*List Acquisition*		*$5,000*	*$3,000*	*$5,000*	*$4,680*
31	*SEM*		*$3,000*	*$3,000*	*$3,250*	*$3,250*
32	*Strategic Account Support*			*$3,500*	*$4,000*	
33	Alliances		$10,000	$19,000	$0	$10,000
34	*BD Partner Marketing*		*$5,000*	*$14,000*		*$10,000*
35	*VAR Marketing Funds (MDF)*		*$5,000*	*$3,000*		
36	Associations		$5,000	$5,000	$5,000	$5,000
42	Translations		$14,000	$18,400	$16,000	$0
45	EMEA Creative		$47,180	$20,280	$47,180	$20,280

Presenting and Defending Budgets

Presenting the marketing plan and the associated budget is one of the most important annual events in the life of a head of marketing. You are ensuring you get the money you need to achieve your objectives, while demonstrating you are an effective leader who can get your team the resources it needs. Despite the vital nature of this function, however, many heads of marketing are not very good at it. This section will explore the best strategies to present and defend marketing budgets, based on my experiences in this area.

The first rule of presenting a marketing budget is to frame it in the context of the company business plan. If the company plan is to expand into Europe, for example, the marketing plan and spend need to reflect and highlight this objective. If customer retention is an issue, then money should be shifted from lead generation to the customer loyalty program. Whatever your company's priorities, make certain the budget is specifically geared toward supporting them.

Unfortunately, many marketing leaders make the mistake of walking into the boardroom with only a spreadsheet of all the line items requested by their staff (something like figure 2). This approach requires your CEO, head of finance, VP of sales, and whoever else is in the room to interpret your data. Be warned: This scenario usually is not pretty. These individuals likely won't understand why you need all of these monies and how everything fits together. Ultimately, your specially crafted spreadsheet will probably look like one big number to them. So, what to do instead? Basically, keep the rolled-up version for the marketing team, and create a budget spreadsheet or presentation for the executive team that conveys the same numbers but also clearly demonstrates how each number supports the business.

Further, come prepared with marketing spend benchmarks for your industry. Better yet, come prepared with estimates of how much your competition is spending. This approach will help you to stave off any broadsides concerning why marketing is spending so much money.

Table 2 below shows an outline for presenting a marketing budget for approval. The presentation should start with an overview of the key objectives for the *business* and how marketing will support them. The next slide should show how well marketing is performing against current goals, and a comparison to the competition. These will give the executives present confidence the function is performing well. *Only after these have been presented should any proposed budget numbers be shown.* The budget should be shown in summary form with a clear tie back to the business objectives. Requests for additional funds should be labeled with the business objective they support, for example "European Channel Expansion" instead of "Increase in MDF." Close with a slide that offers proof your investment will pay off.

Table 2: Essential components of an executive-level marketing budget presentation

Slide	Elements	Comments
Key Objectives	List a handful of objectives that are tied directly to the company's annual plan.	A small list that is consistent with the company plan will serve you well. Use words like "invest," "support," and "grow" to underline the connection to the business.
Marketing Efficiency	Show efficacy stats such as investment-to-revenue, any planned cuts or reallocations, and, optionally, industry or competitor comparisons.	Lead with strength by showing efficacy, which also demonstrates your command of the department. Make your own cuts, as required by overall budget trends, so others don't do it for you. Highlighting industry or competitor comparisons is usually reserved for situations where you are severely underfunded.

Summary Budget	Show summary version of the run rate, the previous annual budget, and incremental items.	Less is more here. Tie back to key objectives. Illustrate that the run rate and previous budget are essential. Depict incremental items as investments in the business. Do not show detail here or enter the budgeting rathole. Illustrate any potential reduction in run rate or previous budget to demonstrate you are a good steward of your money.
Proof	Provide further detail on new investments and how they will achieve the organization's objectives.	Make sure you know your numbers cold and you can back up your assertions on how new investments will drive the business.
Backup	Anything you might be asked or probed about. You will likely need a summary view of program spend, metrics from the previous year, and more detail on competitor spending.	These slides are called "backup" for a reason. If you can seal the deal without them, don't use them. Sometimes bringing up a detail slide can unravel a previous agreement.

Finally, if you are requesting incremental budget, make certain you can point back to results. For example, if your company needs to grow the top line by 50 percent, and you know that a certain program can generate those leads, start by demonstrating how effective this program has been, and then show the math to support how additional investment will grow the top line by 50 percent.

Budget Tracking and Accounting

Spending your money wisely is an excellent strategy to ensure you get more money next year. When companies suspect that marketing teams are wasting money or spending it indiscriminately, closer scrutiny is sure to follow. And, rightly so. After all, CEOs and CFOs are paid to spend investor, donor, and shareholder money wisely.

Also, keep in mind that most people who work in marketing were never accountants, nor did they major in accounting or finance in college. Not surprisingly, then, accounting is not their strong suit, especially the creative free thinkers in the group. Budget planning, process, and reporting are critical skills that need to be instilled in each member of a well-run marketing organization. To make this a reality, an effective marketing leader will devote time to each of the following functions:

> Staff education – Many marketing teams are unaware of how accounting works, including the processes for opening purchase orders, processing vendor invoices, and accruing expenses. Further, different companies do things differently, so prior knowledge acquired in a previous company may hurt, not help. Ideally, then, your company should send someone from accounting over to marketing for a refresher. For whatever reasons, however, few companies take this step.

> Regular reporting – Even if you have a well-constructed marketing budget and your staff understand the process, the plan can come apart without good tracking. Purchase orders that were assumed to have been issued may not have made their way through the full process, and completed work may not have been invoiced. Actual expenses may be greater or less than vendor estimates. Regular *budget versus actual* (or BvA) reports from finance, sometimes called *budget trackers*, can solve this problem. Budget trackers are spreadsheets that show planned spending and actual spending side by side. Some larger marketing teams have a marketing operations role that performs this function.

Use it or lose it – Many companies have a "use it or lose it" policy regarding budgets. The policy is not intended to be punitive; rather, it is designed to encourage teams to spend on plan. CFOs are expected to provide accurate guidance on earnings. Therefore, spending less than what was budgeted may goose up earnings, but it also makes the CFO's forecast inaccurate. Especially in public companies, this is not a good thing. Unless there is a planned reduction or reallocation of the marketing budget, teams should be held to their quarterly budget numbers. Marketers may need to learn the art of "parking" money with a vendor, in other words, paying a vendor in advance for services rendered later. A caveat—CMOs should have a chat with their CFO counterparts to take their temperature on this practice. Some CFOs view parking funds as a violation of financial compliance regulations. Others don't see it that way. Still others just don't want to know.

Holding marketing staff accountable – Even those CMOs who have educated their staff and who obtain weekly BvA reports from finance can still run into problems if there is no staff accountability. For this reason, it is a good idea to build budget management into the MBOs of any manager who manages program budget. A better plan is to tie budget management to each manager's bonus. Ideally, budget spend should be either exactly on target or 1 to 2 percent under target. Objectives that reduce employee bonuses for significant underspending or overspending can be very effective.

So, make sure to cover your bases. Teach your staff and hold them accountable. Not only will your team be able to better explain its actions, but understanding how effective marketing spend is can lead to more constructive team discussions.

Chapter 23

The Marketing Department

With all of the dramatic changes in media, technology, and buyer behavior that we have witnessed in recent decades, CMOs should devote a lot of time to rethinking the optimal structure for their department. Should their team be organized around functions, geographies, customer segments, or something else entirely? How well is their team aligned with the business, and is the team adaptive to changes in the market? Which functions are essential to the success of the marketing effort? Finally, which key activities need to be performed internally, and which can be outsourced?

Marketing is changing. Customers are able to find more information online than ever before. Consequently, B2B marketers are more involved in the later stages of the buyer journey, staying involved longer than they have ever been, assuming responsibilities that historically belonged to sales. Marketing automation is changing the way marketing operates, enabling company executives to track marketing's performance against the company's goals on a daily basis. Analytics—an area most marketers traditionally stayed away from (ran away from?)—is becoming more and more important, both because analyzing user behavior online is yielding new insights and because CEOs are examining ROMI more carefully. The digitization of marketing, in fact, presents opportunities for CMOs to strengthen their ties to the business; to assume additional responsibilities, with the concomitant higher budgets; and even to increase their compensation by being paid "upside" based on contribution to the sales pipeline.

This chapter will start with considerations for aligning marketing with the business. It will then shift its focus to the basic roles and responsibilities of the marketing department, as well as some common alternatives to evaluate. It will conclude with recommendations on how marketing can work effectively with other parts of the organization.

The Marketing Department in the Overall Organization

Before exploring the marketing department and the staff, understanding the specific role of marketing within a given organization is critical. An obvious place to begin is by determining how many of the Four Ps marketing is responsible for covering.

How Many Ps?

In chapter 1, we covered McCarthy's Four Ps of marketing: product, price, place, and promotion. Depending on the organization, marketing can be responsible for some or all of these functions. Managing promotion is a universal marketing role. But, is the marketing department also responsible for product? How about distribution strategy (place)? Does it own or influence pricing?

It is not uncommon for a marketing department to be responsible only for promotion. In fact, this is what many people expect marketing to do. If product management—also known as brand management in consumer packaged goods companies like Procter & Gamble—is part of marketing, then the department probably will be responsible for *product* and *price*. *Place* is determined by go-to-market strategy—which may be owned by product marketing—and by the channel or partner strategy. In situations where sales owns the channel or partner strategy, marketing may be responsible only for the channel program, channel enablement, and channel promotion.

Whatever the organization, understanding which of the Four Ps marketing is responsible for will define the skills that the marketing staff must possess. In some cases, a head of marketing will use the Four Ps to expand the scope of marketing or to better align it with the needs of the market. A CMO should not take the attitude that marketing "gets what it gets." Rather, he or she should press the issue and consider how changes in technology, media, and customer behavior present opportunities for marketing to do more.

Match the Mandate

Regardless of whether your CEO is open to a discussion on the Four Ps, or even knows them, which can be a problem, a VP of marketing or a CMO needs to understand marketing's mandate. The fundamental rule here is to build your marketing department to match your CEO's or board's business goals. This is so obvious I almost didn't include it in this chapter. Having seen it bite several CMOs I know, however, I decided to put it in.

I call this strategy "matching the mandate." As an example of matching the mandate, if your CEO cares exclusively about demand generation, then put your best people there, and make certain it has sufficient staff and budget. Dial back on PR or social media if the executive team is not impressed by your share of voice numbers. Although it may pain you to starve one function or the other—after all, you appreciate the importance of a balanced marketing mix—refusing to take these steps can damage your department's reputation and even limit your longevity in the job.

Be careful not to sound pedantic in your efforts to educate your peers on the importance of brand affinity, social sentiment, or any other inside-baseball marketing jargon. This will only make you appear to be out of touch with your organization's real needs. In addition, make certain you probe your CEO or board to identify goals or needs that may not be written down in the annual business plan. A vital point here is that CMOs are frequently assessed by *unwritten* criteria. For example, a VP of marketing I know was let go even though he had achieved all of his written objectives, because the CEO just didn't feel that the brand had grown sufficiently on his watch. In his book *The CMO Manifesto*, John Ellett stresses the importance of understanding expectations early on. He contends CMOs in new roles should begin setting expectations during the interview process, and early on in their first hundred days should have a clear and agreed-to mandate.

The moral of this story? Simply put, understanding what your executives *really* want can be vital to performing—and preserving—your job.

Marketing Functions and Groups

There are many ways to design a marketing department. The design will reflect the responsibilities (Ps) from above, marketing's mandate and goals, as well as the industry and the overall size of the organization. This section covers common functions, functional responsibilities, and the typical group name applied to the function. In general, groups in smaller organizations perform multiple functions, whereas those in larger organizations are more specialized.

For the sake of clarity, the word "organization" will refer to an overall business, government, or nonprofit entity. A "department" is the highest-level functional separation inside an organization—marketing, sales, manufacturing, HR, etc. A "group" is the functional separation within a department.

Groups Common to Most Marketing Departments

Let's begin by examining marketing groups that are found in most marketing departments, regardless of organization size. Specifically, let's discuss field marketing, regional marketing, marketing communications, product marketing, and—where relevant—channel marketing.

Field marketing is responsible for demand generation and customer engagement at the regional level. It employs such tactics as running events, supporting user groups (for tech), and coordinating promotions with the field sales group. Some field marketing groups also support the channel, or at least serve as the local arm of the channel team, if the organization does not have a dedicated channel marketing group. In larger organizations, field marketing groups function as the local ambassadors of an organization's brand and reputation.

Regional marketing is the marketing arm for an organization in a geographic region. Regional marketing assumes some of marketing communications' responsibilities for marcom in the region, including producing marketing collateral in local languages, refining graphics and messages to suit regional tastes, and running regional public relations. Regional marketing may also inherit some of channel marketing's responsibilities for partners within a region, such as localizing channel collateral and managing partner marketing funds.

Marketing communications, commonly abbreviated as "marcom," is something of a catchall group. Marcom's responsibilities include all of marketing's design, promotion, and communication functions. In addition, it is responsible for advertising, demand generation, direct marketing, graphic design, identity, public relations, and web design and management. As the organization expands, marcom's functions are usually transferred to specialized groups such as corporate communications and brand management.

Product marketing is responsible for the "outbound" marketing of a company's products (as opposed to the "inbound" activities of the product management function), including identifying buyer personas, creating product messaging, creating content for marketing assets, designing sales tools, overseeing product launches, briefing the media and relevant analysts, and training salespeople. It can also be responsible for monitoring the market for the company. In this capacity, it manages competitive intelligence, and it creates *market requirements documents,* which convey a high-level profile of the current state of the market and customer needs. The division of responsibilities between product marketing and product management varies from organization to organization.

Finally, *channel marketing* is responsible for creating and maintaining the partner program. The term *partner* is a broad one that encompasses value-added resellers, OEM partners, consultants, and other affiliates. Channel marketing is responsible for managing the partner portal, creating to-channel and tailoring through-channel assets, running channel promotions, coordinating channel training, and managing partner marketing funds. In some companies, independent of the size of the organization, channel marketing exists within the channel sales organization.

Groups Common in Larger Organizations

As organizations expand, roles become more specialized. The actual functions are the same as in smaller organizations. However, functions that are managed collectively by a single group in a smaller organization are typically dispersed among multiple groups in larger organizations. To cite one common example, larger organizations frequently establish separate groups for branding and advertising, corporate marketing, and online marketing. In contrast, a smaller company might consolidate all of these functions within the marcom groups. Let's take a closer look at some specialized groups that are common within larger organizations. We begin with branding and advertising.

As the name suggests, *branding and advertising* manages the company brand image by creating brand guidelines, maintaining style and usage regulations, initiating brand-building activities, conceiving and delivering advertising, and "policing" the use of the brand by other marketing functions. Branding and advertising can report either to a VP of marcom or the VP of marketing.

Whereas branding and advertising maintains the *company* brand, *brand management* is responsible for planning, developing, and directing the marketing efforts for a *particular* brand or product. Found primarily in consumer packaged goods (CPG) companies, where products are their own "brands," brand managers are responsible for coordinating activities of production, sales, advertising, promotion, research and development, marketing research, purchasing, distribution, package development, and finance.

Corporate communications is responsible for public relations, analyst relations, and influencer relations in general. In some organizations, it oversees e-mail and other written communications sent to existing customers. Finally, depending on the company, corporate communications may be in charge of creating content for and tracking the use of social media.

Corporate marketing is something of a catchall group that supervises branding, advertising, marketing communications, and digital marketing for a corporation, unless the CMO has established separate groups, such as branding and advertising and corporate communications, dedicated to those functions. Regional marketing and Field marketing usually take materials created by corporate marketing and adapt them to suit their needs.

Companies that rely on renewals or increasing share of wallet to grow their revenue frequently have dedicated *customer marketing* groups. These teams are responsible for creating and maintaining customer loyalty programs, measuring customer satisfaction, overseeing user group relations, and creating campaigns designed to incent renewals or expanded purchase.

As mentioned in chapter 7 on social media and word of mouth, having your customers sell for you is frequently the most effective sales strategy. To cultivate this type of customer support, many companies create *customer advocacy* groups. These groups write case studies, record customer testimonials, arrange for customers to speak at industry events, set up customer round tables and user group meetings, and, in some cases, establish online communities or peer networking groups where customers can interact with one another.

Digital or *online marketing* is one of the most recent additions to the marketing family. As its name implies, it is primarily responsible for executing marketing programs that involve digital media, including web design, video production, and online strategy. Digital marketing typically takes over management of an organization's web properties from the marcom team. In addition, it can collaborate with corporate communications to manage aspects of the social media program, such as maintaining forums, overseeing the blogging platform, and managing the organization's presence on social media sites such as Facebook. In a world where everything is going digital and brochures increasingly are downloaded but not printed, careful oversight of digital marketing may be necessary to avoid conflict between it and groups like marcom or corporate communications. In essence, digital marketing should function as a service organization that assists in production of digital assets and promotes best practices throughout the marketing team.

Marketing operations is responsible for increasing the overall efficiency of marketing by measuring performance, facilitating strategic planning, driving budget planning and spend reporting, developing marketing processes, and managing marketing systems. In some organizations, they also own and maintain the marketing databases. The head of marketing operations typically reports to the head of marketing, and may act as a chief of staff, even driving department communications.

Finally, *vertical* or *solution marketing* creates training, enablement, and customer-facing assets around a particular industry or solution area. Vertical marketing is typically associated with large industries that have unique requirements, such as government, health care, financial services, and tele-communications. This function can be located within product marketing, or it can be part of a field marketing team that specializes in the industry in question. The latter arrangement is especially common if the industry has a regional concentration, such as the US government.

Groups that May Be Found in Marketing

There are a handful of functions that sometimes reside in the marketing department, and sometimes reside in other departments, regardless of the organization's size. The reasons vary but are mostly due to the preferences of the executive team.

Product management defines and oversees the life cycle of a product. Product management is a common group in the computer hardware, software, online services, pharmaceutical, and aerospace industries. The group's responsibilities include analyzing the market, understanding the competition, collecting and prioritizing product requirements from customers, creating product requirement documents, collaborating with engineering or manufacturing to develop products to specifications, setting or recommending product pricing, and maintaining the product road map. In smaller organizations, product managers may also take on the outbound activities described above for product marketing. Product managers may report to engineering or manufacturing, to a VP of products, or to the VP of marketing, depending on the organization.

The *e-commerce* group sells a company's products online. Their duties include managing the company's online store(s), creating and managing online advertising to attract customers to the store, and managing relationships with DMRs and e-tailers who sell the company's products on their online stores. Depending on the company, its scale of operation, and the type of product, this group may report to sales or marketing, or it may be its own business unit.

Some companies rely on a small team of *evangelists* to spread the word about their products or company. Evangelists are usually charismatic types who possess detailed product knowledge. They rack up huge amounts of frequent flyer miles attending conferences, meeting users, and speaking at trade shows. An evangelist team may report to the CEO in smaller organizations, the chief technical officer (CTO) in high-tech companies, or to marketing.*

Finally, *telemarketing* follows up on direct mail or inbound inquiries, in addition to directly calling prospects to spark some interest. This team may also be called "telesales" or "sales development," and they are sometimes situated within the sales department. Many companies, however, outsource telemarketing to an agency. When telemarketing is owned by marketing, it prequalifies leads before handing them over to sales as MQLs, thus improving the chances of lead acceptance.

Emerging Functions

Marketing is changing. Much of the change is due to technical advances that allow the marketing department to have a more direct relationship with prospective customers on the web or via their mobile devices. Below are two groups that have begun to emerge in marketing departments.

Customers today progress further in the buying cycle before they involve a salesperson than ever before. Prior to making contact with sales, they rely on written and recorded information to conduct online research and compare products. The result is the emergence of the *content marketing* function. Content marketers are usually found within product marketing or on the PR team. The latter arrangement requires the PR team to shift its focus from running briefings and writing abstracts to creating content that will stand on its own. To successfully navigate this transition, PR teams need to be bolstered by including professionals who formerly worked as reporters or writers, contract writers, and product marketers.

Some companies have a separate *demand generation* group. This team typically manages the marketing automation system and sends out direct mail. In some companies, it also is in charge of search engine marketing. In some cases, it controls the marketing database, and it manages telemarketing

---

* Guy Kawasaki is credited with popularizing the secular use of the word "evangelist." He worked at Apple in the 1980s as an evangelist for the Macintosh computer. According to Kawasaki, "Evangelism is the process of selling a dream."

or sales development reps who follow up on direct mail and inbound inquiries before passing them on to sales. There is a trend toward calling this department "revenue marketing," though most marketers don't appreciate the damning insinuation that the rest of marketing is not contributing to revenue.

Finally, more and more companies are setting up centers of excellence around marketing activities that cut across marketing groups. A *marketing center of excellence* brings together varied people and skills, promotes collaboration, and establishes best practices. Social media expertise, for example, may exist within the PR team, the product marketing team, the web team, the customer advocacy group, and even within the engineering and technical teams. Three of the more common marketing centers of excellence are mobile marketing, social media, and search engine marketing.

Outsourcing – Agencies, Contractors, and Vendors

We have just considered a number of marketing functions that large organizations frequently assign to specialized groups. Alternatively, many organizations outsource these functions to specialized agencies, especially when resources are limited and need for agility is high. The most commonly outsourced activities are public relations and advertising, though there are others. Companies use outside agencies to take advantage of their relationships, creative talent, and specialized skill sets, or to satisfy intermittent needs that do not justify hiring full-time employees. Significantly, companies are increasingly engaging smaller, specialized agencies, rather than a single creative or marketing agency, to handle their needs because they get the skills they need without the often high markup of larger agencies. This trend is especially evident in technical and rapidly evolving areas such as search engine marketing and social media. Here we consider some common agencies that marketing utilizes:

- ◆ Public relations – As we discussed in chapter 5, PR agencies specialize in getting companies in front of the media (and hopefully into it) and other influencers, such as bloggers. They are valuable because they maintain close relationships with the media and they have extensive experience in pitching stories. Depending on how much you pay your agency, they might also provide strategic advice on how to position your company, monitor social media monitoring, and ghostwrite blogs or bylined articles. PR agencies like to work on retainer—typically $5,000 to $25,000 per month, although it can be much higher for larger organizations. CEOs and finance folks often balk at the price, but the agency's relationships and expertise are worth the expense.

- Advertising – The most basic reason to hire an ad agency is that most companies simply don't produce good advertising internally. This is certainly the case with television ads. The creative thinking, copywriting, and production and placement experience of an ad agency are not cheap, but neither is advertising. Ad agencies are paid for their creative work—either on a project basis or a monthly retainer—and they may earn commissions on advertising placements.

- Media buyers – Media buyers are responsible for purchasing advertising time and space. Organizations engage media buyers to obtain better rates and placement than they could get themselves. Media buyers can also identify opportunities your marketing team may not be aware of. Traditionally, buyers worked for advertising agencies, but the consolidation of the advertising industry in the late 1990s, coupled with the emergence of online advertising, spurred the creation of independent media buying agencies.

- Branding and identity – There are times when organizations need help with branding—how they present themselves to the outside world. There may also be occasions when a new product requires just the right name or the company is changing its name. This is the time to bring in a specialist. It's amazing how hard it is to think of a good name that works around the world and isn't already taken. Branding and identity agencies typically work on a project basis.

- Graphic design – Depending on your company size, you may or may not have a graphic design person or team in-house. Even if you do, you may want a stable of outside designers whom you call on either to enhance your team's skill set or to perform certain types of design work—print versus online, corporate versus hip, presentation versus data sheet, to name just a few. Or you may just need their eye to *zhush up* a stale piece. Graphic designers work on a project basis, sometimes hourly.

◆ Writing – Organizations frequently outsource the writing of certain content—for example, white papers or placed articles—to experts. For example, technology companies frequently employ technical writers to make their manuals and other customer-facing documentation more understandable to the layperson. These writers tend to be individual contractors rather than agencies, and they generally work on a project basis. I recommend a good mix of internal writers in a product marketing or content marketing team, augmented as needed with outside professionals.

There are even more specialized types of agencies you may run across: agencies that create names but don't design logos, vendors who create and manage loyalty programs for channel partners, agencies that specialize in list acquisition, PR agencies that specialize in social media. To decide whether the company should perform the function internally or via an agency, a CMO needs to consider the following factors:

◆ Does the talent exist internally?

◆ Should the function be a core competency?

◆ Does it make more economic sense to outsource the function?

Finally, marketing departments are most effective when they treat agencies and vendors as a part of the team. Sharing strategy with them, involving them in team meetings, and even ensuring they are invited to the holiday party can go a long way toward making your vendors loyal. Remember, agencies are comprised of people, and these people need to be motivated—just like employees. Moreover, the better the agency people understand your business, your pains, and your goals, the better they will perform for you.

Marketing Department Design

There are many ways to structure the marketing department. The design inevitably reflects a number of factors: the company size, industry, number of products or business, location, and goals.

The most common form of organization for marketing is the *functional department*. Under this design, functional specialists head the various marketing groups. For example, field marketing manages events and demand generation. Product marketing is responsible for go-to-market planning, product launches, content creation, and similar functions for the entire company. Marketing communications handles graphic design, PR, and other communications functions for the marketing organization. Figure 1 illustrates what I consider to be a bare minimum marketing department for any organization of size. If a company conducts business primarily online, then field marketing may be replaced by demand generation or digital marketing.

Figure 1: A simple functional marketing department

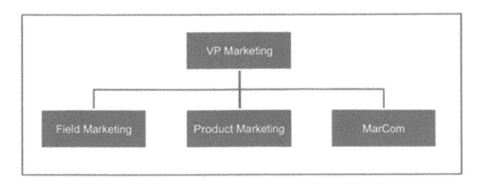

An alternative structure is the *geographic department*. This design is common among companies that sell internationally. As illustrated in figure 2, in the geographical organization, functional specialists head the various marketing activities within a particular region. In contrast to the functional organization, these specialists report to a country or regional manager rather than a head of marketing at the central headquarters. The underlying philosophy is that regional teams can tailor marketing efforts to suit the language and customs of their region. In addition, they are geographically closer to the salespeople and channel partners who actually do the work.

Figure 2: Geographically distributed marketing department organized around regional general managers

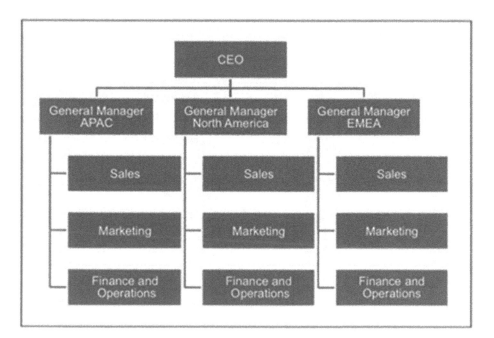

Many large companies adopt a *hybrid department* in which some functions are managed centrally and others are handled in the region. The centralized functions typically report to the head of marketing at headquarters, and the regional functions report either to the head of marketing or to the regional general manager. Dotted-line reporting, a relationship between an employee and a secondary supervisor who provides additional oversight and guidance to the employee, is common. For example, the head of European field marketing might report to the CMO but also maintain a dotted-line reporting relationship to the vice president of European operations, or vice versa. Figure 3 displays a standard hybrid organization.

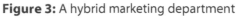

Figure 3: A hybrid marketing department

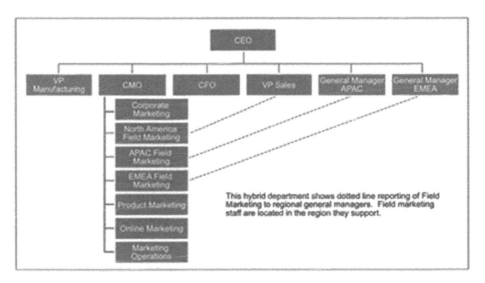

Another way of categorizing department designs is to consider where decisions are made. Based on this model, an organization can be classified in one of three ways:

- Centralized – Marketing activities are directed from headquarters.

- Decentralized – Marketing groups within the business units operate independently within the parameters of the overall corporate strategy.

- Matrix – Marketing groups within the business units operate fairly autonomously yet have a dotted-line relationship to headquarters.

Note how the functional, geographic, and hybrid department designs fit neatly into these three models. Deciding which model is right for your organization requires you to achieve the right balance between maintaining corporate standards and allowing the field to execute in the ways that work best for their markets, regardless of who reports to whom. Marketing departments that are too centralized frequently become out of touch, or even ineffective, in other regions. Conversely, overly decentralized organizations run the risk of diluting the brand or going off strategy.

One common element in all of the above organizing principles is the distribution of decision-making power—whether marketing functions are needed in region, at corporate headquarters, or some combination. There are cases where marketing is organized around products, brands, and customers:

- Product/brand – Marketing groups are focused on product categories or brand groupings.

- Customer – Marketing groups are focused on relationships with key customers or consumer segments.

- Hybrid – Marketing teams are focused on both products and brands.

In the case of brand-oriented marketing, each brand group includes functional specialists. The thinking is to give each brand the specialized marketing support that it needs. The presumption is that the needs of a given brand are different from those of other brands within the company—marketing toothpaste versus potato chips in a large consumer packaged goods company, for example. This structure is common in a "house of brands" company, for example, CPG vendor Unilever, which sells Lipton tea, Hellman's mayonnaise, and Dove soap, among hundreds of other products.

In contrast, in customer-oriented marketing, companies frequently take similar products to market in different ways based on customer type. An example is creating marketing groups oriented toward consumers, small businesses, and enterprises. With different routes to market and varying cost structures, organizing the marketing efforts around buyers can be the most logical strategy.

Writing It Down

Establishing clearly defined roles and responsibilities is essential to maintaining a high-performing marketing department. As simple as this precept seems, however, many organizations neglect to implement it. Moreover, as the department grows along with the organization, responsibilities may change or overlap. Functions that marcom used to perform, for example, may be assumed by branding and advertising. Similarly, channel marketing may drive programs that previously were in field marketing's wheelhouse.

What steps can a CMO take to ensure that the allocation of roles and responsibilities is clear to all of its members? The simplest and most effective strategy is to "put it in writing." The particular format you employ is not that important, though a simple table with the group name shown on top, followed by a list of responsibilities, generally works well. If you are a new head of marketing, make sure to review the organizational model with your team. You may find the meeting interesting. It can involve a bit of negotiating and disagreement, but ultimately it will make your team more efficient and productive.

As you define these roles, make certain they reflect the department's key marketing initiatives, such as product launches, press releases, user conferences, and campaign creation. It helps to define responsibilities, hand-offs, and approvals. Who, for example, runs product launches? Does product marketing simply define go-to-market strategy and messaging, or does it coordinate the launch? Does regional or field marketing require approval from marcom or branding for each piece they produce, or is having an agreed-upon style guide sufficient?

Figure 4 provides an example from one of my previous stints as VP of marketing. One conflict that emerged in this arrangement involved social media. We resolved this conflict by incorporating social media management to the PR director's role, while making product marketing responsible for the content.

Figure 4: Marketing roles and responsibilities

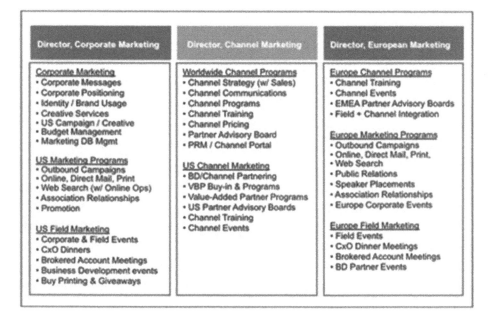

Working with Other Departments

Many people are simply ignorant of the inner workings of marketing, like the VP of sales who asked me to compliment the PR team for the great-looking billboard he saw in the airport. Because marketing departments vary from company to company, the best strategy is to circulate the roles and responsibilities as widely as possible. You can use the same chart or table as you use within your team, such as figure 4 above.

Friction sometimes emerges between groups in different departments who feel they should be responsible for certain functions. Three common examples are (1) telemarketing versus inside sales, (2) web design versus development, and (3) channel sales versus channel marketing. The point of contention is usually who "owns" talking to customers, building or updating the website, and who communicates with channel partners, respectively.

The easiest way to clear up any tension between the telemarketing team (in marketing) and the inside sales team (in sales) is to create an agreement with the head of sales concerning the MQL criteria and when and to whom an MQL is handed over to become a SAL (this is the "hand-off" covered in chapter 11). Likewise, telemarketing will want an agreement back from sales on how soon they will be following up the lead.

Another common source of conflict involves who should own the corporate website: marketing or IT. If your organization's business *is* your website, then product management and engineering can become involved as well. One effective method to defuse these conflicts is to clearly define who is responsible for identity and content and who is responsible for functionality. Also, in cases where IT is your only counterpart, a clear SLA needs to be in place for time-sensitive web content like press releases and new product content related to launches.

One final example involves the channel program. Sales may want to run the entire program, while marketing probably wants to control how marketing dollars are spent.

These scenarios represent only a few common sources of interdepartmental disputes. There may be other conflicts as well. Whatever the specifics, the preferred strategy is to clear them up before they become points of friction within your organization.

The centers of excellence mentioned in the previous section can also help cooperation among groups from different departments. Forming these teams will help to foster innovation, cooperation, and participation across the organization.

"Marketing" Marketing

Funny enough, many CMOs are really good at marketing their brand, company, or product, but they are really bad at marketing their departments, their people, and themselves. "Marketing" marketing is very important. Creating dashboards, circulating an internal newsletter, maintaining an internal marketing blog, and ensuring that company HQ and branch offices get signage for important product launches are just a few strategies for promoting the marketing function.

"Marketing" marketing is critical for the company to understand what marketing does and how it contributes to the business. It can also be a lot of fun. So, don't blanch at the idea or think of it as blatant self-promotion. Employees are just like consumers—you have to hit them over the head with the message. Don't just assume they know what's going on, especially outside HQ. Finally, make sure to call out the marketing team members who were responsible for a successful campaign. You always look good when you praise your team, and your employees will appreciate it.

Learning More

◆ John Ellet, *The CMO Manifesto* (2012).

Afterword

S urely, just one minute after I hit the publish button and graduate this manuscript to a book, some new technology will emerge that promises to change the future of marketing. Not seeing this latest innovation covered, some reader will no doubt bellyache that the text is out of date.

But change in the marketing mix is constant. Some new medium has always appeared and changed the game. Radio. Bulk-rate mail. Television. Toll-free numbers. The Internet. Social media. Smartphones. More will come. You can bet on that.

Despite these changes in media, the practice of good marketing hasn't changed as much as you might think. So-called "growth hackers," from tech start-ups in Silicon Valley, are touting the power of A/B testing. Yet Les Wunderman drew attention to A/B testing in the 1960s and 1970s, selling everything from rosebushes to eight-track tapes via direct mail and print advertising.

Great marketing ideas—ideas that are as relevant as ever—can be found throughout marketing's history. The advice of David Ogilvy, circa 1985, holds up as well as any you might get today (in fact, I wish more copywriters would study his books). The techniques of the big data team at the Democratic National Committee, hatched for the 2008 election, will be used not only to get your vote for years to come but also to sell you all sorts of products you don't know you need. And when we have all tired of hearing about social media, the importance of word of mouth and social connectedness will not diminish.

Which is to say, take it all in. Draw from the decades of marketing wisdom. The pace of technological change will only increase, but humans—the ultimate targets of marketing—are not changing that fast, despite what one generation might say about another.

These days, I get in my car and listen to the radio, step on the train and listen to a podcast, glance at the billboards out the window, and read the "paper" on my iPad. My kids watch "television" sometimes on the television set, but also through a game console and on our family PC. Our daily lives are already multimedia, and simply adding another medium is not enough to break through.

Marketing's great power is to inspire, to compel, and these results do not simply accrue from the medium. It's still the great visual or arresting story that grabs us. This is the other risk of spending too much time on new media developments. Many marketers, in my opinion, misinterpret Marshall McLuhan's "the medium is the message" trope. No doubt the medium affects how we consume information, but many marketers feel it's more important to use a new medium than to hone their message. Perhaps some see it as a shortcut. This is a fatal misunderstanding. Media change, as they always have, and always will; the message is the message and is ultimately what convinces.

So don't be a marketer who rejects the past. Don't be a Luddite, either. There were those mavericks who left radio for television, and today's online advertising gurus who endured the snide remarks of the television guys. So paying attention to new developments can pay off. Just don't lose sight of the foundational work done in the 1960s by men like Peter Drucker, Ted Levitt, David Ogilvy, Everett Rogers, and Les Wunderman. Make a habit of keeping up with the latest innovations so you stay at the top of your game. Do not lose sight of the humans in the mix and what makes them want to buy.

Be inquisitive, keep learning, and beware of the shortcuts.

Tim Matthews
Burlingame, California

Acknowledgments

I wrote this book because I wasn't able to buy it, and I felt there was so much that up-and-coming marketers needed to learn. That said, when I began, I didn't realize how much about marketing *I* had yet to learn. For that I owe thanks to a lot of people.

I owe a great deal to all of my marketing peers who held their noses and looked at one or more early drafts of this book. From the critical to the common sense, to the obvious and back to the insightful, their hundreds of suggestions made this book a whole lot better. Thanks to Tristan Bishop, David Bliss, Chas Cooper, Patrick Corman, Dawn Jensen, Maureen Kelly, Martina Lauchengco, Heidi Lorenzen, Doug McLean, Sylvia McLeary, Amy Phoenix, and Peter Spielvogel.

Even though marketers are thought to be self-promoters, a lot of the details on the origins of marketing are tough to come by. I'd like to give a special shout-out to the folks who built Google Books—whoever you are. Without you, so much marketing history would still be lost to me, and I never would have figured out who first created the sales funnel (which was driving me nuts for almost a week).

Many of the authors cited in this book actually took the time to answer questions about their fields or their books. In some cases, they were generous enough to give feedback on prose to an unfamous, unpublished stranger who asked for their time. Thank you to Stephanie Cota, Nancy Duarte, John Ellett, Mark Hughes, Pat LaPointe, Hugh Macfarlane, Jon Miller, Marty Neumeier, Adele Revella, Tim Riesterer, and Emanuel Rosen.

I feel a deep debt of gratitude to the legends who made what I do into a profession—Edward Bernays, Peter Drucker, Ted Levitt, Jerome McCarthy, Geoffrey Moore, David Ogilvy, Everett Rogers, and Les Wunderman, to name just a few. Some I will never have a chance to meet; others I still hope to.

Thanks to my editor, Robert Weiss, whose copious revision marks and comments initially made me fearful to open his edited versions, but who was usually right. Once I learned to take the punishment, I became a better writer, and this is a better book because of it. My wife, Emily, and her green pen—which sometimes spurred a nervous tic—made edits and suggestions that built on Robert's. Her knowledge of marketing and her uncanny ability to spot a stray comma or extra space tuned this book up a lot.

I have no doubt forgotten hundreds of people. Those who taught me. Those who tolerated me. Those who listened to me. Those whom I've never met, but who elicited an appreciative nod for their inspiring ad or clearly written piece. To all of you, thanks. And keep up the good work.

Endnotes

1   Peter F. Drucker, *The Essential Drucker* (New York: Harper Business, 2001), 20.

2   Ted Levitt, "Marketing Myopia," *Harvard Business Review*, September–October, 1975, 12.

3   Ted Levitt, "Marketing Myopia," *Harvard Business Review*, September–October, 1975, 3.

4   Ted Levitt, "Marketing Myopia," *Harvard Business Review*, September–October, 1975, 7.

5   Apple Inc., *2011 Annual Report*, http://investor.apple.com

6   *American Heritage College Dictionary*, 3rd ed.,s. v. "marketing."

7   Al Ries and Jack Trout, "The Positioning Era Cometh," *Advertising Age*, April 24, 1972, 33–35.

8   Al Ries and Jack Trout, "The Positioning Era Cometh," *Advertising Age*, April 24, 1972, 33–35.

9   Al Ries and Jack Trout, "The Positioning Era Cometh," *Advertising Age*, April 24, 1972, 33–35.

10   "Apple's 'Get a Mac' Awarded Grand Effie," http://news.softpedia.com/news/Apple-s-Get-a-Mac-Awarded-Grand-Effie-56898.shtml.

11   David Aaker, *Building Strong Brands* (Berkeley:Free Press, 1996), 8.

[12]   ACSI Press Release, June 2011, http://www.theacsi.org/media-resources/acsi-commentary-june-2011.

[13]   Joseph T. Plummer, "Life Style Patterns and Commercial Bank Credit Card Usage," *Journal of Marketing* vol. 35 (April 1971): 35–42.

[14]   Joseph T. Plummer, "The Concept and Application of Life Style Segmentation," *Journal of Marketing* vol. 38 (January 1974): 33–37.

[15]   International Data Corporation. "Worldwide Smartphone 2012–2016 Forecast and Analysis," March 2012.

[16]   "How GEICO Is Delivering Shareholder Value To Berkshire Hathaway," Seeking Alpha, October 7, 2011, http://seekingalpha.com/article/298261-how-geico-is-delivering-shareholder-value-to-berkshire-hathaway

[17]   Ariana Eunjung Cha, "In Retail, Profiling for Profit," *The Washington Post*, August 17, 2005, http://www.washingtonpost.com/wp-dyn/content/article/2005/08/16/AR2005081601906.html.

[18]   Cited in *DMNews* Magazine, December 22, 1997.

[19]   Don Bates, "'Mini-Me' History: Public Relations from the Dawn of Civilization," Institute for Public Relations, http://old.instituteforpr.org/research_single/mini_me_history/.

[20]   Don Bates, "'Mini-Me' History: Public Relations from the Dawn of Civilization," Institute for Public Relations, http://old.instituteforpr.org/research_single/mini_me_history/.

[21]   Larry Tye, *The Father of Spin, Edward L. Bernays & the Birth of Public Relations* (New York:Crown, 1998), viii.

[22]   Edward L. Bernays, *Biography of an Idea: Memoirs of Public Relations Counsel Edward L. Bernays,* (New York: Simon & Schuster, 1965), 383

[23]   Don Bates, "'Mini-Me' History: Public Relations from the Dawn of Civilization," Institute for Public Relations, 2006, http://www.instituteforpr.org/topics/pr-history/.

[24]   Bradley Johnson, "Not-So-Slow Recovery: U.S. Agency Revenue Surges Nearly 8% in 2011," *Advertising Age*, April 30, 2012, http: //adage.com/article/agency-news/advertising-age-u-s-agency-revenue-surges-8-2011/234421/.

[25]   "Buzz in the Blogosphere: Millions More Blogs and Blog Readers," Nielsen, March 8, 2012, http://blog.nielsen.com/nielsenwire/online_mobile/buzz-in-the-blogosphere-millions-more-bloggers-and-blog-readers/.

[26]   "Zita Cassizzi of Dell on how to turn 'ranters' into 'ravers,'" *The eTail Blog*, August 12, 2010, http://www.theetailblog.com/etail/zita-cassizzi-of-dell-on-how-to-turn-ranters-into-ravers/.

[27]   "History of the Sears Catalog," Sears Archives, http://www.searsarchives.com/catalogs/history.htm.

[28]   Michelle Fox, "Why retail catalogs survive, even thrive, in Internet Age," *USA Today*, May 12, 2012, http://usatoday30.usatoday.com/money/industries/retail/story/2012-05-28/catalogs-in-the-internet-age/55188676/1.

[29]   "Direct Mail Reponse Rates/Email Response Rates/Telemarketing Response Rates: Annual Response Rate Report: The Direct Marketing Association (DMA) / 2010 Annual Response Rate Report," DMDatabases.com, http://dmdatabases.com/resources/interesting-articles/direct-marketing-articles/direct-mail-response-rates#.ULZnC-RlGf4.

[30]   "Coca-Cola's First QR Code Program," *Branding Magazine*, November 14, 2011, http://www.brandingmagazine.com/2011/11/14/coca-colas-first-qr-code-program/.

[31]   Thomas H. Davenport, Leandro Dalle Mule, and John Lucker, "Know What Your Customers Want before They Do," *Harvard Business Review*, December 2011.

[32]   "Facts – E-mail Marketing," Krause Communications, http://www.krausecommunications.com/facts-email.html.

[33]   Sasha Issenberg, "A More Perfect Union," *MIT Technology Review*, December 19, 2012.

[34]   Dr. Pamela Rutledge, "How Obama Won the Social Media Battle in the 2012 Presidential Campaign," *The National Psychologist*, January 2013, http://mprcenter.org/blog/2013/01/25/how-obama-won-the-social-media-battle-in-the-2012-presidential-campaign/.

[35]   Ric Dragon, "Who Created Aida?" *The DragonSearch Blog*, December 21, 2011, http://www.dragonsearchmarketing.com/who-created-aida.

[36]   Arthur F. Peterson, *Pharmaceutical Selling, Detailing, and Sales Training* (McGraw-Hill Book Co., 1949), 165.

[37]   Alex Cosper, "The History of Trade Shows," *SoYouWanna* blog, http://www.soyouwanna.com/history-trade-shows-1432.html.

[38]   William D. Wells, Sandra Moriarty, John Burnett, *Advertising Principles and Practice* (Prentice Hall, 2006), 211.

[39]   Ibid.

[40]   Ryan Singell, "Oct. 27, 1994: Web Gives Birth to Banner Ads," *Wired*, October 27, 2010, http://www.wired.com/thisdayintech/2010/10/1027hotwired-banner-ads/.

[41]   "Mobile Buyer's Guide," 2nd ed., Interactive Advertising Bureau, 2012, www.iab.net/mobile_buyers_guide, 5.

[42]   Ibid., 6.

[43]   Anreas Ramos and Stephanie Cota, *Search Engine Marketing* (McGraw-Hill, 2009), 204.

[44]   "Top 100 Advertising Campaigns," *Advertising Age*, March 29, 1999, http://adage.com/article/news/top-100-advertising-campaigns/62939/.

[45]   Sean Work, "How Loading Time Affects Your Bottom Line," *KISSmetrics* blog, http://blog.kissmetrics.com/loading-time/.

[46]   Kristen Purcell, Joanna Brenner and Lee Rainie, "Search Engine Use 2012," Pew Research Internet Project, http://www.pewinternet.org/Reports/2012/Search-Engine-Use-2012/Summary-of-findings.aspx.

[47] Dai Pham, "The New Multi-screen World: Understanding Cross-Platform Consumer Behavior," *Google Mobile Ads Blog,* http://googlemobileads. blogspot.com/2012/08/navigating-new-multi-screen-world.html

[48] Aaron Elliott, "The Second Largest Search Engine," *Social Media Today,* August 7, 2014, http://socialmediatoday.com/socialbarrel/1650226/ second-largest-search-engine-infographic.

[49] Matthew Dixon, "Challenger Selling: Driving Growth through the Insight-Led Sale," Corporate Executive Board, 2011.

[50] International Data Corporation "Worldwide Data Loss Prevention 2012-2016 Forecast and Vendor Shares," 2012.

[51] Lawrence Friedman and TimFurey, *The Channel Advantage,*(Oxford: Routledge, 1999), 105.

[52] Robert K. Merton, *The Focused Interview,* 2nd ed. (Berkeley:The Free Press, 1990), xviii.

[53] Timothy L. Keningham et al., "Customer Loyalty Isn't Enough," *Harvard Business Review,* October 2011.

Index